Cognitive Analytic Therapy
for People with Intellectual
Disabilities and their Carers

of related interest

Authentic Dialogue with Persons who are Developmentally Disabled
Sad Without Tears
Jennifer Hill
ISBN 978 1 84905 016 6
eISBN 978 1 84642 952 1

**Caring for the Physical and Mental Health of
People with Learning Disabilities**
David Perry, Louise Hammond, Geoff Marston, Sherryl Gaskell and James Eva
Foreword by Dr Anthony Kearns
ISBN 978 1 84905 131 6
eISBN 978 0 85700 225 9

Active Support
Enabling and Empowering People with Intellectual Disabilities
Jim Mansell and Julie Beadle-Brown
ISBN 978 1 84905 111 8
eISBN 978 0 85700 300 3

Cognitive Analytic Therapy for People with Intellectual Disabilities and their Carers

Edited by Julie Lloyd and Philip Clayton
Foreword by Val Crowley

Jessica Kingsley *Publishers*
London and Philadelphia

First published in 2014
by Jessica Kingsley Publishers
73 Collier Street
London N1 9BE, UK
and
400 Market Street, Suite 400
Philadelphia, PA 19106, USA

www.jkp.com

Copyright © Jessica Kingsley Publishers 2014
Foreword copyright © Val Crowley 2014

All rights reserved. No part of this publication may be reproduced in any material form (including photocopying or storing it in any medium by electronic means and whether or not transiently or incidentally to some other use of this publication) without the written permission of the copyright owner except in accordance with the provisions of the Copyright, Designs and Patents Act 1988 or under the terms of a licence issued by the Copyright Licensing Agency Ltd, Saffron House, 6–10 Kirby Street, London EC1N 8TS. Applications for the copyright owner's written permission to reproduce any part of this publication should be addressed to the publisher.

Warning: The doing of an unauthorised act in relation to a copyright work may result in both a civil claim for damages and criminal prosecution.

Library of Congress Cataloging in Publication Data
Cognitive analytic therapy for people with learning disabilities and their carers / edited by Julie Lloyd and Phillip Clayton ; foreword by Val Crowley.
pages cm
Includes bibliographical references and index.
ISBN 978-1-84905-409-6 (alk. paper)
1. People with mental disabilities--Counseling of. 2. Caregivers--Counseling of. 3. Cognitive therapy. I. Lloyd, Julie, 1952- editor of compilaton. II. Clayton, Philip, 1956 October 17- editor of compilaton.
RC570.2.C64 2014
616.89'1425--dc23
2013030765

British Library Cataloguing in Publication Data
A CIP catalogue record for this book is available from the British Library

ISBN 978 1 84905 409 6
eISBN 978 0 85700 804 6

Printed and bound in Great Britain

This book is dedicated to people with intellectual disabilities, in gratitude to what they teach us and in the hope that their lives continue to improve.

Contents

Foreword   11
Val Crowley, Consultant Clinical Psychologist and CAT Psychotherapist

ACKNOWLEDGEMENTS   13

Part 1 Overview of Cognitive Analytic Therapy and People with Intellectual Disabilities

Chapter 1 Introduction   17
Julie Lloyd, CAT Practitioner, supervisor and trainer and Clinical Psychologist, Surrey and Borders Partnership NHS Foundation Trust and Southern Health NHS Foundation Trust and Steve Potter, psychotherapist, coach, trainer and supervisor

Chapter 2 The Adaptation and Adoption of Tools in Cognitive Analytic Therapy for People who have an Intellectual Disability and Their Carers   42
Philip Clayton, CAT Psychotherapist, Calderstones Partnership NHS Foundation Trust

Chapter 3 How Cognitive Analytic Therapy is Being Used in Services for People with Intellectual Disabilities   54
Julie Lloyd and Hilary Brown, Professor of Social Care, Canterbury Christ Church University

Chapter 4 Formulating and Working Therapeutically with the Concept of Intellectual Disability in the Cognitive Analytic Therapy Model   68
Jo Varela, CAT Practitioner and Consultant Clinical Psychologist, Sheffield Children's NHS Foundation Trust

Chapter 5 Relational Intelligence   80
Steve Potter and Julie Lloyd

Chapter 6 The Helper's Dance List　　　　　　　　　　　89
Steve Potter

Chapter 7 What Aspects of Intelligence are Needed to
Understand the Concept of Reciprocal Roles?　　　　96
Julie Lloyd

Part 2 Using Cognitive Analytic Therapy in the Community

Chapter 8 The Problems of Caring and Being Cared For
(or How to Get Your Shoelaces Tied For You)　　　　109
David Wilberforce, lecturer, therapist, trainer and consultant

Chapter 9 Using Cognitive Analytic Therapy in a Systemic
Context with Staff Teams: Reflections on the Process of
Facilitating an Intervention　　　　　　　　　　　　122
Helen Elford, Clinical Psychologist, Cheshire and Wirral Partnership NHS Foundation Trust and Zoe Ball, Chartered Clinical Psychologist, Cheshire and Wirral Partnership NHS Foundation Trust

Chapter 10 Cognitive Analytic Therapy and Behaviour
that Challenges　　　　　　　　　　　　　　　　　136
Jo Varela

Chapter 11 Heroic or Stoic: Why Do We Try So Hard, or Give
Up So Easily, in Helping with Severe Autism?　　　　153
Julie Lloyd and Steve Potter

Chapter 12 What is the 2005 Mental Capacity Act and How
Can Cognitive Analytic Therapy Help Us to Make Sense of the
Decision-making Process at its Heart?　　　　　　　168
Hilary Brown and Julie Lloyd

Part 3 Using Cognitive Analytic Therapy in Forensic Settings

Chapter 13 'Behind the Mask': A Case Study　　　　　181
Michelle Anwyl, CAT Practitioner, Calderstones Partnership NHS Foundation Trust and Pamela Mount, Clinical Nurse Specialist, Calderstones Partnership NHS Foundation Trust

Chapter 14 Cognitive Analytic Therapy Integrated
into a Therapeutic Community Approach　　　　　191
Philip Clayton and Simon Crowther, Clinical Psychologist, Calderstones NHS Foundation Trust

Chapter 15 A Group Approach: The Brooklands Offender
Relationship Treatment Programme   203
*Nicola Murphy, Senior Clinical Psychologist and Cognitive Analytic
Therapist, Coventry and Warwickshire Partnership NHS Trust*

Chapter 16 The Application of Cognitive Analytic Therapy Used
Therapeutically for Personality Disorder and Offending
Behaviour and Contextually Within a Secure Service   216
Nicola Murphy

Chapter 17 Cognitive Analytic Therapy in Forensic Intellectual
Disability Settings   227
*Perry Morrison, Consultant Lead Psychologist,
Southern Health Foundation Trust*

AFTERWORD	235
APPENDIX 1 THE PSYCHOTHERAPY FILE I	237
APPENDIX 2 THE PSYCHOTHERAPY FILE II	244
APPENDIX 3 THE PSYCHOTHERAPY FILE ADAPTED FOR PEOPLE WITH INTELLECTUAL DISABILITIES	256
APPENDIX 4 ADAPTED PERSONALITY STRUCTURE QUESTIONNAIRE	270
APPENDIX 5 '1:1 CAT CARE PLAN' WITH NURSING STAFF	272
APPENDIX 6 THE HELPER'S DANCE LIST: A LIST OF TYPICAL INTERACTIONS THAT CAN AFFECT THE HELPING RELATIONSHIP	275
APPENDIX 7 SEQUENTIAL DIAGRAMMATIC REFORMULATION	280
APPENDIX 8 REFORMULATION LETTER	281
APPENDIX 9 GOODBYE LETTER	284
APPENDIX 10 SEQUENTIAL DIAGRAMMATIC REFORMULATION	286
APPENDIX 11 SEQUENTIAL DIAGRAMMATIC REFORMULATION WITH EXITS	287
APPENDIX 12 REFORMULATION LETTER	288
APPENDIX 13 SEQUENTIAL DIAGRAMMATIC REFORMULATION	290
GLOSSARY	291
THE EDITORS	298
THE CONTRIBUTORS	299
REFERENCES	302
SUBJECT INDEX	314
AUTHOR INDEX	319

Foreword

Val Crowley

Over the last 20 years in the NHS, there have been major changes in the assessment, delivery and treatment of mental health services. These include the closure of the large institutions for people with psychiatric problems and intellectual disabilities. This, and improvements in medical treatment and the development of community services, has led to a greater interest and use of psychological models and interventions for people with mental health problems and complex needs.

During this period Tony Ryle has been developing an integrated, time-limited psychotherapy that incorporates not only the cognitive, behavioural and analytic models, but also a dialogic model, which has added a relational element. This model has increasingly drawn on the need for a dialogic rather than monadic understanding of psychotherapy. Cognitive Analytic Therapy (CAT) was originally used with people with emotional problems within mental health services, but as the model has developed, it has also been used for clients with more complex problems and been embedded in services.

The development of the relational model has given therapists the opportunity to work in a more collaborative, non-collusive way, enabling them to explore the possibilities of working both individually with clients and, where this has proved difficult, with community teams and carers.

This has led to clinicians/therapists working with people with intellectual disabilities becoming interested in the potential of the model. In particular, the work of Vygotsky and the concept of the Zone of Proximal Development seemed to offer a different way of working with clients, where one could look at and work with what they could do with the assistance of another and how they understood the concept of disability.

Historically, people with intellectual disabilities were not offered a full range of 'talking therapies' and it seems as if their mental health problems were overshadowed by their label of intellectual disabilities. This lead to their voices not being heard and they became disempowered. CAT has been willing to work with this client group whose needs so great.

Over the last 15 years, CAT therapists have been using and extending the CAT model for this client group. The tools of CAT psychotherapy have been adapted in many imaginative ways, which are illustrated in this book. Where work with individuals has not been possible, CAT has been used with care teams, families and community teams. The CAT model has also enabled therapists to work with transference issues as they arise. Examples of this work are movingly described in this book.

Despite all the work that has been done and the progress that has been made, the phrase, 'but is it still CAT'? has been voiced. This book gives the answer to that – yes it is. This book shows how to use CAT.

The phrase 'I don't have the words' is often heard in therapy sessions as the therapist tries to attune to the client and their needs. So often, emotions have been seen as overwhelming, unmanageable and hidden away. This links to Vygotsky's concept that what a child does with the assistance of another today, they can do on their own in the future.

Thus, the adapted tools of CAT can be helpful for any situation where the client and therapist are struggling to begin a conversation, where it feels as if there are no words to use or where the therapist feels useless, stupid or stuck. One can truly say that you can work relationally with clients from an IQ of 50 to 150, but the client can only progress as far as they and the therapist believe they can.

This book has been long awaited and now the client's voice is beginning to be heard as the conversations commence. I can wholeheartedly recommend this book to anyone who seeks to learn more about CAT and how it can be used wherever words cannot be found or the conversation is faltering.

Val Crowley
CAT Psychotherapist, Accredited Supervisor
Consultant Clinical Psychologist, retired

Acknowledgements

We would like to acknowledge the people with intellectual disabilities and their carers who made this book possible, by showing us how we could work side by side. We have been helped by enriching conversations with colleagues, both within intellectual disability services and within the Association of Cognitive Analytic Therapy, which also advised us on how to approach publishers. We would like to thank Lindsi Bluemel who re-drew many of the illustrations in a format suitable for the book and Irram Walji who also stepped in to re-draw a couple of the illustrations. Both artists assisted in a creative and efficient way. We would also like to acknowledge our families who supported us to write the book. Particular mention is made of one set of children, who, on hearing their mother had got up several hours before they were due to get up, helped her to put on hold her boring plan of writing a bit more for a chapter to join in with their fun of building a humongous Lego model.

Part 1
Overview of Cognitive Analytic Therapy and People with Intellectual Disabilities

Chapter 1
Introduction
Julie Lloyd and Steve Potter

How encouraging that you have opened this book, despite the label 'intellectual disabilities'! Labels like this are so powerful; you may already be tempted to close the book, thinking it is not for you. Finding a voice – starting a conversation – is really difficult, especially where one of you is thought to have the words, but the other is not always recognised as having a means of communication. Having a language puts us into a powerful place. In this book, we search to give people with intellectual disabilities, and those working with them, a voice. However, this book is not just about intellectual disability work; not having the ability to express emotions is a much more common problem than having a cognitive impairment. Many people do not have words for emotions and for reflecting on what early life brought them. Other people, particularly those with personality disorders, struggle with thinking about and seeing the bigger picture in a joined-up way.

This book is about creative uses of Cognitive Analytic Therapy (CAT) and offers ideas about ways of working with people whose life stories, problems and help seem complex. Using inventive ways to work with our relationship with the world and ourselves, this book describes how we can develop helpful and practical conversations together. In it we celebrate how we do this, in particular how CAT helps us to work together safely, carefully and constructively.

Most people in intellectual disability services describe their work in terms of their client group rather than their particular brand of therapy. This suggests that what matters are the people we work with, not the school of therapy. So why CAT? It is popular and useful precisely because it offers an understanding about human relationships, both with others and how we relate to ourselves. This means that, as a therapy, CAT not only offers skills development and explicit learning, but also gives people an experience of healthier relationships, both within therapy and indirectly through working with staff teams. This chapter introduces CAT, and concludes with a brief summary of the contents of the rest of the book.

What is CAT?

CAT's relational approach

CAT involves working with our relationships with ourselves, with others and with the world around us. The agent of change is not merely cognitive, behavioural or experiential; it is relational. Holding a relational stance means weaving flexibly between possible meanings, conversations and silences. It means trying to attune to the people we are with – sometimes standing back, sometimes getting more involved, sometimes focusing on a detail and sometimes seeing the bigger picture. It means being able to navigate the relationship in the room at that moment, including our own relationships with ourselves. At heart, we are social beings and where people are not adept at being sociable, we sense this limitation and can react in helpful or unhelpful ways. Whilst valuing talking and negotiating, CAT's relational understanding includes holding onto times when there are no words and meaning is communicated in other ways. In intellectual disability work we know many of our clients have little voice; the attraction of a CAT approach includes our encounter with silence and wordlessness. Intelligence is not placed as the property (however limited) of an individual. In CAT, it is the intelligence between us that we can jointly notice and sustain; hence its utility in services for people with intellectual disabilities.

How did CAT develop?

CAT developed in the NHS as a way of working with people who were hard to help. Tony Ryle, who was originally a GP, brought a medical and compassionate commitment to careful description and evaluation of how psychological help might work effectively. He saw that there was far more need for psychological help and psychological thinking than specialist services could cover. He was keen to provide a clearer language that clients could use to make use of some of the rich ideas from psychoanalysis. He put these ideas in a more cognitive language thereby creating the cognitively analytic approach of CAT. He was particularly interested in combining ideas from Personal Construct Theory (Kelly 1955) and

Object Relations (one branch of the British tradition of psychoanalytic thinking Greenberg and Mitchell 1983). He wrote a series of papers in the 1970s based on various research projects he conducted, out of which he developed concepts for describing important relationships in people's lives and the beliefs and actions that people take in or internalise and replay in their interaction with themselves and the world. By the 1980s, a group of people working in the NHS started to explore how these psychological ideas could be used in an efficient and fair way, particularly to meet the needs of hard-pressed psychological and counselling services that had limited resources. Gradually, the group brought in further ideas from outside British practice at that time, as, with the inspiration and help of a Finnish psychologist, Mikael Leiman, they discovered ideas from Eastern Europe about activity theory (which relates to skills development) and dialogism (which relates to the social and psychological context to our communications). Dialogic ideas further enriched the group's understanding of how the internal version of early relationships shaped our present day behaviour.

Reciprocal roles

'Reciprocal roles' describes a core concept in CAT, naming the psychological and social, inner and outer sense of ourselves and others. Reciprocal roles are the psychological equivalent of genes because they are the building blocks of our social, mental and emotional lives. 'Reciprocal' describes the interchange between 'doing to' and 'done to' and the coping response. We have a number of different relationships and at various times hold a range of views about ourselves. For example, if I am with someone who is being kind to me in ways that I welcome and accept then the reciprocal role might be described as '*giving kindness* in relation to *receiving kindness*'. Later, I might be involved in a different reciprocal role with someone else or with myself at a different time. For example, I might subsequently be with someone who is very bossy. In response to their bossiness one person might tend to be a placatory '*good girl*' or tend to be *resentfully compliant*, and another person might appear to go along with them but be *covertly defiant*. A third person might make a stand and be overtly *rebellious*. Whatever position I get into, I am responding to them; we are in a reciprocal role. Reciprocal roles have two faces: one facing inward and giving voice to a way of relating to ourselves, and one facing outward and giving voice to a way of relating to others, or to things (including ideas) and the world around us. Reciprocal roles summarise the forces behind familiar, automatic and habitual ways we cope with the actions that have an impact on us.

All of us tend to get into certain relational roles more often than others. The options I choose and how I experience the impact of their roles on me is influenced by how I have learnt, from what life has brought me, to respond to people in those roles, such as kind or bossy people. I will likely be particularly influenced by the pattern I developed in my early life from how my parents and I related (either by continuing that style or by specifically reacting against them). Although the origins of any particular reciprocal roles lie with people we have known, in CAT the continuation of these roles is emphasised by describing the role and not naming the person we are like. For example, we talk about a nurturing or a hostile role, rather than 'being like my mother'. This is because a role rarely starts and stops with a specific person we have known, but like a ripple in a pond, spreads wider because we take it in as a relationship with ourselves even when the initial person is no longer around. We then play it out, drawing others into responding to the role relationships with which we are familiar and that have become part of our nature.

Playing one role always implies a partnership between two roles where one is being cast or controlled by the other. One is more parental or powerful (we mostly call it the top end of the reciprocal role) and the other is more childlike and less powerful (we mostly call it the bottom end of the reciprocal role). We learn to participate in these role relationships by knowing the actions, voices and intentions of both ends and tend to pull or push for reciprocation from one end or another within ourselves and between ourselves and others. Using behavioural insights, we describe the top end of the reciprocal role as the stimulus, and from psychodynamic insights, especially object relations theory, it is sometimes called the 'parentally derived' top end role. It is the 'doing to' or active point. It often involves words ending in 'ing'.

At the receiving end is the bottom pole. This is the response, the child derived role or the impact position. It is the 'done to' place. This often involves words ending in 'ed'. Many of us may find that people will try to move from the bottom end to the top end, either for themselves or they experience others moving from one end to another. The issue is often: either I am bossy or am being bossed around. Reciprocal roles capture what often becomes our essential character and social style. Ryle and Kerr (2002, p.220) describe a reciprocal role as a 'stable pattern of interaction originating in relationships with caretakers in early life, determining current patterns of relationships with others and self-management'.

We have said that reciprocal roles are simultaneously internally and externally facing. Take the 'bossy' example; a person may end up ordering him or herself around all the time, so there is a part of them that is in the top end. Of course, treating him or herself like this may invite them to put things off endlessly as a secretly defiant way (bottom end of the role) to deal with such a bossy part of their self! Their lack of progress then proves to their 'top end' that this only goes to show why they need to be bossed around. This is an example of a self-to-self reciprocal role. Roles start off as other-to-self (how my parents treated me), and in the process of repetition and learning become self-to-self (how I treat myself) and self-to-other (how I treat others) in a self-perpetuating circuit. If we cannot get out of the dance of being at one end of the reciprocal role or another we may shift to another set of roles from our familiar repertoire.

Tony Ryle, who first coined the term 'reciprocal roles', describes how they are useful as a shortcut that lets us work out (usually without thinking about it), what is going on and what position we are taking up in response. We get a feel for what is going on and select how we are going to react. We deduce reciprocal roles from stories of childhood, current relationships and our interactions with individuals, and use these role descriptions as a tool that allows or assists us to predict relational patterns. Roles are strong because we are kept in them whilst we are unaware of their operation. Tony Ryle wrote (Ryle and Kerr 2002, p.112): 'By learning to link the wide range of acts and experiences to these broad patterns, the patient can reflect upon them and gain control over what has been automatic.' The idea of reciprocal roles is a useful tool for therapists to explore unhelpful relational patterns with clients. Many of our roles are healthy; working using CAT will include trying to help a person to enhance the amount they enact their healthy roles. However, referrals will be about unhealthy roles, or at least unhealthy enactments of roles. Within intellectual disability services, there was some research (Psaila and Crowley 2005) that looked to elucidate what the most common unhealthy roles were for our clients. These are:

- Abusing to Abused
- Rejecting to Rejected
- Rescuing/Caring to Rescued/Cared For
- Damaging to Damaged
- Abandoning to Abandoned (Unloving to Unloved)
- Special/Perfect to Learning Disabled
- Controlling to Controlled/Fragile

- Blaming to Blamed
- Overwhelming to Overwhelmed
- Sheltering to Sheltered.

Of course, these are not the only unhelpful reciprocal roles in operation, but they are common ones. Each of our lives is describable by a limited number of roles; how many we have affects how versatile and flexible we can be in our responses and what roles we elicit from other people. However, it is not just the number of roles that is important, it is also how much we can oversee and orchestrate the right role response to the right occasion. Ryle also argued that we can be damaged not just by limited roles but a limited ability to orchestrate and reflect upon these roles, which in turn then limits our capacity for self-awareness (Ryle 1997a). We often see in our intellectual disability work, that difficult reciprocal roles operating with a client are the same as the ones operating in the support team around that client.

Reciprocal role procedures: traps, snags and dilemmas

Reciprocal roles incorporate beliefs, values, memories and affects/emotions and give rise to or may arise from 'procedures' or patterns of expectations and habitual ways of setting aims, taking action and then evaluating them. Procedures are the actions that are responses to the feelings arising from the feelings in reciprocal roles. They are what you get away from and what you get into. Procedures may be behaviours or a mental sequence within someone's internal life. As a therapy, CAT involves selecting one, two or three target problems to work on in a time-limited way; 'procedures' offer a way of viewing how these problems are maintained or avoided.

The idea of reciprocal roles and the procedures that maintain them overlaps with the idea of procedural sequences or patterns of reflection, action and impact in response to the core feelings generated by being at one end of a reciprocal role. A simple way of thinking about the idea of reciprocal role procedures and processes is to see that something starts with an action that has an impact and an expected response. How the action impacts on the person's experience, or how it feels, partly influences the response. CAT's purpose is to help the person see how they have been pulled into a response because of the impact of the action and how they might make a choice about, reflect upon and change their response.

The issue in CAT is not so much the difficult or unhelpful reciprocal roles a person has, as the way in which the person responds to them in what they do or how they treat themselves. Harmful procedures intensify, turn inward, fly from or make worse one end or another of the reciprocal role. They are automatic and part of our first reactions to some action towards us. If we can spell them out, often by mapping them out with words or pictures and arrows, then we can spot where to change our intentions, our thinking or feeling, or how we evaluate them. In CAT we say that once we can see the dance we do and name the detailed sequence of a harmful reciprocal role procedure, we can go on to identify the sequence of a more helpful procedure. Procedures can be mapped or written out in a loop as in Figure 1.1.

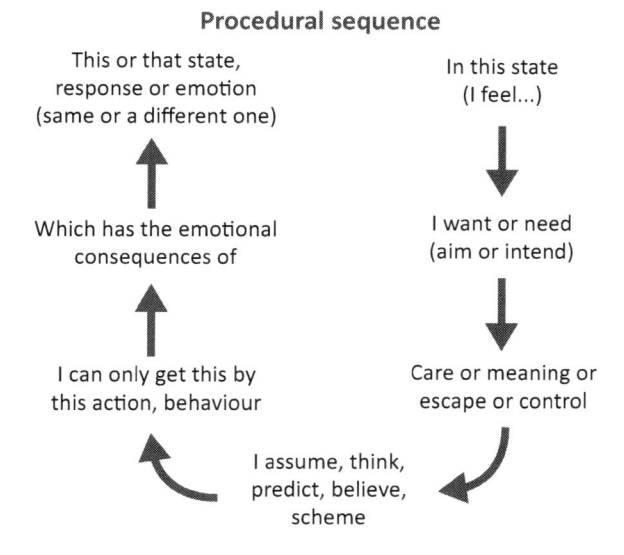

Procedural sequence

```
This or that state,                      In this state
response or emotion                      (I feel...)
(same or a different one)
            ↑                                 ↓
Which has the emotional                  I want or need
   consequences of                       (aim or intend)
            ↑                                 ↓
I can only get this by                   Care or meaning or
 this action, behaviour                   escape or control
            ↖         I assume, think,      ↙
                      predict, believe,
                           scheme
```

Figure 1.1: Procedural sequence

As part of a plan to evaluate whether therapy worked or not, Tony Ryle looked at 27 of his cases to identify the key problem patterns that become the focus of therapy. He discovered that there were several common underlying patterns that could be described in general and ordinary language. Although his interest initially was research, his clients liked these descriptions and they become a key part of making a collaborative partnership in the early stages of therapy, which became the basis of joint reformulation. He concluded that there were three types of procedures that acted to maintain the status quo and were the result of underlying reciprocal roles that caused difficulties. He named these three procedures 'traps', 'dilemmas' and 'snags'. Traps are like 'vicious circles'; once we get into a trap, we just go round and round and it is hard to stop. Traps are self-fulfilling prophecies. Here is an example of a trap from the adapted version of one of the assessment tools in CAT, called the 'Psychotherapy File'.

1: 'Keeping my feelings to myself' trap

I don't tell people how I feel or what I need because I worry that I will upset them

↓

This means that sometimes people ignore me or hurt me

↓

This makes me angry or upset

↓

I think it's bad to be angry or upset, and that I'd better keep my feelings and needs to myself

Figure 1.2: 'Keeping my feelings to myself' trap

Dilemmas are patterns where it seems that there are only two behavioural options open to us, for example, where we assume 'if I do…then…will happen', and where we think 'either I do this…or I do that…' When we are doing one behaviour we may be in constant fear of the 'if then', or 'either or' sequence leading to the other behaviour. It can lead to something like 'black and white thinking' where only two choices of action seem possible. By thinking this way we can make things harder for ourselves by living as if there is not much room to negotiate what we do. Here is an example of a dilemma from the same Psychotherapy File.

1: 'Upset feelings' dilemma

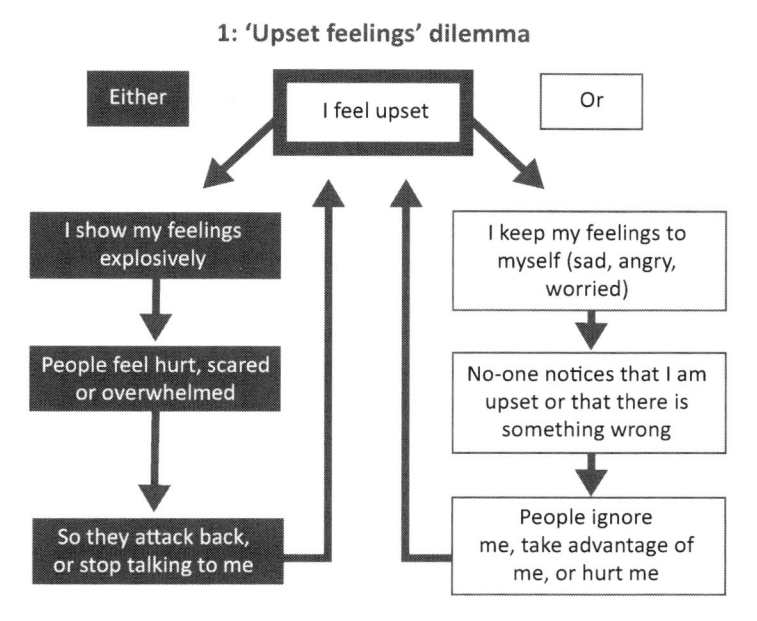

```
Either          I feel upset          Or

I show my feelings              I keep my feelings to
explosively                     myself (sad, angry,
                                worried)

People feel hurt, scared        No-one notices that I am
or overwhelmed                  upset or that there is
                                something wrong

So they attack back,            People ignore
or stop talking to me           me, take advantage of
                                me, or hurt me
```

Figure 1.3: 'Upset feelings' dilemma

The third kind of pattern that Ryle identified that makes up part of the psychotherapy file are snags (or *s*ubtly *n*egative *a*spects of *g*oals). Snags are patterns that get in the way of sustaining progress when we are doing okay. They can be quite deep rooted and might feel like the cul-de-sac or brick wall we come up against as we head off in a successful direction. They stop us doing things that we want to do and stop us making changes in our lives. Snags stop progress as if the effect of gain/success on someone would:

- deprive others, because there is not enough to go round
- make others envious, so they fear attack or rejection
- damage others in some way
- be bound to be spoiled/taken away, so they give it up first
- be undeserved
- never be enough
- set a standard they can't keep up
- be too much for them
- cost what they don't want to give up, so they resist moving forward
- give others satisfaction they want to withhold, in order to keep the power.

We often find in working with people with intellectual disabilities that they understand the concept of a trap or 'circle', particularly when we draw it out. People can see that despite their wishes, they end up back where they started. Dilemmas may be harder for people with intellectual disabilities to understand as they need to be able to think of two rejected options at the same time. It can make more sense to see on a map how we yoyo between a place we want to be in and a place we don't want to be in or fear being in. We end up being stuck in limbo, putting up with something that is not what we want but is better than being where we don't want to be. Many people tend to go along with only one possibility and reject the other option automatically; people with intellectual disabilities may find it harder to think about things they do not do (even if their rejection acts to push them more firmly along the other option). However, dilemmas often appear to be expressed by 'the system' with services exploring the other option of a dilemma that the client does not exhibit and rejecting that option as making things worse. They can involve extreme thinking; for example, 'Either we allow the person to make their own choices and let them go to the pub each night and spend all their money on alcohol so they have no money for food, or we stop them going to the pub and deprive them of their rights and freedom.' In this situation, the system is in a dilemma because the only options are 'all or nothing'.

Snags come in all sorts of shapes and sizes, particularly within services when there are serious economic constraints. A common snag for people with intellectual disabilities is that they would like to be independent, but can only get care if they are needy.

CAT's way of thinking about relationships and being in dialogue

When we spend time with people with intellectual disabilities, we are often painfully aware of the gap between us. We want a relationship where we can be in dialogue but we find it hard to connect. We can try all sorts of helper's dances as described in Chapter 6 and in Appendix 6, which take us in and out of dialogue and offer more restrictive or more enabling relationships. For both the helper and the person being helped, it can, at times, feel very hard to understand what the other wants or is offering or saying. How we live our lives may be very different and one of us may have opportunities, education, paid jobs, a car, our own property and other wealth, and perhaps marriage and children, which are denied to the other. One may have responsibilities and demands the other does not have. One may feel secure in their position within society; the other may experience exclusion, loneliness and great longing. However large these differences are, there may also be lots of things they have in common.

CAT has found it useful to draw on a broad view of how we relate, which comes from contemporary psychoanalytic approaches and the dialogic perspective of people who follow the ideas of Mikhail Bakhtin, which were introduced to the CAT community by Mikael Leiman. CAT offers a way of working with this view that is described in the sections on reciprocal roles and procedures (see pp.19–26). In summary, it sees that there is always an inner dialogue to accompany the interpersonal interactions and that the past history of these internal and external interactions is always in play. Bakhtin thought the differences between people could also be a source of connection and dialogue.

Bakhtin (1895–1975) was a philosopher and literary critic whose ideas have influenced some of the more recent thinking in CAT. His ideas were quite varied but come together in the view that our relationship with words and communication is never fixed but open and personal. He saw language as something that should be understood by its use rather than as labels and words in a dictionary. His idea that a person cannot be fully known, completely understood or labelled marries up with our experience of working with people who are not fully revealed. When we do not fully understand people with intellectual disabilities, Bakhtin would point out that we cannot fully understand anyone else, whether or not they have an intellectual disability. Bakhtin had another important idea about how every person is influenced by others in an inescapable and intertwined way. No voice can be totally isolated; indeed, the words we use have been used by someone else before us. Other people influence how we come to be, how we think and how we see ourselves. This comes alive in a practical way in CAT with reciprocal roles. We can also use his idea to think about the socially constructed nature of the label 'intellectual disabilities' and how some people may feel that using 'difficulties' rather than 'disabilities' somehow makes the label more palatable by giving it a different meaning. Bakhtin's third big idea was that there are many 'voices' in the process of sharing language and communication. This helps us see how our work is with the relationship between us not the individual alone.

CAT's use of Vygotsky's Zone of Proximal Development

Lev Vygotsky (1896–1934) discovered how children use drawings as a graphic form of speech. He showed that drawings offer a method for relating to and working with our internal world and are used to convey a story. The impulse that children have to draw comes out of their wish to tell a story. This is demonstrated in intellectual disability services through the use of accessible communication. In CAT, mapping uses jointly developed pictures, signs and symbols to offer such a means of representation. For example, a person with severe intellectual disabilities may be able to pick out a picture of someone putting someone else in a dustbin from a selection of pictures. This describes how they feel they are being treated, and/or how they treat themselves and others, although they could not put this into words. The picture acts as a tool that gives him or her the use of a higher mental function. CAT uses Vygotsky's awareness of how signs are created between us and act as tools that enable advances in mental functioning. Vygotksy was also acutely aware of how advances in mental functioning can only occur if they are within the Zone of Proximal Development for those involved. This refers to the gap between what a person can do with the help of another person but cannot yet do alone. This 'zone' is constantly moving forward as the person does for themselves the skill that they could only do earlier with help from another person.

A Vygotskian approach means taking on board what is called the behavioural phenotypical presentation of the type of intellectual disability a person has and using interventions that are just within the person's zone of what they can achieve (their Zone of Proximal Development). For example, the desire that someone with severe autism would engage in socially sensitive conversation at a wedding may be outside their Zone of Proximal Development and so in CAT that would not be an appropriate target problem to work on. Working in the Zone of Proximal Development (often called 'ZPD'), means viewing a person not frozen in the present moment, but where they could be with help from others. This help involves giving prompts, clues, modelling and explanations, asking leading questions, discussion, joint participation in the new skill, giving encouragement and bringing the goal to their attention. However, this needs to be done collaboratively in the presence of shared goals. Play is also important in creating Zones of Proximal Development, because it uses objects in a symbolic way. Vygotsky focused on how dialogue and conversations become internalised through those conversations, becoming tools that a person uses to transform their environment.

The structure of a Cognitive Analytic Therapy

Because CAT is time limited within the NHS, doing it involves a structured approach. We will describe how CAT therapists follow this structure quite tightly but with a view to creating a unique relationship with the person whom they are helping. However, there are no session-by-session manuals as CAT involves using a collaborative approach to tackle problems, rather than going through a pre-set menu. Having a general structure acts like scaffolding to hold up and support what happens and to reduce the risk of a therapy getting stuck.

A Cognitive Analytic Therapy is divided into three main phases. The first is the reformulation phase involving assessment and arriving at a joint understanding of what the problems are. This may take at least a quarter of the agreed sessions. Assessment can be complicated as there can be many issues to deal with, such as what the staff team see as the problem in addition to the client's view and how the client experiences the therapeutic relationship. Although many clients may be used to helping relationships, these may include the parental roles found in many support and nursing roles. One of the most useful tools for the reformulation phase is the Six Part Story Method, and we also use adapted versions of the Psychotherapy File, which are described later in this book. The reformulation phase of CAT is very important and is based on careful, accurate and shared description of what the client is struggling with and how help might be focused, planned out and set up, either involving just the client or other helpers as well.

The second of the three phases in Cognitive Analytic Therapy is the active phase in the middle of therapy, in which clients practise and learn to recognise their problematic procedures in relation to target problems. Along with recognising how patterns work, there is the beginning of a process of revising and changing patterns to more helpful and productive alternatives. In CAT, although reformulation, recognition and revision all help each other, it is often important to see that recognition needs to precede revision. In other words, therapists need to hold back from trying to teach useful skills until the client recognises times when their current procedures are unhelpful; this is when they will be motivated to try out a more productive approach. Recognition and revision are very active times in which clients explore new approaches, and this takes up at least half of the therapy.

The final phase of a CAT is the ending. Reviewing progress and saying 'goodbye' is often avoided in intellectual disability services and endings may be abrupt. Often our clients have experienced disrupted attachment and so in CAT at least a quarter of the time is spent working on processing the ending of therapy. This work may also involve finishing work with the staff team. The ending can be a time of sadness, celebration and realistic appraisal of what has been achieved and what remains to be done. It is normally good practice to share review letters or find a structured way of acknowledging what has been done.

Assessment

There may be two elements to assessment. The first about general assessment of what elements could respond to a psychological approach. The second is to consider whether CAT or elements of CAT might be the best way of helping. When using CAT with people with intellectual disabilities, there are a number of tools that can be used, including using the Psychotherapy File (this is described in Chapter 2 on adapting tools). Much of our assessment work involves drawing stick people with our clients as we try to understand what is going on. Most of us are pretty useless at drawing; this serves the therapy well as our abilities can feel more equal.

Reformulation

A reformulation letter is a joint endeavour, written by the therapist and the client. The client's words are used to describe their experience and the therapist makes the progression of actions clear by reflecting on the consequences of those actions. Using language at a level that the client can understand, the letter describes the reason why the client has come to therapy. Then, the letter describes how the presenting problem is linked with their childhood relational experiences of their emotions, behaviour, bodies and thoughts. Sadly, there are occasions in working with people with intellectual disabilities when we do not know anything about their childhoods; at least nothing that is connected with their presenting problem. In that situation, where the client is also unable to inform us, we describe how we do not know how the problem started and comment about what it must be like for them not to have this aspect of their history. We also try to describe how the presenting problem is linked with a 'big picture' about the client's assumptions, roles, identities and self-understanding. The aim of this letter is to concentrate on how the client has now become stuck.

In the letter we try to validate experience, de-pathologise difficulties, elicit repudiated or unappreciated emotion, develop the therapeutic alliance, clarify responsibilities (avoided or incorrectly carried). We identify how current procedures are maintaining distress. We summarise reciprocal role procedures through the concepts of traps, dilemmas and snags. The wish is that by recognising these sequences of actions and revising their consequences, the person develops greater internal emotional health, helping them to be more adaptive and relationally responsive in our intricate world. We then relate these reciprocal role procedures to the therapeutic relationship. Reformulation guides the therapist to avoid colluding with the client's normal reciprocal roles (and to monitor their own), that threaten or help develop the therapeutic alliance. The open and shared process of writing out a reformulation (also helped by mapping as described in the next section) is like having a supervisor in the room.

Writing a reformulation requires particular skill at generating accurate and comprehensive words that offer tools for recognising and then revising specific self-restricting patterns. Our challenge is, amongst ourselves, to develop the flexible relational thinking that can be good enough to write this complex letter.

Letters are usually augmented through Makaton (and other symbols as appropriate) and are often illustrated. Prose does not need to be in text form, and can obviously be recorded if the client has the means to play the recording. The big issue is the client's level of comprehension. For clients who have a level of intellectual disability that would preclude attending to, understanding and being able to think about such a letter as described above, writing one would be counter-therapeutic. Some clients would gain nothing by having a letter; others gain by having a letter that blends the style and content of a reformulation with a Social Story™ approach. Social Stories™, invented by Carol Gray, accurately describes a social process that an individual benefits from learning. The techniques of writing a social story are very helpful to make a reformulation letter accessible. Yet others gain more by being given the letter in small sections over several sessions. A question to be aware of is whose letter is it? For adults who live with their families, it is likely that their parents will take charge of the letter. In this circumstance, a letter might start by acknowledging this and ask if it is being written to the client's parents as well as the client. In other situations, staff may want to 'keep the letter safe' by putting it into a file about the client that the staff keep in the office; this may be disempowering.

CAT uses a jointly developed narrative that is actively shared within the brief time frame of NHS services to formulate and guide treatment. Long after the therapy has finished, the client has the reformulation and ending letters to guide their processing further.

Maps

We have described how CAT values work openly, side by side, together with the client. One idea that has helped a lot is mapping to show how our understanding is developing. This means putting a diagram on paper to show the pictures or words describing reciprocal roles with arrows showing how procedures relate to each other. This section summarises how mapping came to play a central role in CAT. It shows how mapping helps ensure careful, shared description of the three-way relationship between the client, their problems and the systems around them.

CAT trainees learn to make a diagram as part of the reformulation phase at the beginning of therapy; one type of diagram is the Sequential Diagrammatic Reformulation (SDR) (many CAT therapists refer to their maps as SDRs). As its title implies, it offers a way of tracking the sequence of actions, their impact and typical ways of responding. The sequences are called procedural loops and are summaries of coping strategies, interpersonal patterns or self-management patterns that serve to handle the impact of one or more core reciprocal roles.

The reciprocal roles in these diagrams often have a core reciprocal role where the top end described the kinds of powerful influences from parents or adult in childhood. These mainly describe actions and what parents or carers did. The bottom end represents the childhood experience of being treated in this way and is mostly described in terms of feelings. What makes drawing the reciprocal role doubly useful is mapping out the procedural sequence that was a way of coping with these feelings. It is often the harm or limitations that were kept going through childhood and into adulthood that are the focus of therapy. When drawing maps, people often start with a core feeling (or impact) that is felt to be at the heart of the problems and is hard to manage now or in childhood had to be managed in ways that are costly or not helpful now. Some CAT therapists call this core feeling the 'core pain'. Others call them 'unmanageable emotions' to show how several difficult patterns from the past contribute to a mix of difficult feelings, such as sadness, anxiety and anger.

Using the idea of reciprocal role procedures, the typical map traces out who was doing what to create this core feeling and what is done to cope with or respond to it. This creates initial focus points on the map as shown in Figure 1.4. These are the actions behind the difficult feeling – the words that describe the felt impact of the action, for example, if the action is someone hitting me, I feel scared; if they are loving me tenderly, I feel cherished or held. Mapping out the actions, impact and responses with reciprocal roles helps us progress when talking through how patterns that maintain our present problems have become so ingrained.

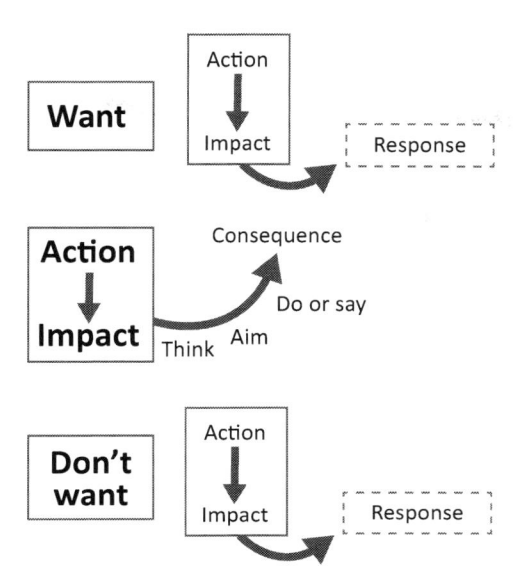

Figure 1.4: Reciprocal role template

Tony Ryle advised that in making these maps it was important to keep them simple for fear of them looking 'like maps of Birmingham's road system' (Ryle 1995, p.33). They need to be understandable – neither too detailed nor tied to one story, but not so general that they seem as if they apply to everything. As we map out the interaction around one reciprocal role we often discover how the response to the impact of this action links into another reciprocal role.

In a further development, the mapping helps to show how some people were faced with quite a fragmented sense of themselves in the world and found it hard to reflect upon and integrate their feelings and actions with their beliefs. The idea is of distinctive states of mind or states of being that are hard to orchestrate together or could be the dominant and exclusive source of a sense of self for various lengths of time. This gives a sense of the person's sense of self being emotionally hijacked (Goleman 1995) by a particular state; in CAT this is called a self-state. Mapping out the interaction of different states through a sequence of reciprocal roles can help us see where there was a gap in awareness of the procedural details of the loops connecting one state to another. This helps map and understand difficulties associated with what are clinically called 'personality disorders' or with the origins and effects of trauma on our emotional sense of self.

All this thinking between therapist and client is more easily achieved and kept track of by mapping it out on a piece of paper. Just seeing it develop and be spread out with a few pictures or key words and arrows on paper helps keep track and check for accuracy and usefulness. It helps promote a sense of shared ownership of the therapy journey. A diagram worked out with the client can help in the following ways.

- It can help therapist and client share in developing their understanding.
- By using pictures it can say what cannot be expressed or understood through words alone.
- Maps show more points of view and make links between the big picture and small detail, between past and present.
- Maps show how problems in one area of life could be connected to problems in another area.
- More complex problem patterns of relating can be more easily kept in mind and tracked.
- Using the map we can share feelings, work at recognising and revising patterns and learn new ways to feel more control and choice over our lives.
- We can check for accuracy and for detail, or make changes here and there more easily.
- Maps can show how several patterns may be acting simultaneously to orchestrate the actual choice of procedure for responding.
- Maps can help to manage the feeling of being exposed too intensely: instead of sitting face to face with a therapist, there is this third object – the map – between them, which creates a triangle.

From this experience of mapping out patterns to help develop the reformulation it is clear that the important goal of working together in an open and transparent way is made more effective by mapping side by side with the client rather than doing the map for the client; mapping as a process of collaboration is popular with CAT therapists.

Maps can be made with staff teams, describing difficult moments, or particularly helpful and therapeutic moments.

In recent years, a growing number of CAT practitioners have put much more emphasis on the process of mapping as an aid to building an open, transparent and developing relationship where an understanding of why, how and what the client's problems are and how the therapy can help emerge hand in hand. This helps to mitigate the ever-present risk of doing the therapy for the client or the client experiencing it as being done to them.

Therapists vary between those who develop the map and write the letter from the map and those who write about the target problems and target problem procedures in detail in the letter and develop the map subsequently and collaboratively from the shared and emotionally focused experience of reading the letter. There are arguments for working both ways, but in any case, in the first few sessions of therapy it can always be a great help to make together sketches of patterns, loops and orchestrations of reciprocal roles capturing common elements to several stories, linking past and present.

Active phase in the middle of therapy

Once reciprocal roles have been identified during a CAT, the aim is to select one or two specific examples of these overarching relational patterns that the client wants to change in the active, middle phase of the therapy. For example, the reciprocal role may be 'Neglecting in relation to Neglected', so a target problem might be, 'I don't know how to be in relationships.' A general aim that would offer an alternative to their neglecting way of life might be, 'I want to have kind and generous relationships.' This would be something a person would like to achieve and is likely to be expressed in fairly general terms, as they may not know how to achieve it. By contrast, a specific exit or way forward from their self-defeating procedure would be a description of something they can actually do, such as, 'I will be generous towards other people and treat myself kindly.' This new procedure will need to be enacted in various concrete ways, such as developing social stories about more adaptive procedures together.

The middle phase of CAT involves moving from rethinking the patterns behind problems to practising recognising the patterns and working at ways of revising them or finding new patterns that are called exits. It can be helpful to spell these out on a sheet of paper as a way of rating progress week by week, or to mark on the map where recognition of patterns and exits takes place.

These can also be drawn on a chart in lots of ways (using pictures or symbols). Clients can be asked two questions: first, whether they remember or recognise the problem patterns, and second, whether they can identify and try out alternative, more helpful patterns or exits from patterns during the week. How much change has occurred can be marked on a line between 'no change' and 'lots of change'. There are many creative ways of devising rating scales; the key is to come up with something together that the client finds meaningful. Using a rating scale each week helps to focus therapy and encourage discussion about what is working well and where the roadblocks are. However, often people find it hard to remember whether or not they have done or noticed something connected with their new procedure. In addition, many of our clients do not have the level of abstract thinking that lets them define and link various events to their new procedure. It can be just as helpful to walk round the map each week and see where a different feeling, thought or experience might have arisen. Within the therapy room, the reciprocal roles from where the client's procedures stem will often be in play; as they recount events in their life, or as they relate to the therapist, links between these events and accounts and the relevant replacement procedures can be spotted. The therapist can then relate this information to the therapy goals and support clients to fill in a rating scale. Discussions may become enriched if clients then associate doing this with other events.

How change is achieved in the room and with the wider team

Vygotsky's work on the process of change sees change occurring through activity; people are not frozen in the moment but are active beings who can show us what they are like through their actions and movements. Instrumental action (learning) may issue from a diffuse, vague and unordered feeling about how a person is positioned, which then is brought forth into action or a higher mental activity. Learning Theory describes how change occurs at a pre-linguistic level, outside higher level thinking. Change occurs through associational learning. When the felt experience of the therapeutic relationship offers new ways and wider options, when the client experiences being able to be with the therapist in a way that is not trapped by previously frustrating procedures, then change happens. Most research into change in therapy shows that life events outside the therapy are a major factor, and the next most influential factor is the therapeutic relationship. CAT tools help therapists to stay in a therapeutic relationship. Ruptures also are a key factor. If the therapist is able to address something going wrong in a non-defensive way, clients can see how change can occur constructively.

When working with complex clients, one hour a week for a limited number of sessions may be insufficient. The therapeutic leverage may be the staff team; staff may have unwittingly been nudged into unhelpful reciprocal role procedures that originate with the client but also resonate with them. This is often why difficult relationships get stuck and the client does not seem to change or develop. Therefore, in CAT, a lot of work is aimed at staff teams. This work involves using CAT tools to help the staff become more aware of the limited roles they may have slid into. Recognising their own reciprocal roles with the client lets them develop more flexible and versatile approaches that enhance their client's opportunity and ability to try out healthier options.

Goodbye letters

Ending therapy is an essential part of CAT and is talked about throughout the therapy. A way of helping this conversation to happen is to use a pie chart to mark off each session as it occurs. At the end of therapy, letters to say goodbye are exchanged. These letters should include a summary of the therapy, what has been achieved and further work identified if necessary. It does not repeat the reformulation letter, but reviews progress, what has changed and what has been achieved. It also acknowledges the 'work in progress' nature of these achievements and expresses realistic hopes and encouragement. The letter also refers to the therapeutic relationship and how this developed, including threats and ruptures, as well as acknowledging disappointment, sadness and anger because of it ending.

Clients are encouraged to write a goodbye letter back to the therapist. Hopefully, the therapy will have been experienced as a trustworthy and respectful place, so these letters not only inform the therapist of the client's experience of therapy but also can offer ideas for service improvement.

There are major issues in using goodbye letters in intellectual disability services and a lot of adaptation is often necessary. The majority of our clients cannot write. Most of us have found that asking support workers to help clients write such a letter is often unsuccessful because support workers believe they need to write an appreciative letter; these polite letters lack the intimacy of many therapeutic relationships. We can give our clients the opportunity to tape or record their comments, which is useful for clients who can get together an overview of their therapy and express their experiences, but others would struggle with this. In this situation, in the CAT Special Interest Group in intellectual disabilities (see the next section for more information) we found that adapting the Six Part Story Method (6PSM) worked well. Both therapist and client in the therapy room each write their own 6PSM:

- Drawing one: therapist and client in the therapy room
- Drawing two: what the client wanted to achieve in therapy
- Drawing three: what hindered this
- Drawing four: what helped this

- Drawing five: a pivotal event
- Drawing six: how life will be now that therapy has finished.

Information about the CAT Special Interest Group for people working or supervising in intellectual disability services

A group of people using CAT in services for people with intellectual disabilities started a special interest group. This process first started in 1999, and since March 2004 the group has been meeting four times a year, at first led by Val Crowley. The March 2004 meeting was attended by a number of the authors of this book, such as Michelle Anwyl, Hilary Brown, Philip Clayton, Julie Lloyd, Pamela Mount, Nicola Murphy and David Wilberforce. The group has continued to expand (see www.acat.me.uk for information) and is open to anyone receiving or giving supervision in CAT intellectual disability services. At first we concentrated on adapting CAT tools to make them suitable for our clients, but right from the start we found that we learnt from each other as we exchanged ideas about how CAT could be useful. Our interchange of ideas and experiences, the opportunity to solve problems and share frustrations and a place where we can develop our identity as 'LD CAT workers' fuels our enthusiasm for this group. The idea for this book came out of the group when we surveyed the experiences members had in using CAT and realised that we had enough material to fill several books! We run various projects including two-day introduction courses on CAT for people working in intellectual disability services. We have one-day conferences every so often, at which a spread of presentations describe our members' work. We act as a resource for professionals wanting to know more about using CAT in specialist services. We also aim to inform and advise The Association of Cognitive Analytic Therapy not only about our work, but also about how advances made by the group can be useful for the whole association.

The Association of Cognitive Analytic Therapy

The Association of Cognitive Analytic Therapy (ACAT) is a registered charity (no 1141793) (www.acat.me.uk). Currently its UK membership is nearly 800 and it aims to educate health professionals and promote good standards of CAT. It is also a member of the International Cognitive Analytic Therapy Association (ICATA) (www.internationalcat.org).

ACAT has an online library, a printed journal and an online newsletter. It runs a wide range of training courses, from one-day events and two-day introduction courses, through to two-year training. The two-year training achieves the academically accredited award of CAT practitioner (and an extension by research into an MSc) and practitioners are also accredited by the Centre for Workforce Intelligence (Department for Health), as psychological therapists. ACAT also runs a two-year further psychotherapy training following which people may apply for registration as psychotherapists, as well as accredited supervisor training. Many members of the CAT Special Interest Group in intellectual disabilities have become accredited CAT practitioners, doing most of their accredited and supervised cases with people with intellectual disabilities. ACAT also offers other special interest groups, as well as regional groups. There is also an annual residential conference and every two years ACAT members can attend the international conference held in a range of countries.

About this book

This book is divided into three main sections. The first section describes using ideas from CAT to inform working with people with intellectual disabilities. In Chapter 2, Philip Clayton gives information about adaptations of useful tools that originated in mental health work for assessment and treatment and some tools developed in CAT specifically with intellectual disability work in mind (see Appendices 1, 2 and 3 for examples of the tools). Adapting and inventing tools to assist using this approach is ongoing, so it may be worthwhile contacting ACAT to see what the current state of development is, if you are reading this chapter some time after it was printed. Chapter 3, by Julie Lloyd and Hilary Brown describes how CAT is being used in services for people with intellectual disabilities and includes a survey of CAT practitioners' experiences of this approach. The chapter also contains a case study about working with a parent of a young adult with intellectual disabilities. Chapter 4, by Jo Varela, explores ideas about how the concept of intellectual disabilities is a mix of neuro-cognitive and social construction. Varela considers the effects on people and services of the predominantly negative concept of 'intellectual disability' and how such labelling may lead to people being offered different and often fewer opportunities. She contrasts this with CAT's therapeutic stance. Chapter 5, by Steve Potter and Julie Lloyd, explores the idea of 'Relational Intelligence', which places intelligence as a shared property or limitation between us, rather than an individual's possession or absence. This idea stems from CAT's radically social view of 'the self' in which a person's ability or disability is seen to function in relation with other people. This is followed in Chapter 6 by a description of a checklist developed by Steve Potter, which describes the typical relationships helpers can be pulled into or push their clients into. Chapter 7 is an account of some research by Julie Lloyd in which she sought to discover what type of intelligences were required for people with severe intellectual disabilities to understand the concept of reciprocal roles and obtained results that she did not expect!

The second section of the book looks at the application of CAT when working with people with intellectual disabilities in community services and examples of applying CAT in common areas of community work. It opens with a chapter by David Wilberforce, which explores the problems faced by people who require care and how we relate to this. Wilberforce illustrates his journey towards finding out the meanings of being cared for and of being a carer through a number of case studies, both from his clinical work and his reflection on a tiny everyday incident that happened whilst he was out walking. Chapter 9 by Helen Elford and Zoe Ball, describes a CAT approach to working with staff teams, especially staff in assessment and treatment services and staff working in community services, with people whose relationships and behaviours are challenging. CAT is used here to help staff hold in mind what they long for and what they dread, with an example of how a team moved towards offering realistic care that was good enough. Chapter 10, by Jo Varela, looks at what CAT can offer to staff who are faced with managing people with challenging behaviour. Staff working in challenging behaviour services have the most stressful and difficult tasks within intellectual disability services and seeking to address the unhelpful reciprocal roles that can unwittingly develop within the staff team is proving to be one of the most useful applications of CAT. Chapter 11, by Julie Lloyd and Steve Potter, is a reflection and discussion of the roles helpers can get into when working with people with severe autism and how a CAT understanding can help when working with people who are unable to dance the relational dances we long for. Chapter 12, by Hilary Brown and Julie Lloyd describes common difficulties in implementing the Mental Capacity Act and how CAT can help to make sense of the decision-making process at its heart.

The third section of the book focuses on CAT approaches to offenders who have intellectual disabilities. Chapter 13 raises an issue that is rarely referred to in the case histories of people with intellectual disabilities who end up in specialist forensic services; that many have a history of domestic violence. Michelle Anwyl and Pamela Mount consider the relationship between domestic violence as an often-ignored history and subsequent offending from a CAT perspective. Chapter 14, by Philip Clayton and Simon Crowther, looks at the development of a CAT therapeutic community for detained offenders with personality disorders and intellectual disabilities, and describes the impact on patients and staff of relational perspectives within the ward. Chapter 15, by Nicola Murphy, describes a treatment programme that combines the relational approach of CAT and the skills development approach of the Good Life model for offenders, including some of the creative methods used to explain concepts of CAT to the group members who have intellectual disabilities. Chapter 16, also by Nicola Murphy, contains a case study describing CAT with a detained offender with mild intellectual disabilities. This case presented many relational challenges, which Murphy writes about in a thoughtful manner. Chapter 17, by Perry Morrison, continues this theme with several case illustrations of working with community clients who are attending services for offenders with intellectual disabilities.

In the afterword, the authors reflect on their experiences of writing the book and their central message. Last, there is a glossary to help readers cope with both CAT and intellectual disability service jargon and appendices with copies of useful CAT tools.

Chapter 2

The Adaptation and Adoption of Tools in Cognitive Analytic Therapy for People who have an Intellectual Disability and Their Carers

Philip Clayton

Introduction
This chapter will outline the developments that have been made in the adaptation and creation of tools and the incorporation of 'off the shelf' materials that have helped in the process of delivering the Cognitive Analytic Therapy (CAT) model to people who have an intellectual disability and in measuring change. I will also attempt to place this in the context of the therapeutic relationship, however I would recommend that further training and reading should be pursued if greater exploration, clarification and integration is required.

A brief background
It is well known that the written word and the complex use of language presents as a real problem when conveying material in therapy for people who have an intellectual disability. CAT is no exception and although the use of language is central to the overall therapeutic alliance and the understanding of enactments, it is important to consider the way in which language is presented and how material is used in order that true meaning is experienced in therapy. As in all therapies it should not be assumed that because the therapist understands what he/she is talking

about, the patient also has the same understanding and vice versa. CAT therapists are constantly aware that the relational manifestation of problematic reciprocal role enactments are more than likely to be acted out in the therapy room, and this might include such roles as 'Criticising – Criticised, try to please'. The patient may nod or say yes to questions or enquiry for fear of criticism without perhaps truly understanding what is being 'discussed'. It is well known that suggestibility and acquiescence are interpersonal attributes (Gugjonson 2001, 2003) that may skew what might seem a collaborative process, particularly with people who have an intellectual disability. There may also be other manifestations of a confused communication, such as the 'secondary handicap', in which the person exacerbates their disability as a defence against the original disability or trauma (Sinason 1992).

Summarising during sessions may indeed be seen as a way of the therapist confirming what has been talked about in session, however it is clearly important that the patient has the same understanding. Helping the patient to be able to convey his/her own version of the therapy session can be incredibly empowering for the patient, but it can also be a clear indication of mismatch between patient and therapist, time to perhaps rethink what is happening in the room. It is therefore imperative that the therapist is cognisant of possible mismatches in understanding as early as possible.

Several attempts have been made to simplify the tools used in CAT to make the framework accessible to people with an intellectual disability whilst at the same time maintaining adherence to the model. These include the rewriting of the psychotherapy file, a rewritten paper and computerised Personality Structure Questionnaire (PSQ) and the more fundamental but equally important simplification of language, examples being the use of the word 'map' to replace sequential diagrammatic reformulation and 'patterns' for procedures.

The adoption of technology and graphic support through the use of common tools available on the internet has also been a rich resource that the CAT Special Interest Group (SIG) (for people who work in the field of intellectual disabilities) has been quick to exploit, as well as the more obvious such as speaking a CAT letter onto a compact disk or onto a voice memo or Dictaphone.

Pictures and drawings have to be the most valuable asset in the toolbox for the clinician working in this field (indeed any modality), and within the model of CAT there is a real sense that the relational can be captured in an instant by using drawings and images that depict the client in a relational position with 'the other' in a way that is immediately understandable.

For example, in the following 'map' (courtesy of Lynsey Nuttall, trainee Art Psychotherapist and Karim Baxter, trainee Clinical Psychologist) there is a clear depiction of a 'bullying – bullied' reciprocal role with the dilemma of 'When I am feeling bullied I get into a state where I feel I only have two options; either I hide and bottle up my feeling so much so that I begin to feel as though I will explode (and I do) *or* I do and say things to make people feel uncomfortable. Either way *I* end up being the bully.' There are loops out of the 'not knowing what to do state' that enables the person involved to have a visual representation of exits. These include interpersonal skills, self-soothing, getting help from others, distraction and anger regulation. Clearly the prerequisite to using these exits is a recognition that the problem is occurring and following a period of 'hit and miss' in not finding the most useful exit (perhaps too high an expectation loomed!), change might occur. The ability to communicate with the person who was bullying was the main relational exit. I will let the reader try to work out the patterns and exits!

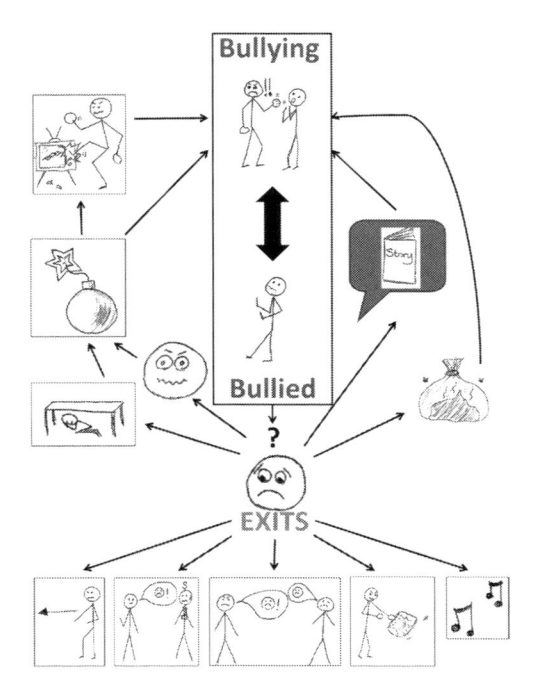

Figure 2.1: A 'map' describing a 'bullying – bullied' reciprocal role with 'patterns'

'In the beginning' and links to the therapeutic process

Dr Roz King was one of the first practitioners to develop a simplified version of a CAT tool. Her psychotherapy file (see Appendix 1) was rewritten in a way that made seemingly complex structural sentences more understandable. It also allowed the therapist to help the person with an intellectual disability adopt a more straightforward approach to thinking about their own target problem(s). A recognition that people with an intellectual disability can engage in the pouring over of a seemingly complex tool and make sense of a relational conceptualisation of their difficulties was immediately apparent. And so, the CAT Special Interest Group was born.

As the Special Interest Group continued to meet and share stories about how CAT could be used, it soon became apparent that this versatility of tool inventiveness, alongside relational attunement with the client in the room was the key. This is, of course, not to say that this is not the intention of all therapists, but the belief of the practitioner has to be that an understanding can be shared, and this can only be done if the therapist is truly aligned to the patient's Zone of Proximal Development (ZPD), in terms of the coming together in understanding. Winnicott (1990, in Jacobs 1995) referred to this relational containment as the 'facilitating environment'. There is a sense that the therapist is recreating that which the (good) mother might have created, thus suggesting a collaborative (playful) context; this he called the 'potential space'. In attachment theory, Bowlby (2005) coins the term 'secure attachment figure', the capacity of the caregiver to remain in the position of the balanced provider of emotional boundaries. Stern (1985) has written extensively on the process of attunement, an empathic connection between the mother and child, which nurtures growth.

So, presenting tools to people who are confused by them may have limited value. Indeed this might have a paradoxical affect of distancing, perhaps reinforcing unhealthy reciprocal roles and causing ruptures to the therapeutic encounter. It is as if the 'snag' of 'I want to be with my therapist but he/she is making me feel that I don't understand; so I give up' is created. It is the working through with the person in identifying relevant and useful tools that is the initial objective of therapy.

Further to this and in alliance to this thinking, Beail (2013, p.9) refers to how psychodynamic psychotherapists should consider the individual cognitive development of the patient. He writes that 'Therapists need to work within the client's vocabulary, facilitate communication by alternative means and help give meaning to what they are trying to communicate'. Again, the notion of being with the person, in time and space, and developing a consensus regarding the 'problem' is the essential goal in the early stages in therapy and necessary to return to when perhaps the focus is avoided.

Of course, there are difficulties when considering how much the therapist nurtures the patient. Dependency could be fostered in the relationship if the therapist is unaware of his/her own needs and is enacting, for example, an *ideally caring to perfectly cared for* reciprocal role. However this is most likely to be evident in the supervisory process and considered, as Bowlby (2008) did a necessary process to be worked through.

Naming the difficulties

Reformulation, the process by which CAT therapists rephrase relational concepts into a narrative, is the next difficult conceptual tool that requires imagination in order that the therapist and patient have a truly collaborative representation of the target problem (the initial aim of therapy) and the underlying procedures (patterns) that maintain the problem. It is very well understood that people who have an intellectual disability struggle to think abstractly (Kirkland 2010) and that it is far more probable that a visual representation is likely to make sense (Lloyd 2013, Chapter 7, Wells 2009), particularly if the person doesn't have the ability to read or write. The use of other tools that reinforce or give added value can be used, however caution should be exercised as confusion might result, i.e. 'which one do I use'. Maintaining clarity, focus and keeping this simple and understandable in the early stages of therapy is essential in sustaining collaboration and maintaining containment.

Augmenting pictures with an audio version of reformulation is especially useful, as the therapist might be focusing on a particular pattern, which could be referred to in the audio and linked to a drawing in the pictorial representation (and vice versa). Further to this, a possible sequencing limitation, which would otherwise be left to the conceptual abilities of the person, can be visually represented, step by step on the 'map', 'picture' or 'diagram' (SDR) to aid in the process of reformulation.

It has to be said here that the term 'intellectual disability' crosses a rather tricky terrain in terms of what to use and adapt. Many people with an intellectual disability have language, can read, can write and have the skills to manage written reformulation and reasonably complex maps, whilst others may need significant help. It is left to the skills of the therapist (with the person in the room) to ascertain what is needed, pushing where it moves into a shared understanding at the right time and with the tools at his/her disposal.

Therapists of all persuasions have encountered difficulties in the naming of target problems as the focus of therapy with the telling of the story perhaps being too difficult, and although the skills and attributes, training and supervision of therapists all contribute to maximising the potential of the client to tell his or her story, there are clearly times when this requires a different approach. The use of story books, reference to favourite films, heroes, villains and metaphor are not outside the imagination of anyone, including those of us who have an intellectual disability. A favourite tool used by many CAT therapists is the Six Part Story Method developed by Dent-Brown (described on p.296), which enables the therapist to explore more indirectly, the relational positions through what I would consider (as in all visual enterprise) a sign mediated method and consistent with the CAT model (Vygotsky 1978). The storytelling encourages the exploration of identification with the characters being described and to perhaps think about otherwise warded off or disavowed feelings.

We have all, in our practice, experienced the use of metaphor that described a situation, wish or idealised dream far better than ordinary words could ever have described them. We have also witnessed the effects of marginalisation, hate crime and abuse and the internalised role identification, all of which are likely to be described either literally or in metaphor. As in all therapeutic settings, it is the meaning that is important. As in all therapeutic settings, it is also the supervision that allows the therapist/carer to make sense of his or her transference and counter-transference feelings (reciprocal role processes/enactments) that may distort the meaning. As the reformulation process progresses it is essential that these feelings are discussed in order that the eliciting or recruiting role played by the patient is not being enacted by the therapist or carer.

Specific adaptations and other tools[1]

Appendices 1–3 contain three adapted psychotherapy files. King's file makes simple adaptations to the language used with simple choices, whilst Steward and Clayton have similar language interpretations with additional colourful illustrations. Bancroft uses diagrammatic representation with language to illustrate each trap, dilemma and snag (see example of snag in Figure 2.2).

---

[1] Psychotherapy files (King 2002, Steward and Clayton 2004 and Bancroft 2009, available at www.acat.me.uk)

The pie chart[2]
This is used to orientate the patient to the duration of the therapy. A chart of 16/24 segments indicates the number of sessions and at the end of each session a segment is coloured in.

I want to...
but...

Figure 2.2: 'Snag'

The adapted Personality Structure Questionnaire (PSQ)[3]
This adaptation (see Appendix 4) was made from standard PSQ, as there was a clear need to make this more understandable. Nicola McNamara, a speech and language therapist, was instrumental in this adaptation, changing the language to make it more accessible to people who had a moderate intellectual disability. David Glasgow, a Consultant Clinical and Forensic Psychologist collaborated and placed the assessment on a computer with additional voice accompaniment. The original PSQ is validated with reliability but the adapted assessment is not, however Tony Ryle in reply to the author suggested that the tool should still be used as it helps clinically.

The Six Part Story[4]
This is not an adapted tool but an adopted/incorporated tool that has found great popularity and utility with CAT therapists. It can be used to help reformulation and goodbye letters.

The process is a co-created enterprise between therapist and client. The dynamic nature of the story means that the character's task leads them to action to which the environment responds. This sequence is paralleled

---

2 King 2002, available at www.acat.me.uk
3 Clayton *et al.* 2003, revised 2013, available at www.acat.me.uk
4 Dent-Brown 2011; Lahad 1992

in the reformulation letter and maps as well as other CAT elements such as the Target Problem Procedure (TPP) or 'patterns' (Dent-Brown 2011). The six drawings involve:

- a make-believe character and setting
- task
- problem/unhelpful factors
- helpful factors
- main action
- final outcome.

Asking questions may provide further information. What leaps out to you about your story? Describe the story from the point of view of each of the objects in it. What would you call the story? Is any of this story familiar to you in your life? Which character or element in it is most like you? What does it teach us? Answers can help us understand our client's beliefs, affect, social aims, imagination, cognition and physical sense of themselves. From this we may get information to develop a map of their main reciprocal role procedures.

Draw on your emotions and draw on your relationships[5]

Again this is not an adaptation, but again these two books have become firm favourites in helping therapists depict relational difficulties in a vivid, clear and descriptive format. They use 'creative ways to explore; express and understand important feelings/understand and work through important relationship issues' (Sunderland and Engleheart 2012, Sunderland and Armstrong 2011). There is a comprehensive selection of figures, images, contexts and metaphor presented through the use of line drawings, pictures diagrams and connected activities that can be adapted for use in many different settings.

Working with objects

King (2005) has worked with objects as a way to understand the person's individual subjective experiences. She describes how buttons can represent relational 'positions':

> Kim, when choosing a button to represent herself, selected a very small button because she felt that she could not do anything, whilst she chose a very large button for me. It was as if in facing the cognitive difference between us she felt completely worthless and useless. It was

---

5 Sunderland and Engleheart 2012; Sunderland and Armstrong 2011

good to see that when she repeated the exercise towards the end of therapy she chose buttons of much more equal size. (pp.10–14)

The significance of a perceived differential in power relations is strikingly apparent here.

The helper's dance[6]

Potter expands our thinking in relation to the 'dances' we engage in with our clients and the systems within which we work. His ideas can be extended through the use of shared case formulation and reflective practice. There is a sense that we are all in some form of reciprocal dance (which of course we are). In the helper's dance, we are invited to consider this from three relational positions (see Chapter 6).

CASE STUDY: INCORPORATING 1:1 CAT INTO INDIVIDUAL CARE PLANS[7]

This is similar to the shared case formulation but has structured tasks that enable the staff team and patient to remain in dialogue. Murphy writes:

> *Arising from 'staff awareness sessions' came the development of the 1:1 CAT care plan. On asking a patient how the nursing staff could help him to recognise his difficulties he made an excellent suggestion of incorporating all of the pictures from his symbolised SDR onto a 1:1 care plan (see Appendix 5). The patient identified that the nursing team asking him the direct questions would: a) aid recognition of his difficulties, b) involve staff in his work, thereby informing them when he was experiencing difficulties, and c) make it more difficult for him to avoid talking about the things he did not want to, or pretend he was happy ('happy face'), when he was not.*
>
> *With a different patient we used the same concept, but for different aims. At the end of a 16-session CAT, we had only managed to establish recognition. This was partly because the patient had identified that to change his unhelpful procedures of: a) Rejecting people before he perceived they would reject him and b) Keeping a 'brick wall' between himself and others, would mean letting people see the 'real him', and showing his vulnerabilities. He said that 'it is easier to be lonely than let people see the real me and risk rejection'. He also feared that to be vulnerable would lead others to take advantage of him.*

---

6 Potter 2013, Chapter 6

7 Murphy 2012

So, in this case the 1:1 care plan was completed on a weekly basis with a staff team with whom he had shared his SDR in a 'staff awareness session'. Doing this served a number of functions. As well as aiding in the process of recognition and entering into a dialogue specifically around his procedures, it was hoped that he would elaborate and thereby show staff a more vulnerable side, as he had done so in therapy. By doing this he would then come to learn that this did not lead to people rejecting him, or taking advantage of his vulnerabilities as he had feared. A further aim was that the staff team might see a different side of him. He was very adept at keeping people at a distance, and was not well liked by the staff team because of the self-defeating strategies he engaged in, (swearing at staff, sarcasm, sexually offensive rhetoric, attempting to get staff into trouble). I thereby also trusted that by seeing a different side to him as I had in therapy, which was warmer, caring and thoughtful, and other positive attributes, that the staff team would begin to like him, and facilitate more positive interactions, thereby resulting in him feeling that he could reveal more of his vulnerable side.

As the care plan was completed on a weekly basis between the end of therapy and the three-month follow-up session, the aim was also to then enable the patient to move from the 'period of contemplation' where he was considering whether he wanted to/could change to him feeling that change was possible. He could then have a further block of eight sessions for the process of revision.

Symbolised leaflets[8]

These have been developed for adults with intellectual disabilities who have some level of literacy. They are designed as a workbook that the person can keep. One leaflet is for adults living in a community setting, whilst the other is for those detained under the Mental Health Act in Secure Settings. The leaflets explain the process of CAT, how therapy can help, who else will be informed of the work, confidentiality, a decision path to gain true and valid consent, and pages to address any questions or worries the person may have. These leaflets are available from the ACAT website (www.acat.me.uk).

Measuring

The standard CAT rating sheets (see the ACAT website) can be accessible to people who have an intellectual disability (with minor adaptation) but

---

8   Murphy 2012

the use of alternative ways of visualising change is also useful. The use of ladders (indeed the snakes and ladders game board) as rating tools enables the patient to see where they might be in relation to their target problem. Again, the imagery based 'map' (SDR) can be used to create pictorial representations of the frequency that exits are used. Other formal and recognised means of measuring include CORE LD and The Inventory of Interpersonal Problems, IIP 32 or 64 (Horowitz *et al.* 2000).

The use of the contextual reformulation as a consultation tool – shifting the focus[9]

The sharing of CAT formulations with staff teams has become a significant tool in understanding and managing the manifestations of trauma, abuse, domestic violence and social demarcation that many people with intellectual disabilities experience and that may emerge in ways that are confounding to carers. It might be that carers are 'pulled into' reciprocal roles that increase the possibility of conflict, thereby creating an environment that is 'anti-therapeutic'. The carers may become demoralised, confused and perhaps feel helpless and useless. There may be 'splitting' in the staff team, whereby team members become mistrustful of each other, 'orchestrated' by the patient to meet an unmet need. It is here that the shared reformulation is able to help in locating what role the carer is being drawn into and finding a way to describe how the team as a whole can respond; see Clayton (2001, 2010), Fisher and Harding (2009), Lloyd and Williams (2003), Murphy (2008).

Summary

In this chapter I have attempted to illustrate the bringing together of some of the elements required when considering effective work with people who have an intellectual disability (and their carers) using CAT. I have referred to the tools that have proved to be useful to the clinicians who have been in dialogue for the last decade and that are readily available to anyone who wish to use them, but I would also like to stress that the versatility and inventiveness on the part of both the patient and therapist in the room will be what brings the encounter alive.

It is important to consider the following points.

- There may be a need to socialise the person to the model, again using materials that are the best fit to enable this to happen. Bancroft and Murphy (2009) call this the pre-formulation phase.

---

9 Carradice 2004

- The therapist works within the Zone of Proximal Development (ZPD) of the person in the room.
- Pay attention to the timing and complexity of interventions, i.e. reformulation, maps (as in any therapy, but this is more applicable for people with an intellectual disability).
- Assess the attention and concentration of the person in therapy. They may not be able to manage 50 minutes to an hour, perhaps they will need considerably less.
- Think about the number of sessions. It might be that someone who can only manage 30-minute sessions will require eight to ten sessions before reformulation and more space in the working phase.
- There may be other 'diagnostic' or relational complexities that alter the possible process and outcomes of therapy, such as autism (see Chapter 11). For those who find it hard to 'revise', it might be that the goal of understanding is the goal in itself (Bancroft and Murphy 2009). From this may come a greater awareness for those who are the carers, which might then lead to the shared formulation with team support and supervision (Carradice 2004; Clayton 2010; Lloyd and Williams 2003).
- Utilise any adaptations and tools available, using them flexibly and augmenting with media as explored above. It is very clear that visual representation is key to making language accessible.
- Use the tools available to help the patient to work collaboratively.
- Contextual diagrams can help teams with particularly confusing and challenging cases.
- Encourage carers to think about the way in which they 'dance' with those they care for.
- Consider how giving information through leaflets enhanced by images can help the patient be grounded and understand who and where they are in proximity to their environment.
- Give the patient the opportunity to share what they have done in therapy with carers, legal representatives and other providers through the use of care plans. This empowers the patient in a way that engages others in collaboration through their own means and reinforces positive relationships.

Chapter 3

How Cognitive Analytic Therapy is Being Used in Services for People with Intellectual Disabilities

Julie Lloyd and Hilary Brown

Introduction

Cognitive Analytic Therapy (CAT), with its understanding of reciprocal roles and procedures, informs people working in intellectual disabilities in a number of ways. Of course it provides a model for individual therapy that can be tailored to individuals and to their level and style of communication and emotional understanding, but it also informs the way we think about the dynamics of the care-giving relationship in families or paid work settings, and it can help people to name and reflect on dynamics that are otherwise left in a taboo zone where they cannot be managed or mitigated.

Presenting problems

People with intellectual disabilities present with ordinary and with 'special' issues. CAT has been offered to individuals with intellectual disabilities for a range of problems, including trauma (both in childhood and in adulthood), bullying, loss, abuse, mood disregulation, self-harm, morbid obesity and non-compliance with diabetes management, challenging behaviour and also as an adjunct alongside social care approaches dealing with problems with finances, conflicts with neighbours, difficulties with housing and inappropriate calls to the emergency services. Working using CAT for these referrals requires the practitioner to clarify and agree what the target problems are for their clients and often with key people in their support networks. A referral may come about following a specific incident, but a CAT approach involves understanding this incident as an example of a general, wider pattern of a client's interactions and helping others to decode its origins and significance. For example, the presenting issue may have been for shouting and screaming at other people, which, in the course of the assessment phase, comes to be seen as an exemplar of a wider abusing and controlling pattern. That insight may then be shared with family members or with a staff group, with the client's permission or, if that person does not have mental capacity to make this decision (see Chapter 12), if it is deemed to be in their best interests.

CAT approaches are thereby used to enhance the routine work of intellectual disability services and to contain difficult feelings experienced by care staff, family members and service users. Using CAT principles to inform this kind of work is probably more common in intellectual disability services, than individual therapeutic work. Some people with intellectual disabilities need others to hold an appreciation of their history and their ways of managing difficult feelings, but also need help feeding these insights back into networks that can become rigid and unresponsive, blaming or neglecting. Hence, in assessing people with suspected dementia (especially people with Down's Syndrome), in addition to the normal locally developed assessment protocol used in a service, CAT practitioners have found it helpful to think about and describe the relational issues between the staff team, families and carers and when conducting psychometric and functional assessments, CAT ideas about relational intelligence (see Chapter 5) are useful to help the care team think about how the client's functioning is affected by the intelligence that is around them, not just the intelligence that is their own individual property.

One such example of how CAT may be used to enhance standard clinical work is offered here in the form of a network diagram. A speech and language therapist found that CAT mapping was very useful in helping to approach those staff teams who could not follow her recommendations regarding the management of clients with severe dysphagia. Swallowing problems, which occur at a greater rate in the learning disabled population, are associated with two great risks: choking and aspiration (food or fluids entering the lungs instead of the stomach, leading to chest infections and possibly pneumonia). Colomb (Colomb and Lloyd 2012), developed this map to draw out the typical roadblocks to collaborative working that arose between staff teams and speech therapists, with the sought-after collaborative position described in the middle. She said that taking this relational overview encouraged her to challenge her own default position, which would have been to take difficult situations personally, feeling attacked and rubbished, resulting in her becoming defensive and defeated. Instead, she used the map to help her discuss with the staff what they wanted, what they dreaded and what they could achieve practically around her input. By describing their dynamic in these terms she found working relationships improved, becoming more productive and straightforward.

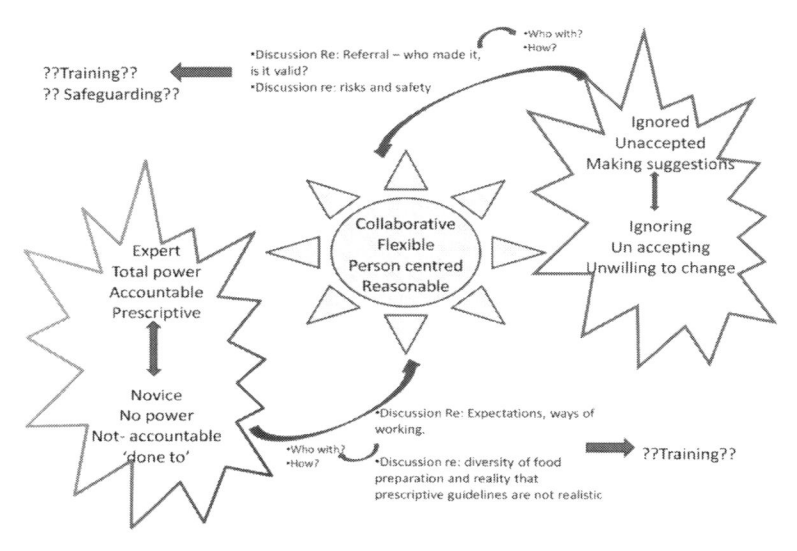

Figure 3.1: Common Relational Patterns for support staff and professionals when dealing with dysphagia

Adapting CAT to the intellectual disability context

So what elements of CAT provide the most useful ways of thinking about the needs of this group? A small survey of members of the Association of Cognitive Analytic Therapy's Special Interest Group for people working in intellectual disability services explored what CAT practitioners found most useful in using CAT. The top feature they identified was CAT's concept of reciprocal roles, particularly as a way of understanding what was going on in the room in an individual therapy, and as a way of thinking about how these same roles were prone to be enacted amongst the client's staff team. In this way, reciprocal roles provide one explanation for parallel processing. One person commented that understanding this allowed work to be done around issues for which the client has no words. CAT practitioners described how they could map out these roles, making use of each person's own idiosyncratic way of explaining things (words, pictures and other images), and how this process helped them to figure out what was happening. However, most of the CAT practitioners surveyed also said that it was essential to avoid language that was too complicated or 'jargonny'. They said that adapting mainstream CAT tools from adult mental health often needed considerable creativity (see Chapter 2 and Appendices 1, 2 and 3 for adaptation examples).

Many people reported that CAT's time-limited approach to therapy was very useful, particularly in the wider context of austerity in the NHS, because offering a limited number of sessions meant that the work needed to be very focused on the target problem. However, most people found that the traditional number of sessions offered in CAT for people in adult mental health services (16) needed extending so that they could work at a pace that was more in tune with their client's needs. They also talked about the importance of individual work being supplemented by working with that client's staff team and of the need for this to be acknowledged in training and accreditation guidelines. Extending the therapy in this way would not result in an open-ended commitment but in a finite number of sessions that would be agreed with the client. So, for example, we would agree on 24 or 32 sessions because one of the most valuable components of time-limited therapy is the opportunity it presents for working with the ending. As many clients have experienced very abrupt endings that are difficult to process (i.e. support staff leaving, often with little warning or acknowledgement), CAT with this group involves careful signalling of the ending in each session and a more intensive focus on it for the last four sessions. The aim is neither to avoid processing the ending nor to prolong the therapy. This can sometimes be difficult – there have been times when well-meaning support staff have not brought the client for their final session as they wished to avoid the client becoming upset, or have suggested extending the therapy because they fear the loss of containment that the therapy has provided; this means that staff may also need help with the ending of the therapy and an explicit 'handover' of the insights and ongoing needs for containment and change that the therapy has uncovered. One approach to this is to assist the client (by acting as the client's secretary) to write their own discharge letter to the staff team about what the client is seeking to change and how the staff could help them to do that. This means that the client shares their own understanding of their difficulties with the staff team, upending their usual dependence on others to articulate need now that the client recognises what has been blocking their development. This means that the therapist effectively writes two goodbye letters, one *to* the client and the other *with* the client for the extended network of family members and carers involved in their lives. This also models the keeping of a boundary, which is often a new concept for the person and unfortunately for their supporters.

Deciding when to offer CAT-based interventions

When making a decision about whether or not they should offer CAT to a client or staff team, CAT practitioners reported taking a number of factors into account. Care staff cannot be expected to know about CAT, so practitioners use an adapted leaflet describing CAT (see Chapter 2 on adapted tools) so that clients or staff teams had sufficient information about CAT and why it had been selected. Some practitioners selected CAT if they noticed that the client appeared to be able to describe their feelings, thoughts and behaviours in some way (such as via pictures, stories and in words) while others would be guided more by the recognition of difficult reciprocal roles, splits or contradictions within the person or their network. All practitioners considered that the problematic issue needed to have a relational or interactional component to it.

If the selection of CAT has been made on the basis of the content then a subsequent evaluation is made about how much of this can be addressed with, and held by, the person themselves and how much of the work needs to be done with their care network. If a person's level of disability is too great for individual direct therapy then work could centre on the care staff. Practitioners responding to the survey spoke of times when CAT would be offered as part of a wider package, such as offering a functional analysis conducted using the principles of Applied Behavioural Analysis to someone with severe autism and then using CAT's mapping techniques with the staff team to help them understand the reciprocal roles that they get caught up in when they relate to the client in the context of their challenging behaviour. Managing one's own responses to challenging behaviour is akin to the work all therapists do in managing counter-transference reactions by resisting being drawn into collusive relating, but in this case with more extreme triggers and 'invitations' to reciprocate in unhelpful roles. Narratives of blame and retaliation can emerge when these processes are not reflected on, and these in turn may fuel abusive responses. Tuning into CAT's dialogic way of thinking and of hearing is therefore essential when reading referrals from, or explanations of, difficult behaviours or unfathomable aspects of the person's responses to their environments, their bodies and to 'others' among whom they live (see Haydon-Laurelut and Wilson 2011; Haydon-Laurelut 2013).

Using maps

CAT practitioners considered that most people particularly gained from the maps that were drawn in therapy, a view confirmed in research by Wells (2009) who asked people with intellectual disabilities who had experienced CAT what they thought of their experience. Practitioners found that clients particularly responded to the idea of getting into a vicious circle (a trap). One practitioner used a picture of a roundabout with 'exits' on it to help her client hold on to the felt sense of 'going round and round in circles' and of not being able to change. Norma's map described how, in response to being ignored, she developed a pattern of 'over-talking' to try to keep people with her, but instead it has the effect of shutting them out and making them go away. Her exits involved stopping and taking in the other person, getting to know them and allowing them into her world. Her therapist worked with her to practise these pauses and to tolerate small patches of silence in the sessions; taking turns and listening were also made explicit as skills and as ways of engaging others. Her 'map' (in the literal as well as figurative sense) is included here with thanks to Norma and to her therapist (Figure 3.2).

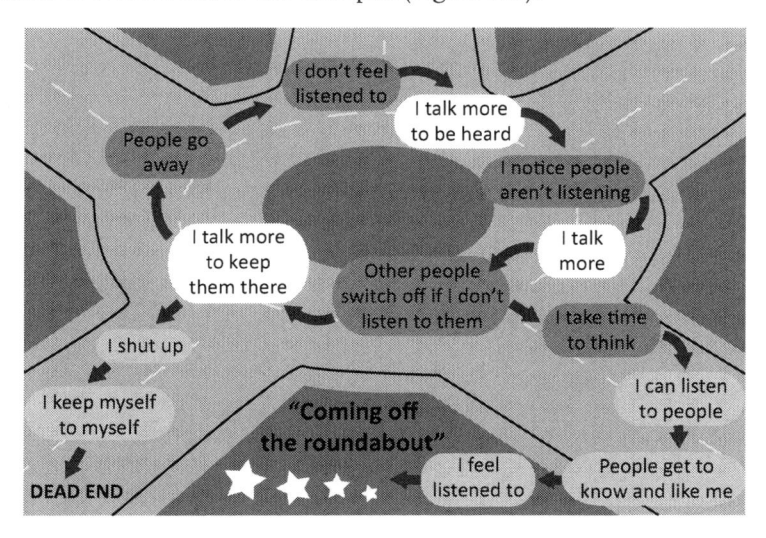

Figure 3.2: Coming off the roundabout

Clients also liked having something to take away and use after the therapy because this helped to remind them that their difficulties could be described. Maps were not the only visual metaphors that operated in this way; clients also liked the process of having drawn flashcards or other visual prompts to remind them of the new alternatives developed collaboratively in therapy.

In the survey practitioners were also asked to name contra-indications to offering CAT and said that they would not usually do so at a time of chaotic crises or where there were safeguarding and serious risk issues. These had to be addressed first so that the client was able to focus on the bigger picture. They also found that it was helpful if staff team members were willing to reflect on their relationship with the client and, where it emerged during the therapy that this was not happening, to challenge this and perhaps start seeking an alternative placement for the person. A poor service acts as a pervasive snag for many people with intellectual disabilities in that the client is pushed into unhelpful states as a result of neglect, control or goading, but is also put down when they try to operate in new ways. A difficulty for staff teams was that, although there were many positive relationships where staff were caring and accepting, advocating for their clients and welcoming of different professionalism, there was a constant pull back into less helpful ways of relating when services were overstretched and stressed. This is especially so in the current climate when challenges are exacerbated by constant radical service 'redesigns', during which there is a real risk that the organisation at large, as well as staff and clients, will fall back on their default positions and operate in their previously unrecognised and unhelpful reciprocal role enactments.

A common theme affecting clients' engagement in therapy was being wary or cut off from services. Building a therapeutic alliance can take time. When clients were asked what they wanted to gain from therapy, quite a few CAT practitioners noticed that clients would quote something they had been taught, such as 'I wish to be more independent.' CAT's dialogic approach helps workers to be aware of the discovery of one of the main contributors to dialogic theory, Bakhtin, that all our words are words that someone else has already said, for example, there is a sense in which we are always quoting significant others in our lives. On hearing a client make such a statement, the therapist may wonder who is actually talking here (i.e., could it be the voice of their care manager at their annual review) so what does 'more independent' mean to this person? Often clients with intellectual disability have experienced a lack of influence over their lives and can feel very 'done-to', and this may be brought into the therapy, so we always have to question whether the client believes they are in therapy to be told off. If the words we use with our clients are outside their Zone of Proximal Development (Vygotsky 1978), they may end up 'parroting' them rather than internalising them as a helpful framework. Similarly, we work with many people with intellectual disabilities who have absorbed hateful and disparaging words that they replay as part of their self to self talk (the conversations people have with themselves) and that leave them little room to feel respected or grown up. For example, one person spoke of how she had heard herself described as a 'piece of rubbish' and carried this with her.

Tuning into the internal dialogue of the service culture

These narratives of dehumanising 'others', of entitlement, blame and retaliation provide the rationale for, fuel and excuse abusive interactions. By framing a person with difficulties as someone who is deliberately behaving in ways that aggravate the staff person, or that defy their attempts to stay in control, they lay the groundwork for punitive responses. By voicing, without reflection, how hard it is to be the one always having to look after others while your own needs go unmet or are put on hold, a person steps into the moral high ground from whence they can grant themselves a kind of absolution, or what Tomita refers to as a 'moral holiday' (Tomita 1990, p.172). A person talks themselves into acting in a way that they would normally regard as out of character. They find themselves responding without understanding or reflection, without brakes or inner censure. Cutting corners, rough handling, depersonalised care, teasing that slips into undermining and hurtful taunts, attempts at containment that tip over into acts of cruelty and brutality and 'joining' the enactment of these roles when they are played out by colleagues may all follow from this kind of reasoning. Recent exposure of bullying at Winterbourne View Hospital provides one example of these dynamics (Flynn 2012).

Students of disability services will recognise that the internal dialogue of the service culture has proceeded through various pendulum swings, which in CAT we can helpfully think about as dilemmas in which the many 'middle-ground' options go un-noted. From infantilising people with disabilities we move to demanding their independence in ways that often lead to lack of appropriate assistance and to isolation rather than engagement or attachment. From a one-size-fits-all grouping of people with disparate needs in institutional settings we have moved to an ethos of 'personalisation' in which it seems appropriate for 24 people with intellectual disabilities to live isolated lives in their own 'flats' rather than be helped to relate to each other or to share any social rituals or activities. It is as if we have moved from making controlling decisions for people as a matter of course to a situation where people are left in situations that they cannot understand or manage in the guise of this being their own 'choice'. We can only speculate about why intellectual disability services are particularly prone to this process of erecting straw men and then shooting them down. Perhaps it provides an illusion of progress or of escape from a reality that is usually static, often challenging and sometimes painful.

Challenging such orthodoxies can lead to splits around seemingly trivial usage of language where people are almost excommunicated for saying 'a learning disabled person' instead of 'a person with intellectual disabilities'. Valerie Sinason, who pioneered the application of psychoanalytic approaches with this group, referred to this as 'changing the verbal bed-linen' (Sinason 1992, pp.39–54) whenever the words seem to be soiled, as if the difficult feelings could be swept away if we outlaw the words that refer to them.

Working with family members

Judged as either neglectful or 'over-protective', mothers in particular usually 'get it wrong' and find themselves cycling back and forwards between the top and the bottom half of a 'criticising in relation to criticised' reciprocal role. They are often left to manage with minimal resources or support but then castigated for doing so. They are idealised unrealistically, for example, one mother was asked to take her son back from a service that could not manage his frequent and often disturbingly violent outbursts with no consideration of the fact that she lived in a high rise flat and was a single parent. At his previous service there were five staff members on duty at any one time, and they had not been able to contain him but considered the fact that she was his mother to be magic solution to the problems that they had been unable to understand or manage. At the other end of this continuum, family members are often left out in the cold, denigrated, blamed for not being able to 'let go' and seen as the source of the person's problems.

CASE STUDY: A PARENT'S EXPERIENCE OF CAT

Cath (a pseudonym) was the mother of a young adult with complex problems known to the community intellectual disability team and as such she would normally receive supportive advice, but not counselling, in her own right. The Royal College of Psychiatrists (2002) found that, despite a third of carers reporting mental health problems of their own, only one per cent have ever received counselling or therapy for themselves. CAT was chosen because it provided a framework for exploring the extent to which Cath's own experiences of being cared for as a child had restricted, or made more painful, her attempts to care for her daughter. As the mother of a daughter with intellectual disabilities she was cast in this role for a longer time and with more intense involvement than she might otherwise have been. This meant that triggers to replay these old ways of managing were frequent and increasingly intolerable. The CAT framework could show how the roles Cath played towards her daughter had come from those she had internalised from how she was treated herself in her own past, and that she now replays internally towards herself, enacts towards her daughter and recruits her daughter to play towards her (other-to-self, self-to-self and then inevitably self-to-other).

Cath was familiar with the supportive advice role of community team professionals who concentrated on how she could manage her daughter's needs, but the referrer had noticed how Cath would squeeze in passing allusions to her own problems during these consultations. Neither party could 'officially' give this full voice, leaving issues unaddressed until Cath was offered 16 sessions of an individual CAT. The community team agreed that Cath's privacy needed to be respected, so on this occasion her confidentiality would remain with the therapist, rather than be held by the wider team. Cath's opening words in therapy were to ask the therapist guiltily to tell her where she was going wrong with her daughter, but she relaxed as they explored the possibility that the therapy could be about herself.

Cath described how her need to be 'super caring' came about because she was so determined to bring her kids up differently from how she had been brought up herself. For Cath, this meant not only not abusing her kids but also protecting them from the harsh side of life. The map drew out how it wasn't possible to be caring all the time.

The therapist and Cath described, using Cath's words, three self-states – the 'Bubble Place', the 'Overwhelmed Place' and the 'Abusing and Neglecting Place' – that were desired, routinely endured or dreaded (Potter 2004). The Bubble Place, as they called the desired state (on the left of Figure 3.3) was not only about ideal caring; it also had a shadow controlling–controlled aspect too. Did seeking to be in control keep her and others safer from the risk of getting abused or neglected, something she had known herself as a child? Was this shadow side to caring because Cath's knowledge of the caring role was based more on desire and fantasy than on the solid experience of having been cared for herself, as she had not had consistent or helpful care in her own childhood? Knowing the Bubble Place never lasts, Cath always had an eye on the dreaded Abusing and Neglecting reciprocal role (on the *right of the map), but was frightened of 'being like my Dad' and, because she easily identifies with the fragile, injured child part in other people, she would seek to be powerfully caring to them as a way of keeping her own demons at bay. She endured being taken advantage of, was ground down into the Overwhelmed Place and, finding her own needs unmet there, would shut off before seeking that 'loving feeling' again as she mustered her energy to care once more. Experiencing herself as exhausted, she would let others know how they put upon her, but then berate herself at the failure of her sacrifice to make everything better.*

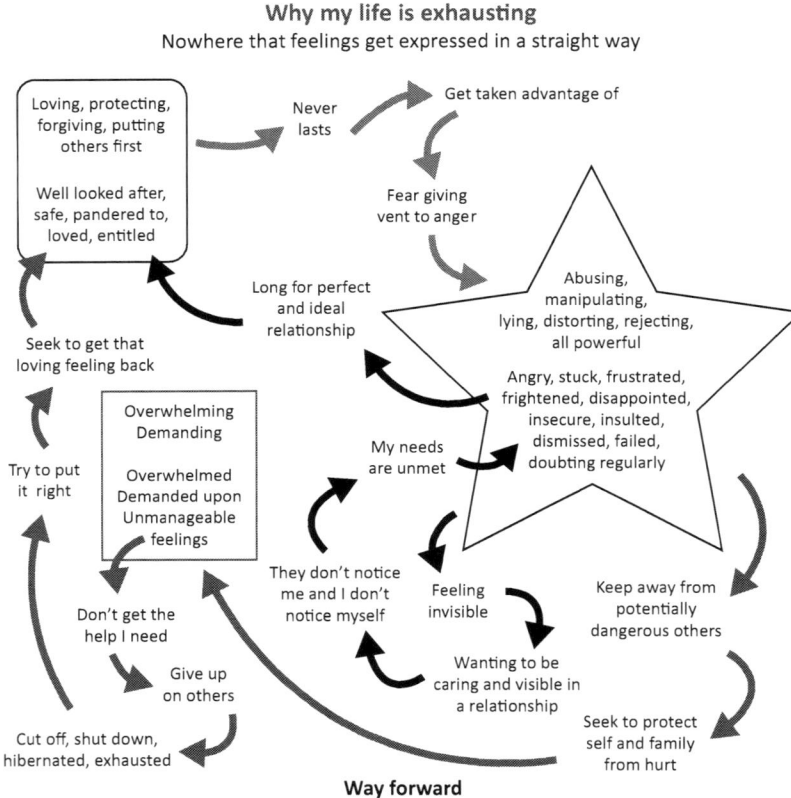

Why my life is exhausting
Nowhere that feelings get expressed in a straight way

Way forward
Being cared for and accepting towards myself, standing up for myself, having a right to my space, and expressing my wishes

Figure 3.3: Why my life is exhausting

Developing this map for use in therapy helped us to engage, 'map and track' and deepen the shared meanings through CAT's way of making relationships more explicit. By working with the map, the therapist had an opportunity to think where they both were, as the risk would have been that well-meaning but unacknowledged role enacting could have stifled their opportunity to think about the realistic limits to caring.

Cath described three target problems that she wanted to address.

Cath's target problems
'I don't matter'
Her daughter would frequently keep her up until 3.30 in the morning demanding reassurance that she was not having a heart attack and threatening to cut herself if Cath left her alone. At one pole of the manipulating, rejecting and all powerful reciprocal role, Cath was surprised when the therapist asked her how she felt about the therapist's two-week Christmas break from therapy, and at the other end of the pole, on one occasion she brought her daughter (on what appeared to be a feeble pretext) to wait outside whilst she had her therapy session, later telling the therapist how jealous and angry her daughter was at being excluded from their relationship.

> The Target Problem Procedure was: 'Believing other people's needs are always greater, I feel selfishly guilty, so I do what they want but then feel resentful and then blame myself.'

'I only get love and acceptance if I please you'
A neighbour who drove her to therapy sessions would comment on how tired she looked, suggesting they went out for a meal. At the meal, which she would pay for, she would end up listening to him talk about all his problems. She came over as very reasonable and rational most of the time. Undescribed, this could so easily have remained an entrapment in which she tried to please and to be acceptable, so the therapist commented that she wondered what happened to the irrational and unreasonable part. Cath replied she that wasn't used to talking to someone nice like her and that she found this scary.

> The Target Problem Procedure was: 'When I make a reasonable choice, others object or sabotage. Either I give in or I stick to my plan and have a miserable time.'

'If I stick up for myself, I may damage you or be rejected'
Cath stated she would like a sexual relationship with her husband but her daughter insisted she did not want them to have sex, avowing that sex is wrong, intruding into their bedroom often and threatening to kill herself or run away if she suspected they were having sex. Cath would talk constantly, continuing as the therapist opened the door to show her out once their session time had

finished, and the therapist worried that sticking to boundaries felt disrespectful.

The Target Problem Procedure was: 'Worrying and feeling guilty about feeling angry, I back down, take the blame and invite others to walk over me.'

We developed aims and then these exits.

- *To listen to myself respectfully and not brush myself aside.*
- *Having time for myself to do something I want to do for myself and to have one-on-one time with others too.*
- *I will negotiate a fair agreement. If others break our agreement I will stick with my boundaries and help them to respect their boundaries.*

The first two exits involved validating and respecting herself and her own needs in a self-to-self procedure. The last two looked at self-to-other procedures in which Cath would be able to offer a more consistent relational approach to her daughter and her friends while enforcing appropriate boundaries.

The first change the therapist noticed was when she arrived excited at a session in new clothes having had her hair cut smartly, and she recounted lots of examples about how she had been doing things that respected and valued herself. They looked at the map and Cath told the therapist how she used to try hard to be invisible with her clothes to avoid predatory men; they agreed that this strategy was valid 20 years ago, but no longer necessary and discussed how a new role could leave her freer to move in her appearance as well as voice and script.

Cath contrasted the rather idealised relationship she and her therapist had when telling the therapist that she had been shocked to realise that she often had friends who were similar to her family in that they used her to provide things they wanted. In a rhetorical question Cath asked sadly 'Why has this crept up on me?' She then said how she would have liked the therapist to be her friend but that she knew this wasn't possible, and then went into one of her sensible, coping modes. This led naturally into thinking about their relationship as good enough and how, as a parent and carer, her aim could be to offer good-enough parenting (as described by Winnicott 1965 and Hannush 2002). Gradually the content of sessions calmed down, becoming more a space for reflection and less an attempt to get everything sorted.

In the last few sessions Cath became able to describe how angry she was with her daughter and other members of her family who constantly walked over her and she started to express thoughts about it being time for her daughter to move out of the family home into Supported Living. She was able to put in place firm and appropriate boundaries so that her daughter did not continue to intrude into her mother's bedroom or private life. The therapist and Cath both wrote moving goodbye letters, which echoed each other in content. Their last piece of work was to explore how she was going to let other community team professionals help her to continue the work she had started in getting the balance right between her own and her family's needs. Cath said: 'K [her daughter] now needs to move away, get her own life, to learn how to look after herself.'

Concluding remarks

This chapter has set out the many ways in which CAT can be offered to people with intellectual disabilities, their family members and their paid carers. We have argued that CAT does not need to be limited to one-to-one therapeutic encounters with people with intellectual disabilities but that CAT tools can be shared with the person's wider support network so that the understandings that come from the therapeutic work can be shared and held by them on the person's behalf. We have described how family members also need help to allow them to set realistic limits to their own involvement and to mitigate the possibility of revisiting painful scenes of control or neglect from their own childhoods. Liberating parents from the burden of being 'special' provides a space within which their sacrifices can be honoured without denigrating them for the intensity of their involvement.

We have also argued that tuning in to the internal dialogue of the wider service culture and naming the reciprocal roles that are enacted in care settings can alert those responsible to the potential for poor practice as carers find themselves cornered into either switching off or unhelpfully stepping into controlling roles that can so easily tip over into neglect or abuse. Engaging intelligently with this dialogue enables painful feelings to be addressed and managed, mitigating against extreme reactions or violent switches and enabling networks of people committed to people with intellectual disabilities to hold to the middle ground, which is containing, enabling, nurturing and properly protective.

Chapter 4

Formulating and Working Therapeutically with the Concept of Intellectual Disability in the Cognitive Analytic Therapy Model

Jo Varela

Cognitive Analytic Therapy-informed models of intellectual disability

Historically formulations of intellectual disability are predominantly negative, focusing on damage, contagion and blame. This has led to a slow development of accessible and ethical interventions for this group of people. Few therapy models have integral to them a structure within which the effects of an intellectual disability can be understood as part of a psychological experience. This chapter looks at whether Cognitive Analytic Therapy (CAT) can help an individual understand the impact of an intellectual disability both socially and 'neuro'-cognitively. Core components of the CAT model are described and explored in relation to understandings of intellectual disability.

Intellectual disability as a label

Most texts on intellectual disability start with a chapter on nomenclature and categorisation. These, it seems, are very important in the having of an intellectual disability. The 'condition' has undergone many renamings in the past, almost all of which have become more stigmatising and unhelpful with time (Sinason 1992).

The label of intellectual disability is often deeply unhelpful to the person with an intellectual disability except as a way of accessing services based on that category. It is given usually by professionals to help describe an aspect of the person and help people understand why they are struggling to relate to the person with intellectual disability in a way that positively supports their growth and independence. However, the label itself does not help carers and others to know how to support the person in these aims. Carers still often struggle to know how to present information, adapt conversation and engage in mutually beneficial activities, despite the label (Bartlett and Bunning 1997). It would seem important to be able to understand and address the intellectual disability in order to support the individual as a whole, rather than merely provide a label or description of deficit.

More worryingly, the label may lead to problems in seeing the true difficulties faced by the person with an intellectual disability. For example, mental health and emotional problems, such as grief and pain-related behaviour, may be missed due to 'diagnostic over-shadowing' (i.e., all behaviour is due to the label of intellectual disability rather than distress). It is known that nurses' sympathetic attitudes to a patient depend on the diagnosis or label that they use (Markham and Trower 2003). People with intellectual disability may lead very different lives because of the label given to them. Distress that, in any other individual, would be seen as an indication that something is wrong in life and needs putting right, is given another label, 'challenging behaviour'. Moreover, the behaviour is treated in potentially a very different way than if seen as an expression of boredom, loneliness or preference, or as an *aim-directed activity or communication*, (as could be understood using the Target Problem Procedure (TPP) of the CAT model).

In therapy, people's experience of their disability leads to them labelling themselves with terms full of social and emotionally painful meaning, such as 'stupid', 'thick' or a 'failure' rather than the more emotionally neutral labels, such as learning disability and intellectual disability. Indeed when asked about their understandings of these terms or whether it is an identity that resonates, they struggle to define it, or actively reject the label (Beart 2005).

If we are not careful with them, 'Labels have the power to oppress, by stealing a person's individuality and then a collective stereotype replaces the personal consideration' (Lovett 1996, p.6). In helping an individual understand the nature or impact of their disabilities, labels are not always useful. Their difficulties are more usefully reformulated using personal language, experiences and concept of self. CAT's narrative approach and Sequential Diagrammatic Reformulation (SDR) offers just such a possibility.

Rapley, Kiernan and Antaki (1998) state that the identity of 'intellectual disability' is present in people with the label, but from their research they suggest that it is created in dialogue between two people and is fluid and negotiable. To CAT practitioners, this is an obvious concept. One can only be disabled in comparison with an able other and one can experience both poles of the reciprocal role. For those without the label, intellectual disability is a 'master identity'. This is not so for the individuals who may see themselves (as most people do) as having other identities that are important to them (Beart, Hardy and Buchan 2004). Emerson quotes Wolfensberger (1992), describing how people could only be valued by others if they developed more 'normal' roles, and although thinking has moved on since normalisation, there is something to be said for enabling people to reflect on the various roles and relationships they form with others and society and the impact this might have on feelings and personal growth.

Rapley (2005), in arguing that the concept of intellectual disability misses the true competencies of people with the label, demonstrates that an analysis of everyday dialogue enables us to see these competencies in actively negotiating the social world. He looks at two scripts that show that the subjects are all too aware of the roles they are expected to play and are skilled at negotiating them. The importance of dialogue within CAT as a tool for constructing or negotiating the internal and social world would seem, therefore, to be a useful tool in assessing, accessing and developing the abilities of the individual, regardless of their intellectual disability.

In addressing the use for CAT with someone with limited language skills, Fitzsimmons (2000) recommends using the patient's own language as a way of drawing on the patient's skills to develop a new self, rather than teaching a new set of language skills that might confirm feelings of uselessness. If people are encouraged to use their own language to describe their personal world, it may deepen their ability to engage in joint reformulation and diagrammatic representation and give the client a voice. The world of people with intellectual disabilities and their families is awash with complex labels that are ever changing. CAT offers an approach where these complex labels may be put to one side in the pursuit of a collaboratively generated language around a person's difficulties and hopes for the future. The lack of a need for labels in a CAT reformulation also reduces the power relationship difficulties that are generated by the professional's ability to give a permanent and life-changing label (Oakes 2012).

CAT is an effective model for processing distress associated with difficulties in finding a comfortable identity. Studies show that people with intellectual disabilities are not sure of the meaning of the term intellectual disability and this has led some to suggest that they are unaware of their identity as people with intellectual disabilities. Jahoda, Markova and Cattermole (1989) and Davies and Jenkins (1997) suggest that people are aware of this identity but differ in how they articulate it. They found that people did not engage with common definitions of intellectual disability but were aware of their differences, and defined these in relation to the power differences between themselves and others, and in comparisons with others to whom they wished to be more similar. The emphasis on reciprocal roles and the way in which these relationships and their negotiation are mapped in the SDR, makes the expression of a person's self-concept and their difficulties more accessible and provides them with a way of exploring their 'disabled' identity.

Intellectual disability as a cognitive impairment

Definitions of intellectual disability focus on an Intelligence Quotient (IQ) that is two standard deviations below the mean (i.e., significantly below the normal range that could be expected in a population), which affects people in various functional aspects of their lives and has its onset in childhood. Intellectual disabilities include a 'slowness in analysing information, difficulties holding this information, in defining the relevant aspects of given situations to attend to applying strategies, in manipulating and expressing information and selecting strategies to solve problems' (Clements 1998, p.42). Areas affected include language and communication, executive function and social cognition (Clements 1998).

Different ways of describing or categorising the intellectual disability focus on IQ with labels such as mild, moderate, severe or profound; the differences being the extent to which the person is able to score on tests of intelligence or perform in their world (however, Lynch (2004) has suggested that individual assessment can help determine a person's strengths and difficulties and therefore any required modifications to therapy).

This may not be how the person themselves would describe their experience of their disability. When asked, people (and their carers) usually say 'I don't understand' or 'my memory is not great', 'I can't think very fast' or 'I get confused', rather than using this categorical system.

People are, it seems, sometimes much better at describing the real nature of their difficulties than professionals.

The CAT model has embraced a number of models of learning about how people understand and experience their world and process information through the Procedural Sequence Object Relations Model (PSORM) (see Chapter 1).

These concepts may support a person with intellectual disabilities to make the most of their abilities and potentially and successfully negotiate their difficulties. The Procedural Sequences are important for understanding the difficulties one might have in the cognitive arena. It considers the formation and maintenance of aim-directed activity involving three phases:

1. mental processes (perception, memory, appraisal and aim-formation beliefs and expectations in light of expectations about personal efficacy and anticipated consequences)

2. behavioural (enactment of chosen action based on the above)

3. consequences.

(Ryle 1994)

The Procedural Sequence provides a meaningful description of where someone might be having difficulties in the appraisal, planning and evaluation stages due to difficulties in attention, concentration, working memory, organisation and manipulation of constructs, or processing speed, all of which are aspects of intelligence. This model is not intended for use outside of the relational world and it is usually briefly expressed in diagrammatic reformulations as a procedural loop such as 'wanting to please'. It may be useful to explore how this model may help a person with intellectual disabilities and others understand the difficulties they experience.

It would be valuable to clarify and elaborate within the PSORM by bringing what is known of cognitive processing to enhance therapy for people with intellectual disabilities. In particular, evidence from neuro-rehabilitative psychology in the areas of problem-solving, decision-making and self-regulation would enrich the use of PSORM and would place these difficulties firmly in the social/relational world. Rice-Varian (2011) quotes Yeates *et al.* (2008) and discusses developing a clinical formulation linking CAT understandings with a neuropsychological model of acquired brain injury to good effect. Harvey (1993) also proposes that CAT could benefit from artificial intelligence and cognitive theories in supporting people to be more effective social problem-solvers.

Formulating and Working Therapeutically with the Concept of Learning Disability

CASE STUDY: 'MAPPING' THE INTELLECTUAL DISABILITY TO IMPROVE THE RELATIONSHIP WITH THE STAFF TEAM

David lived in a house with four others, had a job and a good social life and was part of a self-advocacy group. Occasionally he would become really angry and shout and swear at people, taking himself to his room following these 'outbursts'. David's support team and family were hurt and confused by this, as they were behaving in ways that were in line with modern service philosophy and David's Person Centred Plan. A reformulation was completed with David, which explored how, in attempting to be consistent with these life goals, he became panicky when 'things were too fast' and he perceived people to be 'talking gook'. On assessment he found that he needed more time to process information but that his comprehension was good. He also needed a little more help to break decisions down so that he could be successful. In reformulating his difficulty using CAT rather than just providing a psychometric report, David was able to convey his difficulty in his own words but also place them in the context of very valued support. The 'desired' reciprocal role was, in his words, 'great staff team', with each person named, to David's 'happy, in control'. David was also able to use the diagram to describe to his staff how important their empathic response was in making things right again.

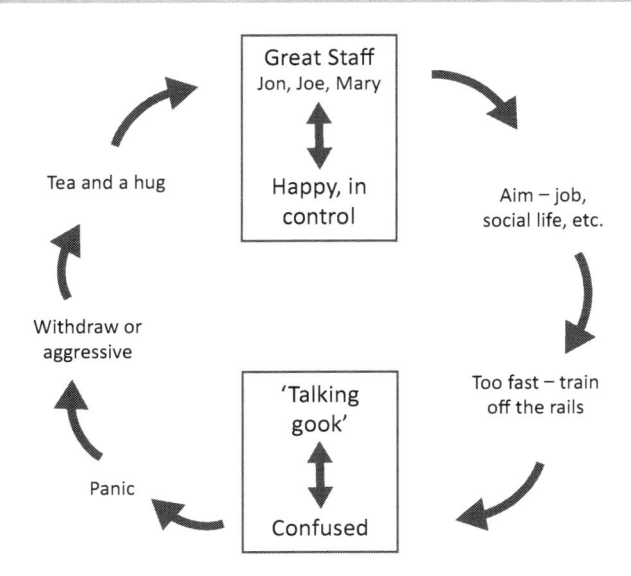

Figure 4.1: David: mapping his experience of his learning disability

Other models of difficulties in assimilating information about the world around us can be found in CAT. Ryle's model of borderline personality disorder (1997) suggests three levels of difficulty in the development of a 'procedural repertoire' (the number of different ways of coping):

1. restriction and distortion of the procedural repertoire due to genetic factors, biological damage and abusive or neglecting relationships in early life
2. disruption of integrating procedures concerned with selecting and mobilising appropriate strategies
3. deficient and disrupted self-reflection focusing on attending and reflecting on changes in the world or one's own behaviour.

This construct may also be of use in establishing where the person with disabilities might be having problems revising problem procedures, whether it be due to intellectual capacities, deficits in problem-solving skills and evaluation, or reductions in experience (a common occurrence in the lives of people with intellectual disability who are less likely to get married, have a job and have satisfying social relationships and life experiences).

CASE STUDY: RE-FORMULATING INTELLECTUAL DISABILITY: COGNITIVE DEFICIT OR THE EXPERIENCE OF BEING TREATED DIFFERENTLY

Leanne was 22 and had been living in a supported flat on her own for nine months despite her intellectual disability and epilepsy. She was referred by staff concerned that she was letting people into her flat and that her money and belongings were going missing. The referral was for support to complete a capacity assessment about her ability to make decisions around living on her own. On meeting her psychologist, Leanne appeared deferential and uneasy as she felt that she had done something wrong. She could, however, explain why she had been referred and could describe the difficulties she had had. This marked power difference in the session was remarked on by her psychologist. Leanne's intellectual disability seemed to have a small impact on her ability to manage the situation she found herself in, but other issues relating to her experience as a person with an intellectual disability were equally important. The above model was used to look at some of the reasons for her difficulties.

Leanne had restricted experiences of relating to others, mainly comprising contact with more able people to whom she was expected to defer (parents, teachers, staff, social workers, doctors). She had not had much experience of reflecting on her perceptions, actions and choices in order to judge whether to defer to others in any given situation. She had a restricted experience of how to be more assertive and problem-solve. An SDR was drawn with her and her staff to explore her dominant reciprocal roles (able-to-disabled and victim-to-bully) as well as her TPPs (placate and defer to other). This was used to encourage exploration of other more competent roles and responses in the context of a more valuing relationship. A small amount of problem-solving skills development was offered to help her structure her thoughts. The focus of intervention moved from making decisions about her, to informed support around enabling her to experience making these decisions in her life.

The Zone of Proximal Development (ZPD) and the development of intellectual functioning

CAT theory suggests that learning must take place within a benign relationship characterised by collaborative, empathic reflection. It relies on activity theory, 'the high level thinking, doing and being within a social context...that leads to development, particularly intellectual development through the process of internalisation' (Ryle 1991). Studies have shown that if this learning within a healthy social and relational context does not take place, intelligence, as measured by IQ, suffers. Given the amount of research on the effects of relationships and experiences on intellectual development, it is crucial for any model of support for people with intellectual disabilities to also be able to formulate within this arena as the PSORM is able to do.

The concept of IQ measurement and its application to the lives of people with intellectual disability has long been questioned. More recently, concepts such as intellectual competence have been postulated as more useful than IQ. These models (Chamorro-Premuzic and Furnham 2005) focus on potential future achievements as the criterion rather than IQ (reflecting ZPD concepts) and cite this to be the product of cognitive intelligence and non-cognitive factors such as personality. This gives rise to the possibility of supporting the non-cognitive factors through therapy to help people with intellectual disabilities be 'intellectually competent' in their world. King (2005) notes that the concept of the ZPD is of particular importance in working with this client group, and that it aids the establishment of the therapeutic alliance. It supports the person to understand the mechanical processes of what is happening as well as the emotional assimilation of experiences. It also gives meaning to the psychometric tools used to assess intellectual disability. Instead of an unhelpful, incomprehensible label of IQ, psychometric tools can be used to determine a person's starting point within their ZPD. This may be the number of abstract concepts they can grasp and work with, key words they can process or their ability to use numbers and language to scale and compare experiences.

There is no clear relationship between emotional and cognitive functioning. An individual with limited cognitive abilities can be capable of great emotional understanding and knowledge (Waitman and Conboy-Hill 1992; Sinason 1992) and develop enriching relationships. The vulnerability factors associated with psychiatric disorders in the intellectual disability population include not only biological factors, but also issues around rejection, deprivation, poor problem-solving strategies, poor self-acceptance, disempowerment and family issues, such as poor adaptation to the child's disability, parental difficulties with 'letting go', negative attitudes, poor social networks and stigmatisation (Holt, Hardy and Bouras 2005). These all also have an impact on the emerging self and intellectual functioning.

The interrelationship between intellectual functioning, social relationships and development is clearly complex. CAT has an integrated model of cognitive and social and developmental processes and this is key to providing complex and useful formulations for individuals, which can support them in all levels of functioning. CAT's model of personal development and self-reflection taking place within a therapeutic relationship is also important here.

Intellectual disability as a coping strategy

Intellectual disability may also be seen to be a procedural coping strategy. The concept of secondary handicap (Sinason 1992) describes the process by which people 'go stupid' as a way of cutting off from emotional pain.

Intellectual disability as a social role

Intellectual disability is culturally defined in terms of what is 'normal' ability. There are other ways of understanding intellectual disability as a social role or construct instead of an inherent characteristic. For example, Hatton (1998) suggests that intellectual disability is socially constructed in terms of the demands a society places on an individual. The AAIDD definition now used by the World Health Organization (WHO) and Mencap suggests that intellectual disability is a condition 'arising as a result of society's failure to adopt attitudinal views to meet the growing expectations of the quality of life of all people's needs thereby disabling rather than enabling some people' (Commision for Healthcare Audit and Inspection 2007).

The place of people with intellectual disabilities in society has an uneasy history. They have been forced into roles that have been severely limiting, segregating and abusive. Over the years they have been seen as holy innocents or infants, a threat to the health of others, cursed, victims or the archetypal fool. Intellectual disability is a powerfully stigmatising identity (Beart, Hardy and Buchan 2004). Responses have been isolation and segregation, eugenics and sterilisation or paternalistic teaching to reduce the difference. When our understandings of ourselves are developed through interaction with the world and are reflected back to us using derogatory labels and negative evaluations, this has a significant effect on how we see ourselves and how we see our position in society.

One would hope that society is now more enlightened, but people with intellectual disability are still seen as 'different' (Oakes 2012); people who are different are feared. Abuses continue, with bullying, victimisation, stigma and segregation still common (Winterbourne report, Department of Health 2012; Valuing People Now, Department of Health 2009). People with intellectual disabilities do feel stigmatised (Jahoda *et al.* 1989) and devalued in social relationships (Davies and Jenkins 1997). In engaging in CAT, the person is given the opportunity and means to explore the reciprocal roles they experience as part of being seen as different by society. These experiences may include the pain of being avoided or unseen in the street in a 'Does he take sugar?' way, as well as having life dreams dashed due to the prejudiced low expectations of others. I am reminded of the joy of a young man with intellectual disabilities who had achieved real success in his job at a supermarket, only to be informed in the same week by a usually empathic acquaintance that I should not go shopping that night as it was 'mong night' and things were bound to be inefficient or weird.

It may be argued that the emotional difficulties of having an intellectual disability chiefly come from the reciprocal acts of others in prejudice and societal (paternalistic, segregational) attitudes that impact on a sense of worth and belonging rather than the condition itself.

Intellectual disability as a relationship and a dialogue

The IQ concept of cognitive impairment leads us to believe that it is solely an attribute of the person but also leads us to ask what is wrong with the person, and the use of the term disability invites us to make it right. But for Vygotsky (1978) intelligence and learning are created in dialogue and interaction with the 'other'. This interaction is internalised and emerges again in dialogue to be repeated on one's own. Intelligence is a socially mediated ability and can be constructed and understood as such using the CAT model in the use of the reciprocal role, with others and oneself. That one can know one's abilities (and disabilities) through the relationship with others resonates with other studies where people have been found to be aware of the disability regardless of parental disclosure (Cunningham *et al.* 2000).

Lovett (1996) suggests that we should see intellectual disability as lateral (or relational) rather than hierarchical, and by doing so invites us to think about our (reciprocal) role with people with this label. In describing an intellectual disability he invites us to think about our 'teaching disability'. Disability is not therefore an inherent characteristic of a person but a dynamic created in the relationship between two people. The disability does not, in a relational model, always reside in the individual who is labelled as such. Most therapists and others have had the experience of feeling disabled and 'not getting it' when in conversation with a person with an intellectual disability who clearly has a concept in mind and is articulating it in their own words. We feel the discomfort of this disabled experience and wish that we are somehow more knowledgeable or expert, or refer on for more expert assessment to help our understanding. King (2005) stresses the importance of acknowledging the difference in intellectual capacity as a relational issue in CAT therapy. CAT focuses on reformulation in a collaborative manner, starting with what the client brings, making a unique model of joint skill and exploration in which the intellectual disability as a relationship between the client and therapist is material to be explored and negotiated together. Bates (1992) felt that working therapeutically with people with an intellectual disability was only different in the sense that the processes though which one works have a different time span and rhythm. While these issues are important (and addressed in the CAT model through the concept of the ZPD), the CAT model takes into account the cognitive problems and differences in ability between the client and therapist. Only when these are acknowledged and collaboratively worked through, can the client enter into a relationship where both client and therapist comprehend and participate equally in the therapy. Differences in comprehension and communication that are not acknowledged will interfere with the development of a benign helping dialogue and lead to enactments such as seeking to please the powerful other.

Conclusion

There are many definitions of an intellectual disability, and perhaps the term will become redundant as we realise that we need to include those we label in the discussion of how they see themselves (Beart 2005).

By inviting people to engage in a CAT-informed dialogue, we are able to generate many individual and useful descriptions of the experience of intellectual disability.

CAT places cognitive impairment firmly within a social and relational context in a way that leads to the development of interventions for the individual. In being able to describe, within a formulation, the impact of the intellectual disability on a person in terms of the difficulties they and their carers are experiencing, it is possible to support this area more effectively.

CAT is able to develop a shared understanding of psychological difficulty related to intellectual disability and therefore generate exits at all levels of functioning including thoughts, feelings, behaviour, thinking, learning and relationships.

Chapter 5
Relational Intelligence
Steve Potter and Julie Lloyd

In this chapter we introduce the idea of relational intelligence as a way of informing work with people with intellectual disabilities. This notion of intelligence being relational fosters a view of the practical interaction between different sources and dimensions of intelligence. We argue that through a relational view of intelligence and a relationally intelligent view of the world, we can better understand our approach, support and education when working with people with intellectual disabilities, particularly people with autism. We describe a relational view of intelligence and how using the concepts from Cognitive Analytic Therapy (CAT) of role reciprocation, role procedures and role orchestration we can make relationally intelligent maps that track our working routes and describe roadblocks.

In the 20th century, intelligence was psychology's big idea. Originally seen as a general and stable competency measured by language use, arithmetic, reasoning, logic, memory and pattern recognition, this notion does not describe how bright people can do silly things, or how people with low IQ scores can show compassion or giftedness in other respects. It is not good science to act as if IQ measures the sum of intelligence; IQ only measures those capacities that can be captured by pen-and-paper tests. Since we experience the IQ 70 'eligibility' boundary cut-off as insufficient by itself to arrive at a multi-factorial view of learning ability and disability, we need a more pluralistic and versatile view of intelligences.

As Gardner (1985) stressed, intelligence shows up in its multiplicity. Gardner identified seven culturally relevant talents that different societies foster or neglect. He viewed acting intelligently as the management of a plurality of intelligences. 'Intelligence' is therefore seen not as a quality of the individual, but as a partnership between individual minds and the intelligences invested in our languages and cultures. Intelligence is a quality invested over millennia by individuals in the fabric of our societies, cultures and core narratives. In our culture, there is some evidence that the component of general intelligence most relevant to our complex and pluralistic times is pattern recognition. Indeed, according to Flynn (2012) our general pattern of scores on intelligence tests has increased owing to our wider access to culture requiring abstract thinking in particular, whereas our mathematical and linguistic scores have barely changed. Intelligence in practice seems less fixed in the individual and more dependent on shared activity. Working together we can be smarter. This invites a different kind of measurement than that offered by traditional psychometrics. Furthermore, this interactional approach to intelligence incorporates more of the origins of the long history of the evolutionary development of the modern mind (Donald 1991, 2001). It also takes account of the ways in which our earliest feelings, voicing and thinking skills emerge at birth and are only developed through shared interaction with others (Reddy 2008; Trevarthen 2001).

Such a relational view of intelligence points to the plurality of components involved: interpersonal (a meeting between people), dialogic (an invitation of multiple ways of making meaning), interactive (influencing and being influenced by things, events and people), dynamic (replaying old interactions through every new interaction), intrapersonal (a meeting of two subjective experiences between our internal and our external lives) and orchestral (managing, co-ordinating all the intelligences and series of intelligent moments into a coherent experience or event). This last use is particularly important, as it is the orchestral element of relational intelligence that has most bearing on how we manage our complex contemporary lives and how we work alongside people with intellectual disabilities. This list can be freely extended; the main theme here is that relational intelligence is about how we see things and make meaning together with other people. It takes away the notion that intelligence is located in the individual brain.

In the long story of human evolution, culture, tool making and language are often referred to as the 'big brain'. Our individual discovery, development and expression of intelligence are entirely dependent on the joint activity of our little brains with the big brain of culture. Throughout early interactions, both in the long deep history of humanity and in our own early years, we engage with others and the world in the life space around us and participate and reciprocate with what is on offer.

Relational intelligence can be defined as the understanding that there are lots of other things going on simultaneously when we give our attention to one thing in particular.

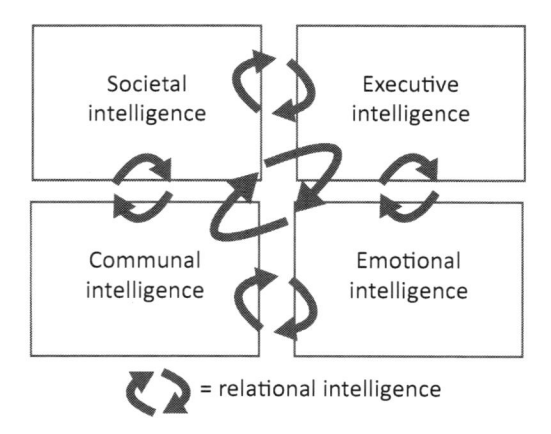

Figure 5.1: Relational intelligence is the orchestration and integration of multiple intelligences through interaction with self and others

As a crude division and simplification, but to help organise our thinking, we divide relational intelligence into four interacting sources. These are: emotional intelligence, communal intelligence, societal intelligence and executive functioning.

Communal and emotional intelligence

Communal and emotional intelligence are at the base of human activity. Our starting point in being human is our reciprocations with each other. Communal intelligence derives from the core network of intimate relations into which we are born and through which we feel our way to memory and identity. It is the source of strength and quality of our attachment experience; the ways we are validated, held and embedded. It is the web of close ties that are part of emotional mapping and unconscious procedural knowledge about the world. Some babies will not get the mix of holding and engagement they need, and yet more will cope with sudden ruptures from holding and engaging to letting go and neglecting. For babies with intellectual disabilities, the mix of reciprocations and how these are orchestrated particularly vary. Those with autism may be unresponsive to parental invitations.

Emotional intelligence is the ability to recognise, express and negotiate emotional meaning (Goleman 1995). It is our entry into participating in and understanding the world. We feel our way into our world. Sometimes this emotional negotiation is seamless; but often it is through tear and repair of the relational fabric around in our community. The newborn baby seeks to engage and the mother responds by engaging back and holding the baby. The holding becomes a source of comfort, food, meaning and control. The baby in time learns to negotiate emotions to get held and to get attention by giving attention. There will be times of friction and neglect in the participation and reciprocation between emotional and communal intelligence. Out of this, our interactive feeling activity becomes feeling skills, recognisable emotions and a language, both verbal and non-verbal, both embodied and mental, for making emotional and then cognitive meaning together. A thorough account of the recent interplay between neuro-scientific, infant research and attachment theory can be found in Knox's excellent account of *Self Agency in Psychotherapy* (2011) and in Reddy's account of *How Infants Know Minds* (2008).

What is it like for the baby whose intellectual disability is obvious at birth? How does the emotional and communal intelligence alter its direction and expression, such as when holding a fragile child with cerebral palsy whose body cannot meld easily in our arms? What does the baby with Down's Syndrome experience when adults look at it with embarrassment, concern, or determination to make up for the visible damage? What is it like being a baby who sees hopelessness instead of the joy that babies usually experience? What about the baby who is too good or too difficult and always screaming, such as the baby on the Autistic Spectrum? Or the baby too fragile to be held and who is kept alive in an incubator supporting its ill-functioning organs? Or, conversely, should we think of the 'emotional' disabilities induced by role behaviour by parents and carers who are damaging, restricting, unpredictable or unavailable, generating hard-to-manage emotions, unmet needs and untried skills in the communal and emotional life of the child?

Societal intelligence and executive functioning

We turn to the other two sources of relational intelligence: societal intelligence and executive functioning. Societal intelligence is what has been invested in our society over thousands of years in our language, rituals, religions, laws and institutions. It is more explicit and more visibly coded than communal intelligence and, as such, is taught (as rote learning rather than procedural knowledge) in schools, churches and the wider social group. Every social rule, word, grammatical injunction, road sign, formula or philosophy is one or another kind of intelligence invested in our society. Built on the foundations of our communal and emotional intelligence, we develop the skills to live in the world by working with and drawing upon societal intelligence. This involves much schooling and guidance. In modern times, our societies have become more complex and more spread around systems and institutions that are independent of us. We manage by appropriating for ourselves some broad rules of thumb (heuristics), and a few relevant areas of detailed expertise. In our commitments to improve the lives of people with intellectual disabilities, we struggle for them to be included in broader society, but we also confront their frequent impairment in developing those social heuristics that allow interactions to occur seamlessly.

The concept of executive intelligence is useful to describe an instrumental, intentional, calculating or prefigured sense of purpose and self. Whereas communal-emotional intelligence is something we own and are, societal-executive intelligence is something with which, and through which, we have a sense of agency and direction. In street jargon we are players; we are on the pitch. It is called 'executive' because it captures the conductor-orchestral way of choosing a line of action, feeling and meaning from several others, in order to make something of the life space in which we find ourselves. It is the ability to know 'this is what I need or want and here is a way of going about it that might work.' It is the ability to orchestrate the various instruments of our personal orchestra of that moment and place and make a good enough coherence or play of the 'music' of sounds, actions and interactions we need. It is the ability to monitor and evaluate progress in an 'executive' way and to steer and negotiate how things turn out. It arises out of and depends upon a mix of shared communal intelligence, emotional intelligence and societal intelligence. It is experienced as a sense of agency or willpower, purpose and motivation. It is highly variable in quality and expression. Overly cognitive views of executive intelligence underplay the flexibility of focus, intensity or perspective involved in choosing to attend to one line of procedural knowledge and action and not another. In this sense, executive intelligence is always expressed and lived within a wider mix of relational intelligence. In autism we see a strong but narrowly defined executive intelligence, which looks for a narrow reciprocation from a circumscribed part of society, cut off from other sources of intelligence. The inevitable mismatch between the person with autism and society's norms often leads to crossed wires and frustration for everyone.

Weak central coherence or executive intelligence in autism

From a multi-factorial point of view, it might be better served to think of weak central coherence as an aspect of executive intelligence. The rapid increase of research into autism, now possible because of advances in neuro-imaging and modelling, includes descriptions of impairments centred on problems within general information processing, particularly reduced central coherence (Frith 2003). This cognitive model, familiar to most readers, describes how people avoid being bombarded by sensory information through developing perceptual and cognitive heuristics and behavioural procedures, which permit a fluent flowing between multiple mental states. Deficits in cross-modal sensory correspondence (Stern 1998) result in reduction in the ability to pull together vast amounts of individual pieces of information. Without a unitary semantic system, much information remains beyond the person's connective or relational reach and is experienced as a surfeit (Rubenstein and Merzenich 2003). Many people with autism focus their energy on reducing the chaos of overwhelming sensory overload by trying to keep everything the same and, as Baron-Cohen (2002) describes, develop extreme systematising. He describes this ability as an extreme version of the 'male' brain in which detailed information about a highly circumscribed system is obtained that offers some emotional pleasure in a predictable part of the world.

Twice a year, when daylight saving causes clocks to be altered by one hour, one man with autism and his staff team experience several weeks of extreme agitation and distress, as he panics and appears to experience a collapse in his sense of the stability of time. Weak central coherence (Frith 2003) – or lack of flexibility of perspective, intensity and focus – causes an inability to see perspective and then patterns, which means events are not linked and neither are incidents, moments and movements in relation to self and others. Weak central coherence also results in a high level of field independence in which the person is far better at spotting figures that are embedded in a context than someone with strong sensory heuristics and the ability to relate detail to perspective (or tree to wood).

In the special case of autism, there is an absence of an ability to link early emotional intelligences to the communal intelligence of the world around (see Figure 5.2). This absence of an ability to regulate the input of communal information creates difficulties with developing theories of minds and regulating intimacy and distance in attachment behaviours, blocking the chance to fully participate in the relationally intelligent richness of early developmental experience.

```
┌─────────────┐          ┌─────────────┐
│  Societal   │          │  Executive  │
│ intelligence│          │ intelligence│
└─────────────┘          └─────────────┘
┌─────────────┐          ┌─────────────┐
│  Communal   │          │  Emotional  │
│ intelligence│          │ intelligence│
└─────────────┘          └─────────────┘
         ⟲ = relational intelligence
```

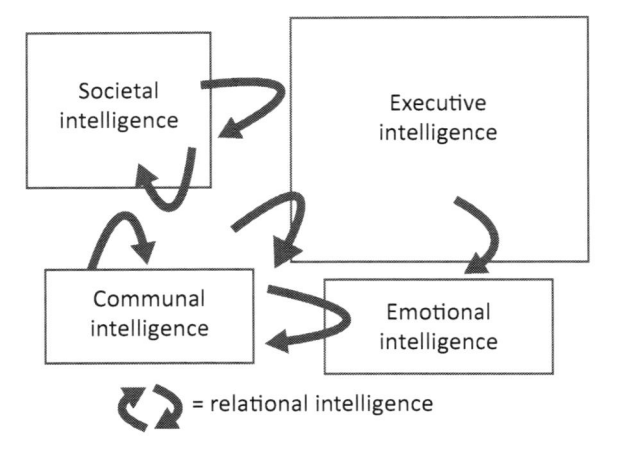

Figure 5.2: With severe autism relational intelligence is filtered through an overdependence on executive intelligence, which inhibits the interaction between the four sources of intelligence

Autism, as a neurological condition, must have been always with us. The persistence and eye for detail that autism exposes would have been very welcome in a Stone Age tool maker, and in the pre-enclosure farming era, the ability to thrive despite social isolation would have been helpful for an autistic shepherd. In more complex, contemporary and radical open societies there are conflicting empathies, competing narratives and exposed hierarchies of power and control. In our complex society, we need to be able to move with enough coherence, attunement and flexibility from one role to another, to be more relationally intelligent and able to multitask more. These are many attributes that are particularly associated with being female. As we gain freedom of control over changing levels of perspective and understanding and vary the intensity of engagement, we find the focus of our attention frequently changes. A person with autism must face such complexity and variety of roles and identities in which they are often exposed as socially inept or as making choices that most people would reject or deride. If, as Baron-Cohen (2002) describes, autism were an extreme version of being male, then the increase in diagnosis in recent years may be the result of autism standing out more in response to dispersed, overlapping, exposing and complex social systems. Mostly we develop group and individual ways of joining and separating (throwing out lots of signals about the dance of attunement and involvement or defence and disengagement). The autistic person has fewer resources for manoeuvre in current times in comparison with more traditional enclosed communities and therefore stands out, triggering secondary responses such as bullying, misunderstanding and derision.

Integrating these separate findings into a pluralistic, multi-factorial model

Relational intelligence views the intelligence of any particular activity, knowledge or interaction as a shared, dialogic intelligence that works between society and us, and within others and us. The idea is to capture the shared experience of doing intelligent things for and with self and others. For example, implicit in the activity of driving, it is the continuously changing judgements and skills (personal, executive intelligence) of the car driver, following traffic signs (societal intelligence) using the internalised knowledge from learning the Highway Code (societal intelligence and executive intelligence combined) with a shared trust or vigilance (communal intelligence) about the patterns of responsiveness of other drivers to be calm, wary or competitive or feel rage, etc. (emotional intelligence). Relational intelligence is simultaneously an expression of the processes of all the above intelligences interacting, the skills of orchestrating them in safe and effective driving and the product in the smooth flow of traffic. When it is enabling in the car-driving example the traffic flows smoothly, the drivers are not over stressed and the road systems are fit for purpose. When relational intelligence is restrictive, the roads are too narrow, the traffic too much and the drivers too competitive, etc. The concept of Relational Intelligence allows a multi-factorial and multilevel analysis of the orchestration of intelligences in any one incident, individual, system or culture. Orchestrating these multiple intelligences requires an appreciation of their reciprocation both from within the person consciously and unconsciously, and from society and culture both explicitly and implicitly.

In conclusion, we learnt our mental abilities and developed the enlarged brain and modern mind in and through joint activity with other humans. The reciprocal relationships between brain size, joint activity (tool making, group life and work, language and empathy) and more complex intelligence is at the heart of human development over several million years. We didn't have a plan and then interact; but through interaction found our plans and procedures for achieving them. The origins of intelligence are relational. The use of intelligence is relational. The sources of intelligence are relational. The management and control of intelligence is relational. The problems with intelligence are relational. When we refer to learning disabilities, or intellectual disabilities, we are referring to something that shows up in someone's interactions with the basic requirements of life in association with others. It is the innately different relationality of their intelligence that often presents the problem. We need to foster a more relationally intelligent response, tailored to the needs of the individual involved and according to the settings they are in. Most people with intellectual disabilities are learning abled on some dimensions, so our challenge is responding with the right mix of relational intelligence and to meet the gaps and conflicts in the most helpful, least harmful way.

Relationally intelligent staff teams

The concept of relational intelligence can be used practically through the method of mapping (also known as 'sequential diagrammatic reformulation') in CAT. Mapping traces out the reciprocal role procedures, which means that it offers a method for thinking interactively in a joined-up way about the multiple factors affecting work with people with intellectual disabilities. By applying this concept of relational intelligence through the tools of CAT, we are guided in developing a common language to understand and improve the quality of care and reduce the risk of harmful and stressful interactions between clients and staff. Mapping these relationships not only helps workers see the relational dynamics that are operating, but also points to the origins of staff's own involvement as helpers.

Chapter 6

The Helper's Dance List

Steve Potter

Introduction

This chapter reviews a list of 20 helper's dancers that can affect the helping relationship. It refers to common human qualities of giving and receiving help, whether the focus is on the caring relationship, the Cognitive Analytic Therapy (CAT) relationship or the treatment or supervisory relationship. Thus, according to the reader's professional role, they might replace the title 'the helper's dance list', with the carer's, supervisor's, doctor's, parent's, nurse's or therapist's dance list. The idea of dance brings to the fore the sense of helping as a joint activity, with a range of ways of carrying out the help and of styles of participation in the help. The aim is to offer an open, reflective but not intrusive framework for noticing when, how and why we join, or create, an unhelpful dance. If we can be more confident in noticing the dance we are in, it is easier to name it in constructive ways and negotiate a better outcome with everyone involved. The dance list is in Appendix 6 and several of its uses are summarised in this chapter. These are concerned with promoting relational thinking along the lines described in Chapter 5 on relational intelligence and go hand-in-hand with the skills of mapping out patterns of interaction using the methods of cognitive analytic therapy (Ryle and Kerr 2002).

Helping is a complicated process

Unless the helping contract is a very straightforward exchange of roles, when we try to help, we can find it hard to hold in mind all the variables involved at once. We tend to focus on one of the following: the goals of help, the recipient of help, the helping relationship, our own failings. When we have difficulty helping, we tend to say to ourselves or to colleagues:

'If only we could understand their needs better, or what they want from me, or work out what I am doing wrong.' Or: 'If only they were more motivated, or more able to make use of the help in some way.' Under pressure of time, the narrowing process of finding a focus is often at odds with the broadening process of gathering a full picture. It is easy to lose perspective as we get immersed in the detail of helping. Famously the task focus can take over from a process focus on the helping relationship itself. Several of the items from the helper's dance list address this. For example question 20: '*Where were we?* I can get so involved sorting out the relationship I forget the reason for meeting' (Q20). Or question 6 '*Lose perspective:* I get so involved in the detail I forget the big picture' (Q6). We can be pulled into saying to ourselves: 'Let's get on with it, forget that psychological stuff. Help me sort this out.' Or dances like the following, summarised by question 1: '*Never good enough:* I have high expectations of myself which makes me think my help won't be good enough, others will be disappointed and I will cope by trying even harder' (Q1).

In this and many other ways listed in the dances, we can easily be so entangled in one style of helping that we neglect, or don't see the need, to talk about the process of helping, in particular the changing quality of the helping relationship between us. Often this is because talking about the relationship in the here and now is uncomfortable, feels a little unnatural and of uncertain outcome and is not so commonly done with good results in everyday life. See question 19 in the dance list: '*Not here, not now:* I see the need to talk about what is happening between us but find it unpredictable or embarrassing and tend to wait and miss the moment to name it' (Q19). In this manner we can understandably fall into some version of saying to ourselves: 'Don't go there.' Whether this is wise or not is an important part of self-reflection, but we need to notice and name the dance before we can negotiate our choice of action. Our patterns of relating, especially our more personal and informal ones, are based on procedural knowledge and ways of reciprocating laid down in our earliest years of life. When stopping at talking about the immediate interaction or our part in helping turns the spotlight on us, we can easily say to ourselves: 'Definitely don't go back there.' This is because to stop and think about the here-and-now relationship is to stop and question personal aspects of our taken-for-granted sense of self.

Caution and a certain amount of reserve are also built into our professional roles. A number of the dances address this dilemma as we struggle between personal and professional sides of ourselves. For example, question 3: '*Genuine and vulnerable or safe but less real*: Either a) I show feelings and feel genuine but somewhat vulnerable or b) I safely hide feelings, appear professional but less the real me' (Q3). Or in a different way, question 13: *'Jump in or hold back:* Either a) I am in at the deep end as a helper and tend to give my all or b) I am not so involved and hold back, miss the moment to help or watch on from the sidelines' (Q13). These dances each have their distinctive kinds of music and detailed steps, which are hard to notice in the blur of active involvement in helping. They are familiar and typical patterns, which can be compassionately described in accurate detail and used to increase awareness and develop negotiating skills to change the helper's dance. Much of the help, regardless of the methods we use, the roles we have or the setting in which we work, depends on working together to establish and maintain the helping relationship. Help often goes wrong because the process of helping has gone wrong.

The dancer's help list offers colleagues and teams an opportunity to reflect together on the interaction between more personal and individual motivations for helping and familiar ways of being pulled into a particular helping role or style. Such shared reflection can foster a more open culture of discussion and supervision combining personal and professional judgement.

The one-third rule of thumb

At the core of the idea of the helper's dance list is the idea of shared responsibility and the notion that one-third of the dance is being led by the client, one-third by the therapist or helper, and one-third by the system, model, context or surrounding culture, etc. This simple rule challenges us not to put all the blame on the system or on the client or on ourselves. Instead we should wonder at the relational dynamics in play. The helper's capacity to reflect and change is helped by having the various helper's dances in mind. The summary descriptions of the dances in the list have been evolved from a repeated process of use and revision involving several thousand people in a variety of helping professions. It seems of particular use in the context of working with the more challenging and complex relationships associated with working with complex needs or in this case of learning difficulties and disabilities.

A scaffolding for building a reflective discussion

Reflecting on the process of helping is not something that we can do on our own. Even the most experienced practitioner needs a bit of backup in terms of theory and a scaffolding that can guide us to building an open way of negotiating how the relationship is going. When we do focus on the helping relationship there are five different approaches that need integrating but are often used as if they can stand on their own. In a very summarised and simplified form, these are:

- the psychoanalytic approach with its focus on the listening relationship and the push and pull of transference feelings from elsewhere on to the helper so as to be explored in the room
- the interpersonal approach with its focus on skilled communication and sensitively creating a collaborative and reflective relationship
- the humanistic approach with its focus on genuineness and authentic, holistic, human-to-human encounter
- the problem-solving approach with its practical focus on solutions, coaching and self-esteem
- the cognitive approach with its focus on ways of making meaning.

Sticking to any one of these approaches has the benefit of giving the helper a clear framework but the risk of narrowing how the helping relationship is managed. From a relational and dialogic point of view highlighted by this book and by the list of helper's dances, each of these approaches has a part to play in orchestrating a full understanding of how help is established and maintained. The helper's dance list contains elements of all of them and offers a hook for reflection and discussion of how patterns of helping are noticed, named and negotiated. A fuller account of integrating these five approaches is beyond the remit of these pages.

Hindsight really is a wonderful thing

It is not easy to achieve awareness of the helping relationship in the thick of helping someone. When things are not working, it is very tempting to blame the client or the system or blame oneself. We can benefit from a checklist that helps us to see quickly what might be going on, develop our self-awareness and not go leaping from the frying pan into the fire when things get hot to handle. It is a familiar lament that 'I can see what was going wrong now (a few hours or days later) so clearly but I had no sense of it there and then in the thick of it.' We are quite good at spotting our mistakes in retrospect. Hindsight really is a wonderful thing. Hindsight comes from seeing something in a fresh light, stepping out of role, hearing and then understanding another person's point of view. We often find ourselves good at seeing what others are getting caught up in as helpers. This is because we are not so involved and can see the main features of the interaction by virtue of being at a distance from it.

Another person who by definition is doing a different dance to different music can see and hear things in ways that we cannot because we are too involved.

Our challenge is to promote a more effective and self-conscious interaction in the helping relationship when we are in the thick of it. We can do this in supervision, or on reflection, by mapping out familiar patterns of help that goes wrong. This can aid our skills in spotting unhelpful interactions as they occur. It is useful to do this routinely and with as much spontaneity as possible without retreating behind professional roles. The skill is to practise the processes of reflection and shared supervision such that they become like second nature. One way of helping this along is *Speed Supervision* (Potter 2012) using mapping tools and ideas borrowed from CAT (Ryle and Kerr 2002).

'It takes two to tango'

The introduction to the helper's dance list, notes that:

> All of us have roles in our lives that involve helping people. Mostly our help is okay but there are a number of unhelpful dances that we, as helpers, can do despite our best intentions. If we can notice them as they happen we have a chance to change. I call them dances to capture the whole interaction between people of feelings, behaviour and thinking summed up by the adage: 'it takes two to tango'. (Appendix 6)

The helping relationship is like a dance in the following ways.

- It is a joint activity involving doing things together, which needs staging. When we agree to dance we need to notice, name and negotiate the dance, the setting and the context.
- It is an interaction that is both genuine and a performance: giving part of self and being in a role.
- There are changes in who is leading and following, changes in direction and changes in the speed, type and intensity of the dance.
- It is something over which we have potential choice, ownership and agency. I can change the dance.
- It is something we do alone, with one other or as part of a group.
- It is something that is transparent, visible and may be exposing and inviting of a response from others.
- It requires a number of competencies and skills that can be learnt but that cannot always be done well but can be more than worthwhile if we can do the step in an okay way.

- Getting the dance wrong and noticing it and practising together to get it right is an important part of the art of dancing.
- It is to be judged by its performance in the moment as experienced and not how it should be on paper.

The helping relationship, like most dances has steps that should be followed or are missed or skipped over. The lead in the dance changes pace and direction, and even the nature of the dance can change. The flow, fluency and direction of the dance will be influenced by the different ways the participants of the dance hear the music. As with dancing, we want to emphasise agency and joint activity and this implies awareness of the skills, needs, context and possible choices involved in the particular helper's dance. No help can be sustained without a certain amount of spontaneity, interpersonal trust and predictability of interaction. Partners to the help need to have some idea of their roles. If we don't know our role or don't take time to work out and rehearse our role then we will tend to fall back automatically on familiar and well-rehearsed positions. This checklist helps increase awareness in the helper and leads to a capacity and willingness to notice, reflect on and change the dance if it is not helping.

Using the checklist

When you use the checklist, keep in mind the list of dances is not set in stone. You can change the words and use it in different ways. Any of us might get pulled into any one of the dances in certain circumstances. With each item it is important that you make the words yours. For personal or private reflection you may think that your home and work responses are somewhat different.

First, just score your first reactions quickly to all the items. Second, go through it again and change or add words to help each item fit your experience if you need to. Third time around, compare your results by talking them through compassionately with a colleague or friend and discuss things you might try and do differently. Not all the items will strike a chord with you. Many may once have been true but are no longer so. Think back to earlier in your current role or career and how you might have scored yourself differently. Think about how you would like to be in contrast to any of the patterns.

The checklist is designed for paired or small group discussion and in particular for team discussion of common and distinctive patterns that they get into. Look for clusters of patterns that seem to link to each other. Usually one or two items will stand out and have a particular reference to one of your work roles or settings. It is also possible to focus on one client, or one professional role, and think through how the relevant dance is being jointly constructed and how you can notice, name and negotiate a number of different steps to the dance or a different dance altogether. As a team exercise divide into small groups, or into professional or mixed groups, and give a score for the team as a whole for each item. Change the first person pronoun to we and us instead of I and me. This use of the dance list to aid discussion can be supplemented by mapping out the pattern as a group using the cognitive analytic mapping methods described elsewhere.

Noticing, naming and negotiating

It is useful as you work together with the list of helper's dances to think of the three-way relationship between noticing, naming and negotiating what is happening. We first have to notice what is happening. This may arise through a feeling, an incident or a gesture between you in the helping relationship.

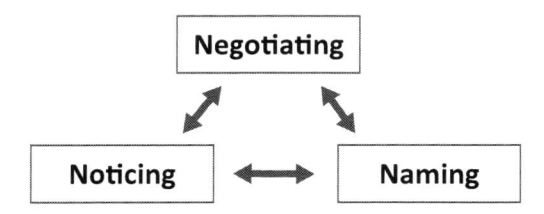

Figure 6.1: The three N's dance

Naming what you notice is a delicate and simultaneous process of finding the words to describe both what you are noticing and how you are noticing it. When naming what you notice, it is easy to go too much 'head to head' and be too direct. The aim is to work side by side. Whilst being direct on some occasions is essential, it often stops the subtle process of noticing something deeper and more fully. This depends upon the shared process of finding the words. As you find the words to name things together more is noticed, (made infinitely easier by mapping to help discussion as considered elsewhere in the book and in particular Chapter 1). Also a quality of collaboration can be built up in how you negotiate a shared understanding. This might be described as meta-dance that can help us negotiate our participation in helpful and unhelpful dances.

Chapter 7

What Aspects of Intelligence are Needed to Understand the Concept of reciprocal roles?
Julie Lloyd

Introduction

In the introduction section of this book, we described the concept of reciprocal roles, a useful shortcut to name patterns of how we get on with other people and how we see ourselves. As therapists, we deduce reciprocal roles from stories of childhood, current relationships and our interactions with individuals and use these reciprocal role descriptions as a device to explore unhelpful relational patterns with clients. Little has been written about the personal or relational lives of people with intellectual disabilities and there is insufficient understanding of their socially derived internal world. As Cognitive Analytic Therapy (CAT) emphasises working within the therapeutic relationship, i.e., involving activity and emotion (contrasted with psycho-educational approaches that depend on verbal skills), one of the central questions is whether reciprocal roles is a meaningful concept for people with intellectual disabilities.

The fundamental importance and efficacy of the therapeutic relationship is common to all psychological therapies, (Frank 1961; Luborsky, Singer and Luborsky 1975; Shapiro and Shapiro 1982). It is characterised by attentiveness, empathy, consistency, warmth and non-intrusive concern. Too often, people with intellectual disabilities have had early relationship experiences that were rejecting or lacking intimacy, leading to them expecting to be devalued or disliked. One of CAT's aims is to offer a direct experience and description of more helpful reciprocal roles, assisting people to learn they can make changes leading to improved relationships.

Do people with intellectual disabilities have a concept of reciprocal roles?

Direct observation and interaction suggest that people with intellectual disabilities do have patterns of behaviour that are likely to elicit reciprocations from others. However, do they have a concept of how what one person does to another person influences what that other person experiences i.e., that roles are reciprocal? Although there is some research demonstrating which reciprocal roles often play a part in the lives of people with intellectual disabilities (Psaila and Crowley 2005), we do not know whether they have a sense of relational patterns, as they have not yet been asked. We also do not know whether the development of being aware of relational patterns depends on a particular level of intellectual development. Therefore, I conducted some research to start answering this question.

Design
Participants were shown drawings of one pole of nine reciprocal roles (selected from Psaila and Crowley's research) to see whether they could select the other side of that role, from a choice of three.

Method

PARTICIPANTS

The participants were adults at a day centre for people with severe intellectual disabilities. People with severe autism or profound and complex needs were excluded. Thirty participants were needed in order to get sufficient numbers to be fairly sure that any results were reasonably representative. Participants were approached following discussion with their key worker.

OBTAINING CONSENT

The Arscott, Dagnan and Kroese (1998) protocol to assess consent for people with intellectual disabilities to participate in research was used. Only if participants obtained a full score did the retrieval of data continue. Formal ethical approval was granted.

ASSESSMENT MATERIALS

The first two assessment tools are standardised.

1. *British Picture Vocabulary Scale: Second Edition* (BPVS) (Dunn *et al.* 1997) was used to assess verbal mental age. It is designed to assess receptive vocabulary in children aged 3–16. Whitaker (2011) found this assessment tool was specifically connected with language ability but not with visual ability, which means that the BPVS is very specific and does not measure general intelligence.

2. Ravens Coloured Progressive Matrices (RCPM) designed for 5–11-year-olds was used to assess the ability to generate (usually non-verbal) schemata that make it easier to handle complexity. As a 'paradigmatic' measure of fluid intelligence (Mackintosh 1998, p.228), recommended uses include measurement of a person's ability to form perceptual relations. Spearman considered Raven's Matrices was the best measure of general intelligence, as it is a test of inductive reasoning; a view confirmed in a majority of the later studies (e.g., Raven, Raven and Court 1998).

   Both these scales, although normed for children, are frequently used when assessing adults with severe intellectual disabilities because of a lack of age-appropriate alternatives at the required cognitive level. Occasionally, a drawing in the BPVS does appear more suitable for children, but most are not directed to any particular age. The RCPM drawings are appropriate for all ages.

3. The feeling-event matching task was tailor-made. This used Makaton symbols depicting five key emotions (disgust, happy, angry, sad and fear) (Ekman and Davidson 1994) and five line drawings depicting events (dog faeces, a Christmas tree, a man hitting a dog with a stick, a grave and a ghost) to assess whether participants could match up feelings with events. A small, informal pilot sample of five adults with milder intellectual deficits, showed they could easily match up these cards.

Line drawings in Makaton style were used depicting actions involved in nine reciprocal roles:

1. Abusing in relation to Abused
2. Rejecting to Rejected
3. Rescuing/Caring to Rescued/Cared for
4. Damaging to Damaged

What Aspects of Intelligence are Needed

5. Abandoning to Abandoned (Unloving to Unloved)
6. Special/Perfect to Learning Disabled
7. Controlling to Controlled/Fragile
8. Blaming to Blamed
9. Overwhelming to Overwhelmed.

The same five adults from the previous pilot study could also all select the correct cards to form these roles.

Figure 7.1: The feeling-event matching cards

PROCEDURE

The stimulus pole of the reciprocal role was offered together with three cartoons in a random order. One was the anticipated response pole, another an opposite and the third a distracter.

Figure 7.2: The top pole of the abuse reciprocal role i.e., abusing

Illustrating the reciprocal role 'Abusing to Abused', the first drawing shows someone with a cross face holding a raised stick apparently in the throes of hitting (abusing). This is the top pole of the reciprocal role, i.e., the stimulus, doing to, or parental position.

Three possible responses were then offered.

Figure 7.3: The bottom pole of the abuse reciprocal role i.e., abused

1. A person cowering with their hands over their head, (abused).

    This is the bottom pole that matches up to form a reciprocal role as the response, done to, or child position.

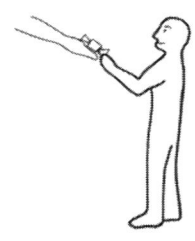

Figure 7.4: The bottom pole of the abuse reciprocal role the antonym to abused

2. This next picture showing a smiling person being offered a sweet (supportive and nurturing) depicts an antonym.

Figure 7.5: A distraction picture unconnected with abuse

3. A person standing, not doing anything but smiling (random).

   Participants were then asked verbally about each card
   - What is happening?
   - What does the person feel?
   - What does the other person do or feel?

If participants were unable to say, they were told what the drawing was meant to show. Participants then selected which of the three possible response cards fitted the stimulus scene best. Using the five emotion pictures, they were also asked how the responding person might feel.

STATISTICAL ANALYSIS

Statistical analyses were performed using SPSS (Statistical Packages for the Social Sciences, Version 17.0, SPSS Inc.). In order to decide whether any results were meaningful or not, this analysis used the traditional cut-off point for psychological research of this size, weighing the risk that 1 in 20 results may be significant by chance.

Results

Descriptive analysis

BPVS and RCPM scores showed an even spread of verbal and visual abilities amongst participants. BPVS range was 27–128 months with a median of five years, and raw scores on the RCPM range were 4–80 with a median of 13. RCPM norms are too outdated for an IQ score to be valid. Participants' results from the two intellectual assessments were compared to see if they were linked. If there was a link, then these two tests did not, in fact, measure totally different aspects of intelligence. A second task was to see whether their scores on either of the intellectual assessments were linked with whether or not they could do the feelings-event pairing task. As expected, scores on the BPVS were significantly associated with scores on RCPM (there was only a 1 in 200 chance that this result was just a fluke). However, how participants performed on both the intellectual measures did not predict whether or not they could match pictures of feelings with pictures of events.

In Table 7.1, the left hand column gives the numbers of matches, which subsequent columns show as the Percentages of reciprocal roles (RR) correctly identified, antonyms or distracter cards selected and the number of correct matches between feelings and reciprocal roles. For example, this table shows 33.3 per cent of participants identified correctly six reciprocal roles and 76.7 per cent could correctly identify five or more of the reciprocal roles.

Table 7.1: Frequencies (rounded to 1%)

Number of matches	% correctly identifying RR	% selecting opposite	% selecting distracter	% selecting possible correctly associated feelings with the RR
0		23.3	10	
1		26.7	46.7	
2		36.7	23.3	
3	13	6.7	13.3	13.3
4	10	3.3	3.3	6.7
5	16.7	3.3		Page	1010
6	33.3			13.3
7	10			6.7
8	16.7			13.3
9				6.7

Were these responses on matching pairs of specific reciprocal roles just caused by random luck (such as could be achieved by tossing a coin) or were participants really able to match the pictures showing both poles of reciprocal roles? A statistical test called Chi^2 was used to answer this; seven out of the nine reciprocal roles produced results that suggest their ability to match these pictures was down to more than luck, meaning these results were significant.

Linear regression

A more practical approach to finding out whether different factors are linked is to explore whether results on one assessment *predict* the results obtained on another. Linear regression is a mathematical technique that explores whether a person's assessment results can be drawn as a straight line that predicts how they will do in another assessment. The question here is whether participants' results from the intellectual assessments or the feelings-event pairing test could predict whether they could match pictures of the common reciprocal roles encountered by people with intellectual disabilities into pairs. Results of this statistical test showed that how participants performed on the verbal assessment (BPVS) or the feelings-event pairing task did not predict whether they could match up pictures to make reciprocal roles. However, what turned out to be the intellectual key to whether or not they could match reciprocal roles was how well they scored on the pattern-making tasks RCPM. At first sight, this result is surprising, especially if therapists assume that 'psychological mindedness', i.e., whether or not a person might benefit from a talking therapy, is based on verbal comprehension or the ability to link feelings with events. However, perhaps seeing patterns and links is even more important.

In Table 7.2 the first three columns describe whether scores on the matrices test predicted what responses were selected to the stimulus pole of the reciprocal roles, and the fourth column describes whether scores on matrices predicted the capacity to assign correct feelings associated with the reciprocal roles.

Table 7.2 Linear regression from matrices score to RR identification

	RR correctly identified	Opposite selected	Distracter selected	Link with correctly associated feelings
Predictor variable	0.464	-0.509	-0.137	0.645
P =	**0.010***	**0.004***	0.478	**0.001***

Reciprocal role identification

This table shows that we can be 99 per cent certain that scores on the visual pattern-making task RCPM predicted whether people could match up reciprocal roles and correctly assign feelings to those reciprocal roles. Furthermore, scores on the RCPM significantly predicted the overall tendency to assign an antonym to the stimulus pole of the reciprocal roles.

How consistent or reliable is the idea that these nine reciprocal roles do represent different roles, or are they, in fact, simply nine different labels for just one or two roles? This was checked using a statistical test called Cronbach's Alpha to explore whether the nine reciprocal roles represented a single unidimension or nine multidimensional constructs. The score showed that these nine reciprocal roles did represent nine *different* roles (the score was 0.107; 0.7 or higher is needed to show that ability to spot one reciprocal role is associated with the ability to spot another).

Discussion

This research explored what cognitive abilities are needed to understand the concept of a central tool in CAT: reciprocal roles. The findings indicate that the ability to recognise reciprocal roles does not depend on verbal ability but appears to draw more on fluid, general reasoning and the ability to form abstractions, as assessed by RCPM. This finding is consistent with the non-verbal, pre-linguistic nature of being in relationships. It suggests that when we look at feelings, we are more likely to succeed if the pattern of feelings and their links is presented or developed in map form alongside the talking.

Why is the ability to discern reciprocal roles linked with RCPM?

As there are so many potential specific image patterns, it would be impossible for these to pre-exist as templates at a genetic level (with the exception of a preference for human faces). What does appear to exist is the predisposition to observe and synthesise such image patterns, and to engage emotionally with others. For example, Damasio (1994) defines the mind as a process of developing neural representations 'of which one can be made conscious as images' (p.229), not requiring language.

Discussion of the selection of opposite drawings

The results showed a significant number of opposites were also matched with the stimulus part of the reciprocal role. This selection might be based on how a person might cope with the stimulus end of a difficult reciprocal role.

Ryle considers someone whose reciprocal role is Neglecting to Neglected would know that care exists, seeking it as a part of the neglecting reciprocal role: 'Thus, the self-neglecting person, who cannot care for himself, may also hold on to an image of an idealised, caring parent' (Ryle 1975, pp.12–13).

How does the visual basis of reciprocal roles relate to the practice of CAT?

One of the important components of CAT is the development of a 'Sequential Diagrammatic Reformulation'. This is a map depicting the client's typical unhelpful roles, which tracks how people move from one role to another. Wells (2009) interviewed people with intellectual disabilities who had received CAT and found that participants used their diagram to internalise their therapy. It is possible the Sequential Diagrammatic Reformulation assists internalisation because it taps into the ability to abstract patterns used to understand reciprocal roles.

The contrast between the intellectual requirements to benefit from Cognitive Behavioural Therapy and CAT

Research conducted within Cognitive Behavioural Therapy explored what intellectual abilities are required for people with mild intellectual disabilities to benefit from it. Most people with mild intellectual disabilities (typically a BPVS score above seven years) can identify pictures of basic emotions. However, only 10 per cent can understand 'cognitive mediation' (Oathamshaw and Haddock 2006), an important approach in Cognitive Behavioural Therapy requiring the ability to identify what emotion would be experienced given a specific situation and belief. This ability is linked to language comprehension (Dagnan, Chadwick and Proudlove 2000). This suggests that in Cognitive Behavioural Therapy, as a psycho-educational approach, verbal abilities are important, contrasting with relational therapies such as CAT.

Conclusions

This small research project explored whether vocabulary (assessed by BPVS) or a general ability to make sense of stimuli through constructing patterns (assessed by RCPM) is more influential in understanding the central tool in CAT: reciprocal roles. However, this is an initial study. If future research does confirm this initial suggestion that the ability to make visual patterns could be useful in being able to understand social relational patterns, there are implications for developing tools that tap into this for therapeutic interventions. It supports the CAT idea of how mapping side by side with someone with intellectual disabilities might help a therapeutic conversation or interaction by enabling and supporting some of the dimensions of relational intelligence.

Part 2
Using Cognitive Analytic Therapy in the Community

Chapter 8
The Problems of Caring and Being Cared For (or How to Get Your Shoelaces Tied For You)
David Wilberforce

Introduction

> 'One must first of all take pains to find him where he is and begin there, in order to help another effectively I must understand more than he – yet first of all surely I must understand what he understands…'
> *Soren Kierkegaard (2000)*

In this chapter I aim to explore a subject that I have always struggled to fully understand; from my early years as a nursing student working in a hospital for the 'mentally handicapped' through my time as a community nurse working with families and up to my years as a psychotherapist: the meanings of being cared for and being dependent and of being the carer one's self.

Each time, my perspective altered as my role changed. Initially I was mostly curious about my helping role and that of colleagues as members of staff; I then focused very much on the needs of parents and family in relation to the 'burden' of caring; and finally, I became much more aware of the struggles of individuals themselves, by now labelled as 'learning disabled', in being the recipients of all this help and care.

There are a number of relationships in which the descriptive term 'caring' might be used: parental and romantic love, friendship, pets, we may care about our work or hobbies, whether our football team wins or loses, our garden or house and so on. Such a breadth of usage perhaps makes it difficult to pin down a meaning that is specific to this particular area of work.

Perhaps more specifically, it is the 'helping' aspect of caring that I find the most problematic.

It is relatively easy, with good intention, to strive to be 'helpful' and to convey a helpful attitude. Indeed, in the short term, people may actually experience our actions as 'helpful' and then it may make both them and us feel better. I fear, however, that in the long term such 'helpfulness' may be of less benefit and significance than we imagine.

There are a variety of ideas or 'lenses' one might use in order to examine and think about this issue; in this case I am utilising the 'lens' of CAT (in particular the analytic aspects) and being true to CAT, I feel I must stress that this process clearly does not pertain to everyone and nor can it entirely define any one individual. In addition, my experiences are inevitably skewed by the type of referrals I have received – mostly troubled individuals with at least some level of independence – and the focus upon problematic procedures.

However, I do believe that there are particular 'problematic procedures' that may well be of general interest and relevance to many whom, like me, may be struggling with the meanings of this 'caring' paradigm that inevitably pervades this area of work.

This chapter then, is a reflection upon certain aspects of the work of 'caring' and the implicit hypotheses we use to understand why others, or we, may have thought or done a particular thing. I wish to attempt to articulate and develop some further understanding of these processes – some more in awareness than others – in the hope that others will be encouraged to reflect upon and examine for themselves the meanings and consequences of both caring and being cared for – with whichever 'lens' they so choose.

Context

> Umuntu ngumuntu ngabantu. (A person becomes a person through other people.)
>
> *Zulu proverb*

This saying from an African Humanist philosophy suggests that personhood is a process; the product of our interconnectedness and relationships experienced in the context of community. From a CAT perspective such thinking is not out of place alongside the dialogic ideas of Vygotsky (VDV and Valsiner 1991) and Bakhtin (Holquist 1990;

Bakhtin 1981) on the development of identity and the relationship between self and others, namely, that identity is socially constructed. The concept of 'umuntu' also stresses our connection with ancestors as well as those yet unborn, thus also accommodating the idea that certain procedures or 'hot potatoes' – often shame related – can be passed on and acted out through the generations.

From this constructionist standpoint the idea of a 'intellectual disability' (as an identity) must also be a social construct (Dudley-Marlin 2004) and therefore to be seen as an actively negotiated status that can change depending on circumstance.

In this sense, it is not a fixed object in an unchanging social world – the 'condition' of intellectual disability is brought into being interactionally. In other words, how others perceive and respond to our actions impacts greatly on how we see ourselves and our place in the world. We are constantly recreating our sense of identity – positioning ourselves in relation to others – both externally in those we meet and internally in those we carry with us.

Similarly, 'caring' must be seen as an inter-subjective phenomenon that will have different meanings between different individuals, depending on context and circumstance.

This process of status or identity negotiation is not so easy from a position of little power; the person with an intellectual disability can become trapped by the definitions of more powerful others. 'In the minds of people there are many understandings, in the minds of professionals there are few' (Suzukis 1973, p.21).

Franz Fanon, a revolutionary psychiatrist and philosopher born in Martinique in 1925 – a French colony at the time – was particularly interested in colonisation, oppression and power in relation to mental heath and identity. He said that we 'may expect distressed persons to give up their own understanding of their own experience and effectively refuse to accept their right to self determination *unless they accept the professional diagnosis and prescribed treatments*' (Fannon 1961, p.166). He believed that their only choice was to conform and be validated or affirm their own beliefs and be perceived as a troublesome rebel. I believe that this still is, despite good intentions, very often the case today within our mental health, and to some degree intellectual disability, services.

One might just substitute the terms 'care' for 'treatment' and 'challenging' for 'rebel'. I have worked with a number of clients who have been only too aware of this 'choice' within even their own family and, unsurprisingly, have chosen to be the passive recipient of care – the 'good girl' or 'good boy' – rather than be perceived of as 'bad', 'challenging' or worse: unloved and unwanted. After all, to be not cared about is to be disregarded and ignored.

In one reformulation, from a woman in her late 20s, this was described as like being a 'cat without claws', the corollary, the 'cat *with* claws' was perceived as dangerous and filled with murderous rage – a state best avoided. What often lies behind the sense of helplessness, dependency and vulnerability associated with being a 'recipient of care' is indeed a primitive rage.

Furthermore, these powerful and difficult emotions are unlikely to be fully attended to within some families; they can be too dangerous and painful and thus become highly taboo. Unfortunately, when the source of a person's feelings of rejection and rage cannot be directly articulated or explored and understood, painful confusion is the likely result.

Such taboos and resultant emotional confusion can also apply within 'caring' organisations amongst professional carers and within communities as a whole. The whole system can then become disrupted and unhealthy for all concerned (Bloom 2011).

Consequently, as Fanon suggests, CAT and any other therapy cannot be seen as just a personal enterprise; there will inevitably be these aspects, along with other moral and political dimensions, that have an influence on the therapist – and indeed any worker in the field – which it is important to be aware of and attend to.

In intellectual disability services, perhaps more than in any other field, there has been a constant quest to find labels that are meaningful and non-stigmatising – 'intellectual disability' being the latest and most accepted (in the UK at least). As we have already suggested, the meaning of labels are socially defined and therefore say more about the attitudes of others towards 'difference' than the individuals themselves. As Fanon also postulated: 'The mastery of language affords remarkable power' (Fannon 1961, p.290). From this standpoint perhaps we must also be interested in this all-pervasive term 'care' and the meanings it suggests in this area of work, for instance: I work in a *caring profession*, I have completed many *care-plans,* our clients live in *care homes* in *care services* staffed by *carers* and inspected by *the care quality commission,* parents are called *carers* – and so on, you get the idea.

Whilst caring is obviously of itself not a bad thing, the images of caring that we see inevitably suggest impairment, vulnerability, sickness and helplessness on the one hand and benevolence, commitment and self-sacrifice on the other. W.H. Auden once remarked that writers were guilty of every kind of arrogance except that of social workers, who say, 'We are here to help others.' 'What,' he asked, 'are the "others" supposed to be here for?'(Auden, pp.81–89). Those 'others' with an intellectual disability, very often reflecting an internalised sense projected onto them by family and society, are certainly likely to *feel* helpless and thus invite help *because they then feel unable to help themselves*. Unfortunately, being helped can often be a way of *maintaining* feelings of helplessness.

In another way, perhaps an interaction can only be perceived as 'caring' or 'helpful' if the recipient perceives themselves as in need of such help or care; if not, it may be more like 'interference' or even 'oppression' – parents of toddlers and teenagers will be very familiar with this scenario. Whilst we, as carers, would of course suggest that it is the experience and perception of the client – the recipient of our care – that matters the most, I do wonder if sometimes it actually depends more on who holds the most power?

With regard to our quest for new labels, I would suggest that there might be no escape from the *caring to cared for* relationship no matter what terminology we choose. Whilst CAT, in utilising the client's own language is actually less reliant on such labels, in my experience, howsoever it is named, in the field of intellectual disability at least, this is a relationship that often emerges as problematic. The main problems being just how do people cope with excessive and prolonged dependency? This is on psychological and emotional levels as well as a practical level.

Thinking further about organisational confusion and distress, Stokes and Sinason (1992, p.49) have suggested that societies' (and carers') own psychological defences 'may impede clear definition of [the] difference in order to deny its existence' – in this case the 'difference' being intellectual disability and dependence – and that 'objectivity may well be sacrificed to self-preservation'.

The implicit relationship in *caring to cared for* is, I would suggest, something akin to *healthy expert/healthy 'normal'* to *vulnerable recipient/needy recipient* and thus indeed enables those in the parental derived role to avoid their *own* neediness and vulnerability. Sinason (1992, p.150) supported this view when she suggested: 'The whole network around the handicapped is often equally involved in fighting insight to keep the handicapped individual in his secondary sick role.' Compulsive care-giving and over-involvement can be psychological defences that enable a denial of feelings and keeps others in the 'cared for' role. For parents, for example, staying in a caring role may help to avoid having to face the loss of the 'normal' child or be a retreat from having to face up to their child's actual handicaps; the guilt associated with not being able to make it alright may also fuel a life-long devotion to caring in a way that disrupts the possibility of a healthy separation (Symington 1981). To be cared for then becomes loaded with other confusing dimensions that do not necessarily originate from nor belong to the individuals themselves. It can easily become an oppressive and exploitative process in which the needs of others are used to fulfil our own needs to be 'helpful' and to feel good about ourselves as a result.

Furthermore, the individual's way of coping with the resultant confusion and distress may once again as before, attract the label of 'challenging behaviour' and all *that* entails.

In my work, particularly as a nurse, I have often become aware of my own discomfort and difficulty in finding a way of relating to and of being with individuals beyond the restrictive boundaries of *caring to cared for* – to find perhaps a relationship based more on our similarities as human beings rather than our differences. I am sure that the fact I worked for the NHS compounded my professional difficulties in this area, and whilst I believe in the organisation and value greatly the work of nurses and others, I have always been ambivalent about working under its auspices, simply because of its powerful associations with sickness, care and 'making better'. In addition, having trained as a nurse, I am aware that many perceive 'caring' as central to nursing practice, and whilst I am not sure the problematic nature of these relationships would disappear by merely changing organisations or profession, my psychotherapy role at least afforded me more time and permission to begin to work through this issue with clients.

When co-facilitating a therapy group for people with a 'mild' intellectual disability, I recall noticing, sometime during the early stages of the group processes – which were inevitably characterised by denial and resistance – that whilst I *thought* I liked and valued the group members I somehow could not feel connected enough to want to go out for a beer with them, for instance. You might think, as the therapist, why *should* I? And whilst true, I was still concerned about why I could not seem to respond emotionally beyond a professional 'caring' role. At that time I experienced group members as somewhat passive, egocentric, trying to please (the therapists) and 'empty' somehow. I'm sure at times I felt a vague irritation and disappointment. The therapists were seemingly regarded by the group as the knowledgeable experts, idealised as 'sorted', powerful setters of agendas and rules and so on. I think we were all somewhat frustrated by being seemingly stuck in a *caring to cared for* reciprocal relationship in which we were each defined within very limited parameters.

As the group progressed, the group members began to relate differently to each other – with greater sharing of experiences and more compassion shown for each other, they began to value themselves and each other simply for what they were. I too, as part of this process, changed and realised at some point that now I really *would* like to go for a beer and potentially be friends because I felt genuinely connected to and interested in the group members as *fellow human beings*. For the group members and therapists this was a subtle yet very powerful shift in relationship.

Through the group process of holding and containment, along with the mutual telling and witnessing of stories, we could be with each other in a different way, and whilst there are various theoretical ways of thinking about this process (see Szivos and Griffiths 1992, for example, and others), I wonder if the most important thing was that it had begun to enable our escape from the tyranny of the *caring to cared for* dichotomy in which the other is objectified (see Figure 8.1).

The group members no longer felt that they had to seek our 'help' in order to somehow take care of us in order to be accepted, and as therapists we let go of our unconscious desires to 'make better' or 'make normal'. Instead, we could then engage in finding a more real or genuine way of being together.

My initial feelings of disappointment and rejection were probably more to do with what Corbett (2009) called the 'disability transference' emanating from the group members' own early disavowed experiences.

As Rogers (1958), amongst others, suggests, the goal of all 'carers' and caring organisations should be to care in a therapeutic non-possessive way that is not self-serving (self-protective) but in the interests of the client. I am sure this is the intension of most, however, given the taboos and processes mentioned earlier, this is not so easy or straightforward to achieve and therefore it simply is not the experience of many people with an intellectual disability.

A story

> Whilst I was walking alone in a park one day a small boy – aged about six or seven and something of a ragamuffin – appeared out of nowhere and rather challengingly plonked his foot in front of me. 'Oi mister!' he said cockily, 'I bet you can't tie shoelaces can ya?'

Well, I rose to the challenge of course. 'Bet I can!' I said, and tied his undone laces for him. He grinned at me and ran off happily…

The incident made me smile and also set me thinking about what had actually occurred between us; it seemed to me that the boy had managed to get his needs met whilst rather adeptly avoiding any shame or embarrassment associated with being unable to tie his own shoelaces. I too had felt good in being able to help him although I was also aware of the possibility of shaming him if I had responded in a different way. 'Hats off to him,' I thought. It also got me thinking further about the various aspects and skills involved in the process of getting his needs met in this way.

The shoelace boy: a deconstruction

1. Novelty/complexity is encountered (*lace undone*).
2. Anxiety is evoked (*I can't tie laces!*).
3. Awareness of needing help (*I can get help*).
4. Look for someone who can help (*I need someone more able than me*).
5. Awareness of shame/embarrassment (*they may think I should be able to do this*).
6. Devise a plan which will get my needs met whilst avoiding the shame (*I can't ask directly*).
7. Act out my plan and get help via a 'cover story'.

Qualities needed

- Emotional regulation – containment of anxiety.
- Ability to think – about possibilities/future/problem solving.
- Self-awareness regarding own real capabilities.
- Ability to choose an appropriate helpful/attachment figure.
- Communication skills.
- Negotiation skills/charm.
- Empathy.
- Confidence.
- Risk taking.

I do not think that the problem that this little boy faced was particularly unusual; we could probably all identify situations in which we have found similar ways to avoid the embarrassment of not knowing or needing help in some way. Depending on the qualities and skills in our possession, the pretexts we use in order to get help will either succeed or fail to varying degrees. Unfortunately, many people with an intellectual disability do not possess such qualities in abundance and thus their solutions may lack guile or indeed be self-defeating in that potentially helpful others are actually discouraged or pushed away.

Some words on shame

Shame can be a constructive emotion in that it may well motivate us to achieve, to keep promises or to do good in order to avoid the feeling. However, shame can also be destructive when it is experienced too frequently or intensely or over too long a period; we may be left with a chronic sense of shame, which may lead to withdrawal, passivity and self-denigration.

One definition of shame is: 'The internalization of a particular negative view of the self by powerful others…originally parents then society by extension' (Erikson 1950, p.226).

A colleague told me a story about Jack, a 30-year-old man with Down's syndrome, who climbed into a skip one day and shouted, apparently in jest: 'Look at me, I'm rubbish!'

A joke perhaps, though maybe a rather sad one.

Was Jack acting out his parent's unspoken (taboo) thoughts?

'Having a handicapped child evoked in me a great sense of failure… I thought of killing my child' (father of Down's syndrome baby quoted in Hannam 1975, p.61).

Lloyd (2009) spoke of shame as essentially a feeling of being unwanted and unworthy, one of those 'hot potatoes' that may be passed on to children, its roots being the nebulous shame within a family when one or more of the family members feel ashamed for reasons not clear to the child.

What is focused on during this early development can determine what the grown person will respond to in terms of shame and how they will deal with the feelings that are evoked in later comparable situations.

Shame then, can be taken on and transformed via defensive strategies into a lifelong dysfunctional vulnerability; when this is associated with being cared for (being the 'burden' of care) *this* may become the cause for problems in later caring relationships. The individual may respond with excessive shame when this sensitive area is evoked by even well-meaning others, thus being cared for *in itself* may bring with it unbearable feelings of shame, which *must* be defended against at all costs. Thus, *caring to cared for* has other more complex dimensions:

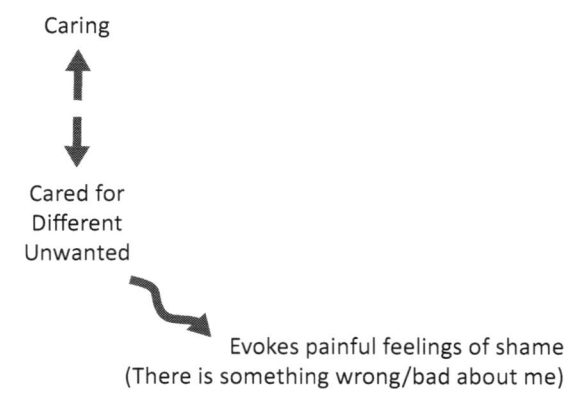

```
            Caring
              ↑
              ↓
          Cared for
          Different
          Unwanted
                  ↘
                    Evokes painful feelings of shame
                    (There is something wrong/bad about me)
```

Figure 8.1: A representation of how the mutually objectified perceptions of both therapists and group members shifted

The conclusion the individual arrives at is that it is shameful to be cared for and to be dependent; the dilemma for many is that they know they *need* to be dependent to some degree and thus cared for, possibly for quite a lot of the time. It's rather like going through life with your shoelaces undone *all the time.*

The 'cover' story

'Any sorrow can be borne if it can be told as a story...'
Hannah Arendt 1958

The idea of the 'cover story' as a defensive procedure related to the getting of 'care', arose for me in a supervision session in which I was discussing the possible motivations behind the words and actions of woman in her 30s with Down's syndrome.

Jenny, as I shall call her, was very focused on being independent and being treated 'as an adult', whilst at the same time placing herself in reckless unsafe situations from which staff at her residence felt compelled to rescue her. She would then be furious at her rescuers for compromising her independence and the process would begin again.

At other times she would profess helplessness or illness in the form of vague areas of pain around her body and seek looking after.

She seemed to vacillate between these two positions and staff felt pulled into either anxiously controlling her or offering protective and rescuing care. Neither position felt comfortable for them, they felt manipulated and unable to offer the 'normal' type of care that they thought of as appropriate to their role. As they saw it, they had no inherent desire to control Jenny and were only responding to her actions when they sought to keep her safe (contacting the police, for instance). Nor could they understand her 'sick' behaviour in order to get the care they were willing to offer her in the first place.

It seemed that Jenny was unable to tolerate such care without, in her eyes, any obvious reason for it to be proffered. In attempting to understand the meaning of her actions we may start with those meanings in her own awareness: 'I am ill' *(rescuing/nurturing to sick/ill)* and 'People treat me like a child and stop me getting what I want' *(controlling to controlled)* and if we then explore and extend her meanings further to unconscious procedures we may get to *disgusted/disappointed to worthless/unwanted.*

Thus, for her to passively accept care would mean acknowledging and accepting the painful truth that she was somehow 'different' and the associations she had experienced in her early (and current) life – such as unworthiness – made this acutely shameful and ultimately unbearable for her.

Her 'solution' was to ensure that she received the care she needed for reasons other than for simply being who she was; hence the 'cover stories' of illness and dramatic risky scenarios (see Figure 8.2).

The cover story or stories had to exist essentially to 'explain' her need for care. This was a process largely outside of her conscious awareness and therefore, in this and similar situations where we are applying meanings to another's actions, our interpretations can only be seen as hypotheses and supporting evidence must obviously be sought through the therapy. This may be gained via the CAT psychotherapy file and self-states questionnaire, use of reciprocal role images and other creative tools such as the Six Part Story Method as well as 'in the room' explorations and interpretations.

Some (Mclean *et al.* 2007) suggest that identity is constructed through narrative and consequently the stories we tell to others and ourselves are crucial to our sense of self. In CAT terms the re-formulation is the re-telling or re-authoring of some of our stories in a more forgiving, understanding or compassionate way. Other therapy models may speak of 'scripts' and 'schemas' but the ideas are not dissimilar.

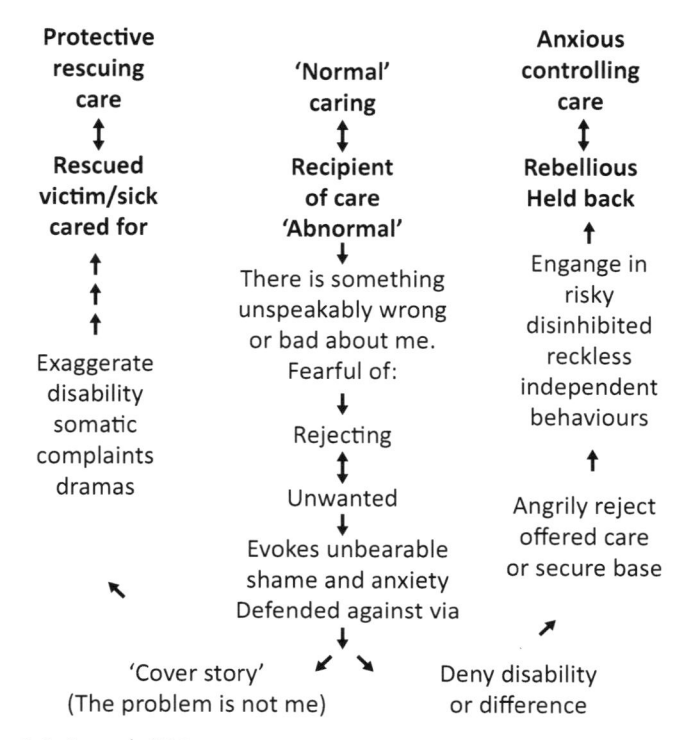

```
     Protective                              Anxious
     rescuing          'Normal'              controlling
       care            caring                   care
         ↕               ↕                       ↕
     Rescued          Recipient              Rebellious
   victim/sick         of care               Held back
     cared for        'Abnormal'                 ↑
         ↑                ↓                  Engange in
         ↑         There is something           risky
         ↑         unspeakably wrong         disinhibited
    Exaggerate     or bad about me.            reckless
    disability         Fearful of:           independent
     somatic              ↓                   behaviours
    complaints         Rejecting                 ↑
      dramas              ↕
                       Unwanted             Angrily reject
                          ↓                 offered care
        ↖           Evokes unbearable       or secure base
                    shame and anxiety
                    Defended against via         ↗
                          ↓
                   ↙            ↘
         'Cover story'           Deny disability
     (The problem is not me)     or difference
```

Figure 8.2: Jenny's SDR map

The quote from Hannah Arendt underlines the importance of having a story to help us bear what would otherwise be unbearable; if we do not have a story to tell, the story will *tell us* through our actions and relationships.

I wonder if many distressed people with an intellectual disability simply do not have or are unable to tell a story to explain the world's relationship with them. They have never been 'helped' to find one beyond having to be an unexplained recipient of care and so, like Jenny and her well-meaning staff – and indeed the wider caring system, they find themselves stuck in acting out a story not of their making. In their struggle to find ways to get her to accept the well-intentioned 'care' they offered, Jenny's staff were inadvertently denying her the option of telling a story that perhaps allowed her to bear her own particular 'sorrow'. Of course she 'rebelled' and became 'challenging'!

Unfortunately, I do not think that this process is uncommon, and the challenge is to re-examine values and ideas such that people with an intellectual disability can develop relationships beyond that of being just 'recipients of care'.

Finally

> 'Perhaps what people with an intellectual disability most long for is the experience of a person to person relationship in which two adults meet as equals.'
>
> *King 2005, pp.10–14*

We have seen that caring activity may sometimes be more in the interests of the carer or caring system than of the clients themselves, and often there are any number of well-meaning others involved, each with their own needs and ideas. This can make it difficult to focus only on the true needs of the client and avoid the imperatives to 'make better' or 'make normal'.

Nevertheless, what CAT and other psychodynamic therapies can offer then, is a space that is containing for both 'carers' and 'cared for' in which they can share, bear witness and reflect upon each other's stories in a way that involves the recognition of the other as a fellow human being – different but equal, worthy of respect and dignity – and wherein each can take some responsibility for the story of the other. There is no blame attached to having or needing a 'cover story' and the aim is not necessarily to get rid of it – sometimes we must just tie the shoelaces, other times we may not – but at least we may strive to understand why (and for who) we are responding in the way we do.

Chapter 9

Using Cognitive Analytic Therapy in a Systemic Context with Staff Teams

Reflections on the Process of Facilitating an Intervention

Helen Elford and Zoe Ball

Introduction

This chapter aims to reflect on the process of facilitating a Cognitive Analytic Therapy (CAT) intervention with staff teams in a systemic context in an intellectual disability setting. It is based on experiences from work undertaken in two intellectual disability inpatient units, but could be considered relevant to any piece of work undertaken using CAT with staff teams, for example, in a community-based setting. A CAT 'mapping' approach (similar to that used in the work) will be used to describe the process and reflect on an overall framework of 'desired', 'dreaded' and 'OK' states. The aim of the chapter is to reflect on the process rather than describe the specific intervention. In doing so, we hope to highlight some of the helpful and unhelpful processes that can emerge in such interventions, and identify learning points which could be informative for those undertaking similar work.

Inpatient units (assessment and treatment)

Inpatient units are used to support service users who have reached crisis in their community setting and require a hospital stay. Within intellectual disability services this is commonly due to an increase in challenging behaviour that cannot be managed safely in a community setting. Admissions may take place suddenly, with little opportunity for staff on the units to prepare for this in advance. There is an additional pressure, particularly within the current financial climate, to resolve difficulties as soon as possible and to keep length of stay to a minimum.

The most widely used definition of challenging behaviour is:

> culturally abnormal behaviour of such an intensity, frequency or duration that the physical safety of the person or others is likely to be place in serious jeopardy, to seriously limit use of, or result in the person being denied access to, ordinary community facilities. (Emerson 1995, p.4)

In addition, the British Psychological Society (Royal College of Psychiatrists, British Psychological Society and Royal College of Speech and Language Therapists 2007) offers that: 'challenging behaviour is socially constructed and is a product of an interaction between the individual and their environment. Assessment and intervention must therefore address the person, the environment and the interaction between the two' (p.9).

CAT, emotional states/systemic traps

In the CAT model, the concept of a trap can be identified as 'self reinforcing patterns of thought and behaviour' (Ryle and Kerr 2002, p.222) or an unhelpful way of thinking where perspectives can become polarised between two extremes. A framework for thinking about this that is sometimes used within CAT approaches is that things are either 'great' – an ideal/desired state – or 'terrible' – a dreaded state.

Admission to an inpatient unit is usually a last resort when a situation has reached crisis point, and therefore the client and the system around them are in a 'dreaded state'. Inpatient staff need to engage with the client (and those around them) when a situation is particularly difficult and the client's behaviour is at the most difficult and challenging level. At the point of admission the situation can feel out of control, and it is hard for clients, families or staff in the system to feel secure. The team can feel disorganised, particularly in the early stages of an admission where there is unlikely to be a clear treatment plan. This can be in the context of having to manage difficult and aggressive behaviour where staff may sustain injuries and feel, or be, physically threatened.

It is natural that at this point there are a lot of expectations around the inpatient admission. These may be for the person to be rescued, cured and managed and to return to their community setting. In such a highly emotionally charged situation it is possible to see how criticism may arise if a staff team struggle to manage, or if outcomes do not meet expectations. In reflecting on the kinds of reciprocal roles that can be elicited within the system it is easy to see how these could include reciprocal roles such as 'overwhelming–overwhelmed', 'rescuing–rescued' and 'criticising–criticised'.

The other extreme from the dreaded state is an 'ideal' state with a reciprocal role of 'perfectly caring–perfectly cared for'. Within such a system it could be expected that there is total consistency in approach, the treatment plan is known, established and effective, there are no incidents of challenging behaviour, there is adequate debrief and supervision for all staff, all service users and staff needs are met and the service user is ready for discharge. This is clearly a high expectation and it may take some time to move from the crisis point of admission to such a state, if it is achieved at all. Where this is not met, a staff team may feel that they have failed and can return to a dreaded position.

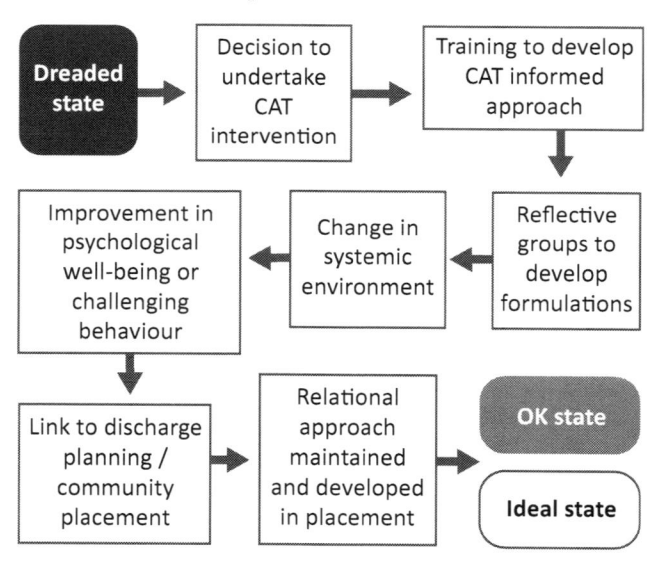

Figure 9.1: Overview map

Often when working with people who find themselves caught between two polarised extremes, the therapeutic goal is to help people to find a middle ground. This helps people to avoid the trap of striving towards a perfect state and failing, and finding themselves in a dreaded state.

A more appropriate goal for an inpatient context might be to have a clear assessment and treatment plan, to have some observed success in treatment and some consistency in approach, to manage incidents well rather than to expect not to have them at all and to provide adequate debrief and supervision for all staff most of the time. This may lead to reciprocal roles of 'supporting–supported', 'containing–contained', 'acknowledging–acknowledged', 'understanding–understood' and 'listening–listened to'.

This framework or trap is used throughout the chapter to reflect on the different stages of the CAT intervention. The polarised extremes of the dreaded and ideal position are acknowledged, with the goal for the facilitator of a CAT intervention to help teams to move towards an OK position. Where this OK position is will vary from team to team and context to context, depending upon the starting point and particular context of an intervention.

This map identifies the various different stages in the intervention process. It works from the premise that often a specific intervention is sought during a 'dreaded' phase (described above).

The intervention in our piece of work involved the majority of the two inpatient staff teams attending training sessions on CAT and developing 'maps' or formulations. These were run by an external facilitator. In order to make this an ongoing process, an attempt was then made to organise regular reflective groups to develop and utilise these. Different CAT interventions may take slightly different approaches in terms of how they are structured, however it is likely that all will involve some initial training explaining the model and some reflective sessions to develop a formulation and shared understanding.

The intention is that this leads to some change in the systemic environment. If such an intervention is working well then this may be demonstrated by some improvements in psychological well-being and ultimately link into plans around discharge and a move into a future setting. The next goal would be to be able to maintain and develop this relational approach in a future placement. Each stage of this cycle involves a number of complex processes and at any stage it could be possible to return to a 'dreaded' state of feeling overwhelmed.

Each of the stages will be considered in turn.

Stage 1: Decision to undertake CAT intervention

Key issues with any referral are why the referral has been made, why it is made at that particular time, and what the expectations are. Not all clients in an inpatient unit would require this type of intervention.

Given that it is resource intensive to have ongoing reflective groups and there are cost implications around this, it is likely that such a decision will be made or approved at a managerial level. If an external person is involved as a facilitator then they may be seen as the 'powerful' person who will 'fix' the situation. In our experience, a key feature of the CAT work was to empower staff to reflect on the relational environment the client is in and their own interactions. As such, the intervention was not about 'changing' the client but instead about changing the relational context of the environment around them. This is important as the goal for an inpatient is to move on, so it is important that it is understood at the outset that the work would need to be carried on into the next care setting. This may need to be considered (and perhaps costed) at the beginning.

Another key issue is that it is important, in our opinion, that CAT is understood as an ongoing approach and that it is not simply the case of doing two days of training and then applying this. For example, this may be within a context where training on a certain issue, for example, manual handling, is bought and paid for and then it is assumed that staff will implement it. It is important that the reflective elements of CAT are understood and that developing the maps and formulations is an ongoing rather than one-off process. Although the CAT intervention may be led and facilitated by a particular person, it is important that the staff team is engaged and committed to it.

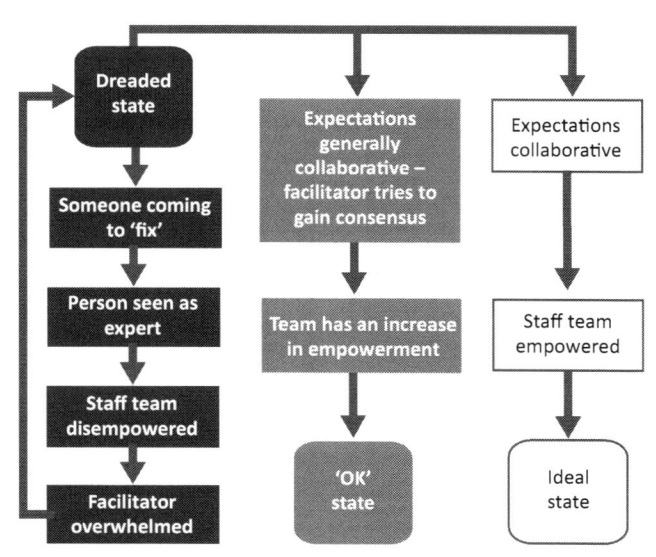

Figure 9.2: Patterns at decision to undertake intervention stage

Stage 2: Training to develop a more CAT-informed approach

A key stage was to get as many of the staff team together as possible to have some training in the CAT approach and using the mapping. The approach taken may vary from setting to setting, but any intervention undertaken with a team will benefit from the whole team being together.

Although this sounds simple, in practice this is not an easy process. Financially it is expensive to get a team together. Clients in an inpatient service require support 24/7 and so cover will be needed on the unit in order for the regular staff to be available. This in itself can lead to difficulties if consistent staff is a protective factor in supporting clients. It is crucial for any plan around training to be supported and understood by the wider system. In our interventions, cover staff worked in the units beforehand and were supported by regular bank staff on the training days.

A dreaded position would be that it was not possible to arrange such cover, it received limited support within the system, only limited numbers of staff attended and there was a lack of motivation and support for the approach. An ideal position would be that all cover and finances could be organised, all staff were able to attend and staff engage with the training and value the approach. An OK position might be that enough cover was provided for enough staff to get to the training (what is 'enough' might vary from context to context) and that the approach is valued and staff have some understanding of it, which is sufficient to be a background to discussions in the continued reflective groups.

Stage 3: Reflective groups to develop formulations

Reflective groups were set up as a way of using CAT on an ongoing basis. On a basic level, it is obviously important that enough staff are available to attend and contribute to the sessions. Depending on the frequency of the sessions, getting the whole team together on a frequent basis is unlikely to be possible. However many staff attend the sessions, this will require cover (and funding) being available on the unit. Situations can arise that mean that the groups may be cancelled at short notice, for example, a new admission or staff sickness. The first task, therefore, is physically getting people to attend reflective groups.

Following this, it is important that staff feel able to talk openly and honestly in the sessions in order to reflect on the issues and discuss the relational environment in which any incidents of challenging behaviour occurred. This may depend on existing dynamics and relationships in teams, and it may take some time to build on. As their reflections are developed into therapeutic 'maps' (or formulations) it is important that staff themselves are given ownership of the maps and that the development of them is not seen as the role of the facilitator. It is also important to consider issues of clinical responsibility, i.e., who is considered responsible for the maps and any implications for direct care that arise from the discussions are documented and translated into care plans. Responsibility for this needs to be decided at the outset, for example, would this be the role of the facilitator or a keyworker?

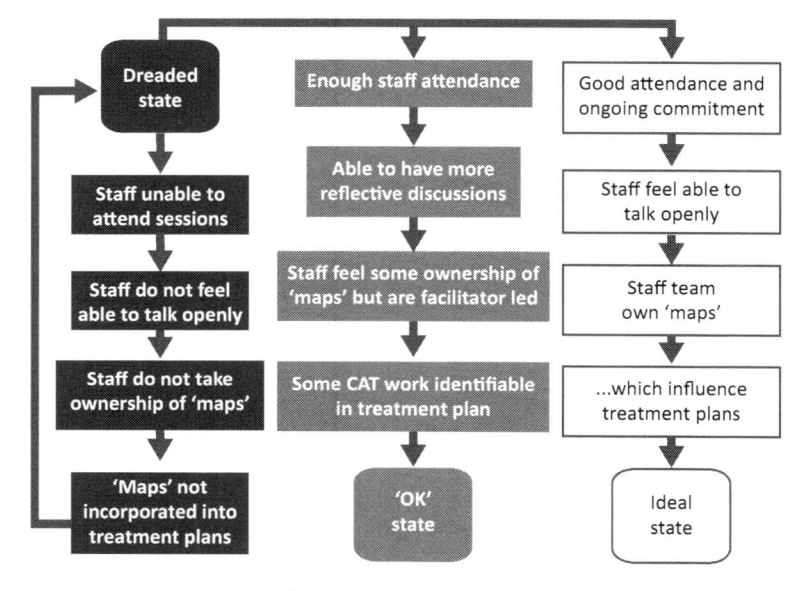

Figure 9.3: Patterns for reflective sessions stage

Stage 4: Change in systemic environment (leadership, consistency, and practicalities)

The hope would be that if the reflective groups are going well, there will begin to be some impact on practice in terms of the relational environment on the unit. The challenge is then how to manage this process of change. For example, a reflective group made up of a small number of unit staff may identify a relational dynamic with a client, which has become unhelpful and could be managed differently. How is this then translated into a change for the wider staff team? Will the wider team agree? How can the proposed change be explained to them? Who takes responsibility for this? These are all issues that need to be considered and are likely to become more complex the larger the staff team involved.

Using Cognitive Analytic Therapy in a Systemic Context with Staff Teams   129

The dreaded pattern might be that there is a lack of time to reflect (productively) and develop 'maps' outside the sessions and no time or process for sharing them. This could potentially lead to inconsistencies in approach between those who have been involved in the discussions and those who have not, which has the potential of being detrimental by creating a divided team. The ideal situation would be that staff manage the sessions without facilitation, there is sufficient time and opportunity to share with staff outside sessions and there is a fully consistent approach. However, although this would be the goal, this is likely to be an unrealistic short-term expectation depending on the complexity of the relational issue involved. The best outcome might be that there is a facilitator available within the team and that some time to reflect and a move towards a more consistent shared approach can then be developed. Mechanisms that might help to assist this are shift handover time, communication books, allocating key staff to disseminate to others and patient review meetings/minutes. It is important to consider members of staff who may find it hard to link into the latter, but who have a relational contact with the client, such as night staff or domestic staff.

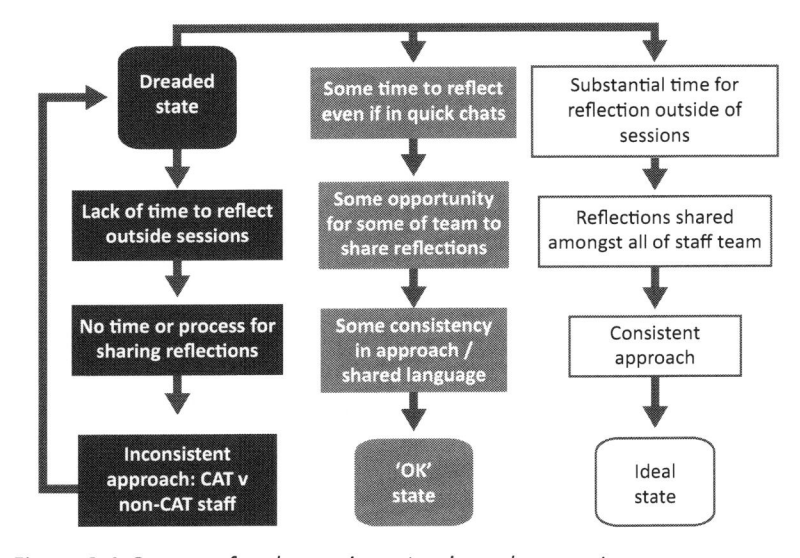

Figure 9.4: Patterns for change in systemic environment

Stage 5: Improvement in psychological well-being and
Stage 6: link to discharge planning and future placement

If all the above goes to plan, the hope would be that the approach begins to have an impact on psychological well-being. We wouldhope that for the client this would be that their relational needs are better met and understood and there starts to be a reduction in incidents of challenging behaviour. For the staff team this may be that they feel contained and supported and have a greater understanding of the client's needs. Inpatient units are intended to be a short-stay environment and once there is a reduction in challenging behaviour and an effective management plan, discussions around possible discharge will begin.

It is here that it is particularly important that the relational elements of the CAT model are understood. An intervention of this type aims to lead to some reflections and changes to the relational environment around the client and does not mean the person is necessarily changed or 'cured'. If that same client returns to an environment that they find relationally distressing then it is likely that similar difficulties will arise again. This can lead to 'revolving door' syndrome where a client is readmitted, which can then lead to feelings of failure throughout the system. Although this can apply in many cases to clients being discharged from inpatient units to home settings, in our view the CAT approach can be particularly vulnerable to this. This is because the discussions and understandings of relational dynamics that can be so instrumental in a CAT piece of work can involve quite subtle issues that can be difficult to capture on paper. In the same way that no one relationship with another individual is the same, the exact same relationship between one setting and another cannot be replicated. The challenge is therefore to be able to transfer and translate sufficient information about that relational context to mean that enough elements of the relational environment are continued. This may be achieved through joint working, i.e., staff from a care setting shadowing or working alongside ward staff, having trial visits with an opportunity to problem solve, or having follow-on support in the community from staff directly involved in the inpatient setting (outreach work).

A transition such as this may take some time to work through and may have resource issues for both inpatient and community settings. It is important that this is built into care planning. It is perhaps inevitable that if there has been intensive work using a CAT approach in one setting, this will become to some extent 'diluted' when translated into another. The challenge is therefore to ensure that there is a mechanism for 'topping up', i.e., ongoing supervision or facilitation of sessions in future placement sufficient to maintain the relational environment.

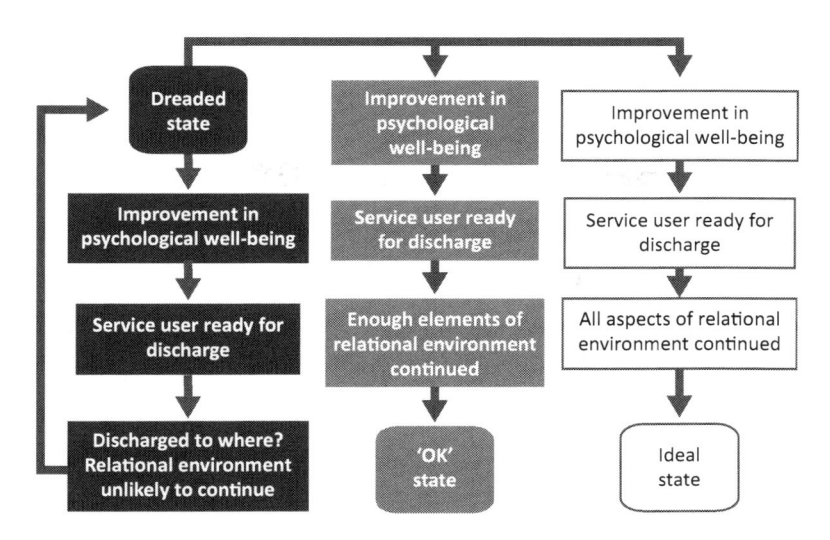

Figure 9.5: Patterns for improvement in psychological well-being stage

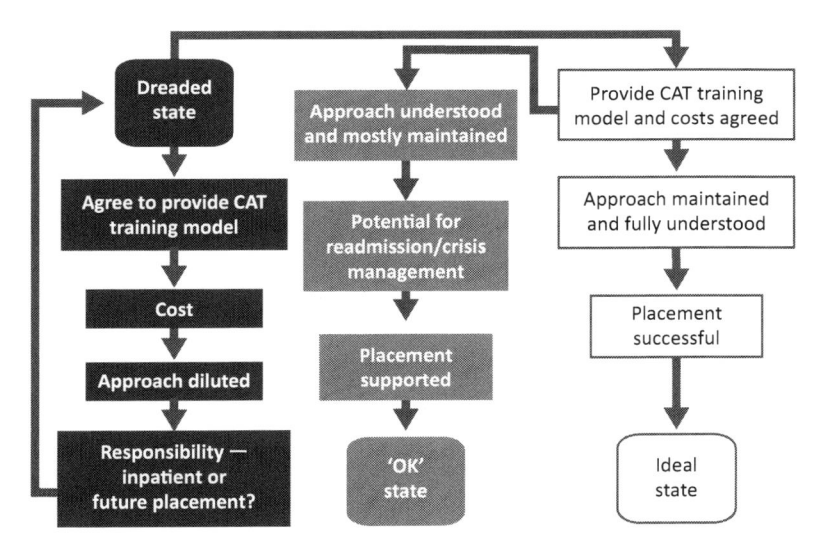

Figure 9.6: Patterns for link to discharge planning and future placement stage

Whilst the focus of this piece of work was with inpatient staff, the approach would also be beneficial to use in long- and short-term community or residential placements that support people with challenging behaviour. A CAT intervention with community or residential staff teams could be implemented when difficulties first become apparent in a placement, which may then lead to a reduction in challenging behaviours, which may avert an inpatient admission.

Stage 7: Relational approach maintained and developed in next placement

The final challenge is to maintain the approach in the next placement. It is important to consider issues such as keeping the approach going so that people continue to reflect and learn from issues that may arise. This would mean that the staff team would need to show enough of an understanding of the CAT model and be able to facilitate reflective sessions independently. There may be the tendency when things are going well, for reflective sessions to no longer be deemed necessary, thus running the risk of the team becoming complacent. However, this may also be explained by the staff successfully working in a CAT-informed way in their everyday work. Challenges at this stage include staff turnover, with the approach becoming more diluted due to staff changes.

Reflections/discussion

In our opinion, one of the most key issues in terms of using CAT in a systemic context with staff teams is to consider the needs of the team itself. Staff may be dealing with situations where they are working with clients with very complex needs and experience extreme challenging behaviour on a regular basis. In order to provide a contained and safe environment for clients, staff need to feel contained and safe themselves in their work environment. If a team is split in their approaches, or if there are high levels of stress or sickness, the CAT approach may be helpful to assist a team to reflect on their own dynamics, prior to or alongside work around client issues.

Consideration of the Zone of Proximal Development is identified as a core concept in CAT (Ryle and Kerr 2002). It is important to consider what a staff team's starting point may be when identifying what the ideal, OK and dreaded reciprocal roles and states may be. For a team that is already struggling and experiencing difficulties, the goal of reaching a 'containing–contained' reciprocal role may feel more of an ideal than an OK state. In contrast, in a team that is already well supported and that has good relationships, staff may feel that they are contained and have some consistency, but wish to build on and increase their effectiveness. For teams that are experiencing difficulties, the commitment to undergo the training may result in them feeling more contained and supported due to

Using Cognitive Analytic Therapy in a Systemic Context with Staff Teams   133

the investment involved in the CAT intervention. Wider contextual factors are also likely to impact on the work and the emotional states of staff and service users; for example, issues such as service restructuring, staff changes and external inspections. The role of inpatient assessment and treatment units for people with intellectual disabilities is currently being scrutinised nationally, following the Winterbourne enquiry (Department of Health 2012).

'Building blocks'

In reflecting on these issues, we have identified a framework of 'building blocks' relevant to using CAT in a systemic context. To a greater or lesser extent, these could be said to apply to any psychological intervention conducted in systemic settings, for example, behavioural approaches. However, we feel that these are particularly pertinent to the CAT approach. These are written with the intention that they might be helpful for those who have been asked to undertake a systemic intervention using CAT or are considering that one might be helpful, because they could be useful for explaining what is required to ward managers or commissioners.

Approach is part of everyday approach

Approach incorporated into treatment plans

Intervention – focus on client or team?

Understanding of the model (whole staff team)
Training itself will not 'fix' difficulties

Reason for intervention
Expectations from the client or team

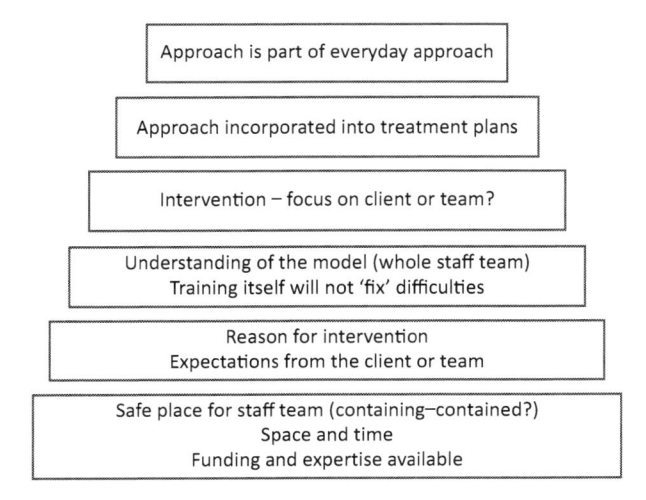

Safe place for staff team (containing–contained?)
Space and time
Funding and expertise available

Figure 9.7: Building blocks for CAT intervention

The building blocks have a similar framework to Maslow's hierarchy of needs (Maslow 1943) in that the larger blocks need to be in place to support future blocks. At the most basic level it is important that there is an appropriate space and enough time to involve a team in such a piece of work. Depending upon the model undertaken, this is likely to involve at a minimum, time to undertake some type of training explaining what CAT is and time for some staff to attend reflective sessions to ensure it is an ongoing approach. This needs to be, as far as possible, protected so staff feel it is a safe time and place.

If this can be met then the next stage is to consider the reason for the intervention and expectations of this. It is important to be mindful here of possible reciprocal roles of 'rescuing–rescued', and ensure that teams are committed to a collaborative piece of work. It is important, particularly at a managerial level, that the intervention is understood as being with the whole system and that it is about understanding the relational environment around the client, not 'fixing' the clients themselves.

If this is met then the next stage is to undertake the intervention, which is likely to involve some work with the team around understanding a CAT approach and some reflective sessions to look at issues. As discussed in this chapter, it may not be possible to reach the ideal goal of having everyone involved in this but it is important to have 'good enough' attendance and engagement.

If this can be achieved then the next goal is for the work to be incorporated into a client's treatment in a meaningful way so that it leads to improvements in psychological well-being for clients and staff. In an inpatient context another challenge would be to find a way to then continue the same work once a client is discharged to a community setting, in order that it represents a meaningful long-term change.

The final block (should the top of the tower be reached!) would be that CAT becomes part of an everyday approach. Referring back to the ideal, OK and dreaded states, this does not mean that every single challenging interaction would be mapped out but that the approach provides a vehicle for a shared language and is used where necessary to assist the team to manage future situations.

Relating back to emotional states

Returning to the initial CAT trap of dreaded, ideal and OK states, it is important to recognise that when facilitating such interventions, facilitators need to be aware of the 'traps' and how they may get caught in them. It is important to gain a balance between providing what may be the hoped-for ideal intervention – for example, the whole staff team attending – regular well-attended reflective sessions may be enough to ensure that a team moves on from a 'dreaded' position, which may be unsafe. Essentially, the goal is to establish a realistic intervention. What is realistic in one setting may, of course, not be realistic in another, but a guide would be: most of the team understanding the approach, staff valuing and holding the approach in mind and it having some impact on practice. It is important to discuss at the outset what the goal is and where the starting point is. This may help to avoid expectations of an ideal state being set too high, leading to a dreaded state where the intervention is not supported or implemented and becomes a piece of training that is forgotten.

The goal would be that the CAT approach gradually becomes part of the culture of the unit and that the emotional states move from what might be the 'dreaded state' at the point of referral to the 'OK state' of feeling contained. As a team moves closer towards an 'ideal state', it will need to recognise the dangers of getting drawn into 'perfectly caring–perfectly cared for' reciprocal role.

Summary paragraph

This chapter has described emotional states and systemic traps that can arise in working in a systemic context with people within intellectual disability settings who display behaviour that is challenging. The chapter has used a framework of 'dreaded', 'ideal' and 'OK' states to reflect on the various reciprocal roles that can arise as part of this work. An overall map of a CAT intervention was presented to consider how these states can arise at different stages of the work. Finally, some suggestions were offered for building blocks to using CAT in a systemic context, with the aim being to inform those who may be considering undertaking similar interventions.

We would like to acknowledge the work of Steve Potter, who facilitated the CAT training for staff groups and developed this framework for CAT interventions, and also the CWP inpatient staff who were involved in the work.

Chapter 10
Cognitive Analytic Therapy and Behaviour that Challenges
Jo Varela

Introduction

Challenging behaviour is described as being present in the lives of 10–15 per cent of the population of people with an intellectual disability (Emerson *et al.* 2001, limited population study). In a study by Qureshi and Alborz (1992) they report that 16.7 per cent of people with administratively defined intellectual disability in the UK have challenging behaviour. The emotional and relational costs of this behaviour are significant. A person with an intellectual disability is at a higher risk of being abused, excluded, restrained and distressed (Royal College of Psychiatrists 2007). They are also more likely to be misunderstood, be prescribed medication and suffer multiple losses as they lose contact with friends and families, are moved far away from their homes in out-of-area placements (Department of Health, 2007) and experience a higher turnover of paid carers. The costs are also high for families and carers in terms of being hurt and emotional distress, with restrictions in the ability to live life to the full with the person they care for (Wodehouse and McGill 2009).

Despite advances in understandings of the causes of, factors influencing and interventions for challenging behaviour at an individual and societal level and several commitments to change from government (Department of Health 2001, 2007, 2009; Royal College of Psychiatrists 2007), the reality is that this vulnerable group of people and their carers (family and paid) are still likely to receive poor services and support. Systemic abuses are still taking place (Winterbourne, Sutton and Merton, Cornwall) despite a number of calls to implement effective services.

Campbell, Robertson and Jahoda (2012) suggest that if these interventions are to be effective, more information is needed about the mechanisms of change and contextual factors that influence outcome. There is some evidence regarding the effectiveness of 'psychotherapeutic' approaches for challenging behaviour (Ball, Bush and Emerson 2004; Royal College of Psychiatrists 2007). This chapter explores how CAT may provide another tool to do this, and help create effective change in the lives of people with an intellectual disability whose behaviour challenges. The aim is to address understandings of what challenging behaviour is from a CAT perspective, explore how to reformulate using the CAT model and explore how to use CAT tools and concepts to design effective interventions for those who are challenged by this type of behaviour, be they the people themselves, families and friends, carers or systems.

Taking a therapeutic stance to challenging behaviour

Challenging behaviour is a term that has come to be used to describe a range of behaviours that may be harmful to an individual or that are difficult for others to tolerate. These behaviours have in the past been labelled as maladaptive, aberrant, dysfunctional, disordered, concerning and disturbed (Farrell, Shafiei and Salmon 2010), the emphasis at first being on the individual and on pathological processes within the individual. Service design mirrored these labels and conceptualisation of challenging behaviour. Those who were labelled 'aberrant' initially were segregated and considered to be a threat to society. Individuals were then given treatment, either in the form of medication or skills training. With these initial understandings of challenging behaviour, the models used implied that the behaviour was a property of individuals and thereby absolved staff from examining their own influence on it (Farrell *et al.* 2010).

A more truly relational and dialogical understanding of challenging behaviour was proposed by Lovett (1996). We were invited to 'Learn to Listen' by Lovett, who supported us to understand that 'behaviour is *communication*'. Emerson (Emerson and Einfield 2011) explains this concept using more concrete examples to show that behaviour may or may not be seen as challenging depending on the social and temporal context.

This shift supported a redefinition of this 'collection of behaviours' by The Association for the Severely Handicapped (TASH), which described it as 'behaviour that challenges'. This challenge was to carers, services and professionals to find more effective ways of understanding the origins and meaning of a person's behaviour, to find creative ways of responding and to 'transfer the demands for change from the individual with severe behaviour problems to the organisation around them' (Royal College of Psychiatrists 2007, p.14).

Defined thus, behaviour can only be challenging within a relationship. By implication there needs to be a person who is challenging and a person who is challenged. Challenging behaviour is relational and can be understood in terms of reciprocal roles.

With this shift in emphasis, behaviour that was once seen as alienating, undesirable and dangerous to others was redefined as existing in a relationship, where one party is in need of help and understanding from another who is interested, hopeful, attuned and supportive. This change enabled the possibility that those whose behaviour challenged might be offered a relationship that was in some way therapeutic.

Redefining challenging behaviour as a dynamic and reciprocal relationship

The most commonly used definition of challenging behaviour is described by Emerson who defined the term as:

> culturally abnormal behaviour(s) of such an intensity, frequency or duration that the physical safety of the person or others is likely to be in jeopardy, or behaviour which is likely to seriously limit the use of, or result in the person being denied access to, ordinary community 'facilities' or 'settings'. (2001, p.3)

Building on this concept, the document *Challenging Behaviour, A Unified Approach* goes some way to addressing the relational. It defines the behaviour as:

> challenging when it is of such an intensity, frequency or duration as to threaten the quality of life and/or the physical safety of the individual or others and is likely to lead to responses that are restrictive, aversive or result in exclusion. (Royal College of Psychiatrists 2007)

The second definition appears significantly more relational in that it defines the *responses* of others as important in defining the behaviour as challenging in the social context. Emerson's definition focuses on a judgement of whether something is culturally abnormal and by participation in a community. The 'judgement' may be 'named' as a response, a 'relational role', which leads to evoked feeling and responses on the part of the other (judging to judged).

The feelings and responses of the 'other' are core to the Royal College of Psychiatrists' (2007) understanding of behaviour. This definition invites an interest in the role of carers in the development and maintenance of challenging behaviour and also suggests an area of potential intervention.

Why is it important to think about the carers when understanding challenging behaviour?
Thinking therapeutically about the challenging to challenged reciprocal role

We know that family and paid carers are incredibly important in the lives of people with challenging behaviour (Felce 1988). Interaction with staff is the main source of social interaction in many people's lives (Felce, de Kock and Repp 1986; Hastings and Remmington 1994). Interaction increases with adaptive functioning and social and communicative behaviour (Felce *et al.* 1991; Felce and Perry 1995), leaving those who are more challenging with more impoverished social worlds.

Carers are important recipients of a powerful communication of distress and are usually the people who attempt to make things right for the individual, to meet their needs and facilitate access to specialist help. Any model of intervention needs to be able to understand and support these carers.

In defining an individual's behaviour as challenging, 'a judgement is made that this behaviour is dangerous, frightening, distressing or annoying and that these feelings invoked in others are in some way intolerable or overwhelming' (Royal College of Psychiatrists 2007, p.14). Families and carers are at times subject to immense amounts of personal distress, strain and abuse as a result of the behaviour from the individual they are trying to care for and, as such, need to be supported by any therapeutic intervention attempted. In thinking reciprocally, we understand that carers need to be cared for. It is clear that we need to address the interactional challenges Emerson describes to enable increased positive support for clients within a more mutually rewarding Carer-cared for relationship (Lloyd and Williams 2004).

Understanding the assessment process as a reciprocal role with associated beliefs and attributions as to the person in distress is important. 'The impact on others, and therefore the characteristics of the observer(s) have to be incorporated in the application and understanding of the term challenging behaviour' (Royal College of Psychiatrists 2007, p.2). Lovett felt that traditional behavioural understandings and assessments were a way of cutting off from the human realities of the lives of people who have intellectual disability and challenging behaviour. The RCP quotes Lovett as saying that 'most of what passes for assessment seems to be a denial about the mutuality of our common condition' and that 'instead of responding to the person we typically react to the behaviour' as a way of intervention (2007, p.2).

Attitudes and staff emotions are important in defining the type of care that they are able to provide. Staff may be less sympathetic to clients labelled as challenging, especially if the person is perceived to be in control of the behaviour (Markham and Trower 2003) and more likely to use seclusion and medication (Duxbury 2002; Duxbury and Whittington 2005) or display a reduction in helping behaviour (Sharrock *et al.* 1990). Negative emotions elicited by behaviour can lead to reactions such as coercion and hostility (Byrne, Morton and Salmon 2001).

Harper and Wadsworth (1993) found that bereaved individuals described their experiences with mainly emotional words whereas their paid carers focused on the behaviours displayed rather than the personal experience or meaning of the loss. Kroese (1997) comments that this is a common phenomenon in the lives of people with intellectual disabilities. Carers may describe behaviour in terms of observed behaviour rather than seeking an underlying motivation, such as fear or sadness. A formulation may be generated that might objectify the person, create confusion and may not lend itself to the generation of positive interventions.

We also know that carers' thoughts, emotions and behaviours are intrinsically linked with the maintenance and development of the very behaviour that challenges them. In studies of paid carers, staff responses are unwittingly socially reinforcing the behaviour (Duxbury 2002; Hastings 1997a; Hastings and Remmington 1994; Whittington and Wykes 1994). An example would be an aggressive behaviour that obtains increased social attention from the carer or pushes others away when social interaction becomes overwhelming.

Hall (1990) suggests we should look at the emotional or attachment state of the carer as well as the actual care act but that professional carers are defined more by their tasks and responsibilities than the care relationship they develop. In thinking about the reciprocal care relationship as the area of 'challenge', both these aspects of carer can be understood in the context of the cared for and their difficulties.

Formulating challenging behaviour in traditional models

Current approaches to conceptualising and assessing challenging behaviour focus on the importance of individual and environmental factors in a person's life and the interaction between them (Royal College of Psychiatrists 2007).

Table 10.1: Elements of assessment according to The Royal College of Psychiatrists (2007)

Individual factors	Environmental factors	Interaction between
The degree and nature of intellectual disability	The characteristics of services	Individual and environmental factors
Sensory or motor disabilities	Number of staff, training and experience of staff	
Mental health problems	Consistency of staff, provision and approach	
Physical problems, including pain and/or discomfort	The working relationship with the client	
Communication difficulties, personal history of relationships and experiences	The working relationship between staff members.	
	Quality of the material environment	
	Opportunities available and ability of the service to understand and respond to unique needs of individuals	

There has been much written on the processes, use and migration of language in the world of people with intellectual disabilities, where language that is used to describe and communicate turns into something that is distancing and derogatory (Sinason 1992). To some extent this is the case in the above formulation of challenging behaviour, where the word 'environment' is used for a predominantly relational aspect of a person's life. It seems odd that in the world of someone with an intellectual disability and challenging behaviour, 'environment' is the word used to describe family, friends, partners and carers rather than 'relationships'. The use of the word 'environment', however 'capable', subtly skews the assessment and resultant formulation so that it becomes less relational or personal and therefore distancing.

Reformulating challenging behaviour in CAT terms

Challenging behaviour is a 'socially constructed and dynamic concept' according to the current definition (Royal College of Psychiatrists 2007). CAT as a model is defined by its relational and dialogical nature, thereby offering a framework for exploring effective ways of understanding the behaviour for individuals and those who support them.

The current formulation of challenging behaviour is that the behaviour serves to fulfil the function of meeting a need, such as sensory, tangible, escape or social attention-based needs (Addison 2013). These needs are not being achieved with adaptive strategies that are understandable to others. The behaviours or strategies used are challenging to understand and therefore meet. Fundamentally therefore, challenging behaviour can be understood as a disruption in attunement and communication between two parties, where neither party in the relationship is having their needs met and where both are distressed.

As laid out above, there are clear relational, emotional, cognitive, biological and behavioural components to any expression of challenging behaviour, which can therefore be understood using reformulation concepts in CAT such as the sequential diagrammatic reformulation (SDR). Within the CAT model, reciprocal role procedures are repetitive sequences of cognitive, behavioural, affective and interpersonal processes, which are rigid, unrevised and therefore prevent change (Ryle and Kerr 2002) and which thus explain the perpetuation of the challenging behaviour. When formulated using the CAT model, challenging behaviour can be as recognisable as the difficulties of any other (Murphy 2008) rather than as a mysterious entity.

Challenging behaviour reformulated as an SDR

Within a CAT reformulation, a focus is placed on the behaviour as a procedure, and the relational and interpersonal aspects of difficulties within the reciprocal role.

The Royal College of Psychiatrists states that:

> We believe that 'challenging behaviour' is a socially constructed and dynamic concept. In order for an individual's behaviour to be viewed as challenging, a judgement is made that this behaviour is dangerous, frightening, distressing or annoying and that these feelings invoked

in others are in some way intolerable or overwhelming. The impact on others, and therefore the characteristics of the observer(s) have to be incorporated in the application and understanding of the term challenging behaviour. (2007)

With the change in emphasis in the 2007 definition of challenging behaviour, it is possible to understand the behaviour in a SDR (Figure 10.1).

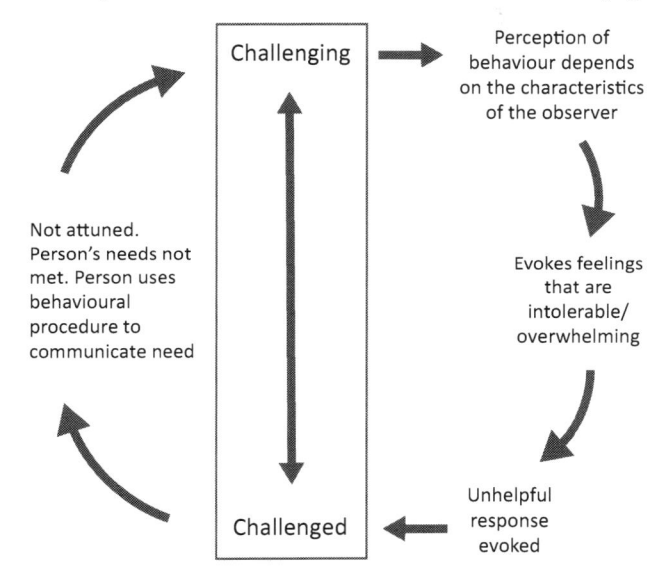

Figure 10.1: Challenging behaviour as an SDR

Both the person with an intellectual disability and the carer are at once challenging and challenged by each other in this cycle.

The traditional and evidence-based approaches to working with challenging behaviour are behavioural. These are not very similar to CAT on first appraisal, but if we acknowledge that a reformulation of challenging behaviour needs to encompass relational/dialogical and attunement/attachment-specific thinking, the behavioural model can be reformulated in these terms.

Understanding the common reciprocal roles in challenging behaviour

Reciprocal roles can be understood in behavioural terms, as mutual stimulus-response (Bancroft *et al.* 2008). In the literature a number of associated unhelpful roles are described. These include:

- Controlling/conditional to crushed compliant or rebellious (Fisher and Harding 2009)
- Neglecting to neglectful (Royal College of Psychiatrists 2007)
- Abusing to abused (Royal College of Psychiatrists 2007)
- Restricting to restricted (Royal College of Psychiatrists 2007)
- a Judging to judged relationship is also implied in the Emerson (2001) definition
- Frightened and Rejecting to rejected and excluded (Emerson 2001; Royal College of Psychiatrists 2007)
- Cut off to misunderstood and alone (Lovett 1996).

In using a CAT formulation, the aim is to develop attuned relationships where the communication of needs is adaptive and dialogical and the impact of distress is acknowledged and worked through in a non-blaming way. This gives the benefit of developing a formulation, not of the person with challenging behaviour but of the carer's interaction with the person, so placing the behaviour firmly in the relational arena. This model of working enables those experiencing difficulties to remain true to the definition of behaviour that challenges. It changes the question from what to do about challenging behaviour (or the person displaying it) to how we relate/tune in to the person and 'revise' how we respond.

Despite the re-emphasis of the Royal College of Psychiatrists' (2007) definition of challenging behaviour on the effects on carers, it would be an unusual referral that stated that the real reason for asking for help was 'John is frightening, distressing or annoying me when he does this behaviour'. CAT makes it possible to name and address the feelings and responses of carers or the care system through the structure of the model (Carridice 2004; Dunn and Parry 1997; Lloyd and Williams 2004).

CASE STUDY: CHALLENGING BEHAVIOUR – WORKING WITH THE RECIPROCAL ROLE

Jason was a young man referred to a community team by his GP for aggressive challenging behaviour. He had significant intellectual disabilities and was unable to self-report as to why he became so distressed. On interview with his mother (Emma), she described how he frequently hit her and pushed her away. Jason would then hit his head and would continue to do this for up to an hour at a time, 'screaming and howling'. At other times she described a loving connection where she felt that she had somehow 'got it right'. In the assessment interviews, Emma found it difficult to recall much about the 'facts' of the behaviour or complete a functional analysis, and instead described how hurt, scared, rejected and hopeless she felt. Emma felt that Jason did not love her and questioned her ability to love him as she felt a mother should. Emma was able to describe the difficulty as a reciprocal role very clearly (Rejecting to rejected) and in doing so was then able to structure her thinking about how the 'good' relationship broke down. We then used the functional analysis to test her theory that he was rejecting her, and established that he had sensory processing difficulties and would become disregulated and distressed. His behaviour communicated to his mother that he needed help to structure and regulate his experience and once she was able to support him to do this, the behaviour decreased in frequency and duration.

Understanding the target problem procedure (TPP) in challenging behaviour

If we understand the procedural sequence object relations model to be a description of aim-directed behaviour, we may formulate challenging behaviour in the same way as any other target problem procedure. The procedural sequence considers the formation and maintenance of aim-directed activity involving the three phases outlined in Chapter 3 including the reciprocal responses of the other (Ryle 1991). Once we add events in the external world we have a way of conducting a functional analysis within the social world.

Table 10.2: Linking CAT and behavioural theory

Procedural sequence	Behavioural theory
Event	Antecedents/setting conditions
Perception	Stimulus
Memory	Personal context – learning theory/ conditioning
Beliefs/meaning	
Aim	Escape
	Social attention
	Tangible
	Sensory
Selection of action	Behavioural response
Consequence and feedback	Consequence

In the words of Lovett, we are now able to 'learn to listen' to the behaviour as a communication of interpersonal importance within an SDR. Traditional formulation of challenging behaviours as 'unhelpful ways of meeting personal needs' may be reformulated using this model (Fisher and Harding 2009).

Integrating evidence-based approaches
Functional analysis and CAT

Evidence suggests that interventions for challenging behaviour are more successful when based on a functional analysis and formulation-driven approach (Campbell *et al.* 2012). It is possible to combine functional analysis with CAT formulation-based approaches. The antecedents and consequences of challenging behaviour can be formulated as 'reciprocal role procedures between the client and support system' (Moss 2006, p.25).

Attempts have been made to construct CAT-informed functional analysis (Greenhill 2011). Establishing the individual's aim forms the important role of empathising (Ryle and Kerr 2002). This aim is usually understandable or 'benign and is a result of intolerable states of mind from which the individual seeks a solution'. This addition to traditional 'ABC' approaches generates a more empathic formulation from the perspective of assessment than traditional ABC type assessments allow.

Using this aim-based approach, we are able to reformulate behavioural thinking as CAT traps, snags and dilemmas. We can also conceptualise the complex long chains of behavioural sequences as TPPs. These are, in essence, circular procedures that are resistant to revision because of the difficulties of the person or care in revising their aims, perceptions or responses.

Table 10.3 is based on Greenhill's approach.

Table 10.3: CAT and ABCs; an integrated approach to recording and recognition

Date	Antecedent	Aim	Hypothesised cognition	Action/behaviour	Consequence
	Alone	I want to be cared for	If I hurt myself people will come and care for me	Self-harm	Staff came and we chatted
	Noisy environment at tea time	I am overwhelmed, I want some relief	If I push others away it will make it better	Hurt others	Staff give me time out, and put me on my own table for tea
	In lessons at school that are too hard	I am bored, I want to have meaningful activity	I don't understand the lesson, I am bored. I know that self-stimulation works	Self stimulation	This disrupts others. Given some staff attention, or given 'time out' to engage in self-stimulation

Table 10.4: A CAT approach to helping carers recognise and revise problem procedures

Behaviour	Client TPP	Staff response	Recognised?	Revised?	Successful?

Client TPPs

Trap

I become frustrated when unable to meet my own needs and do not have the words to ask for help. To gain attention I become vocal then shout and throw things in my frustration. I am then isolated and punished and my needs remain unmet, increasing my frustration and behaviour.

Snag

I am bored and alone. I do not mention this as I don't expect others to listen or respond, I bottle things up until I am unable to contain my pain any longer and express my frustration in ways that label me as challenging. My world and experiences are narrowed due to my challenging behaviour, leaving me again bored and alone.

Dilemma

In the face of overwhelming stimuli, either I withdraw into harmful self-stimulation to block things out or I hit out, pushing the other away, but then am unable to gain the help that I need to regulate my experiences so start the cycle again.

Carer TPPs

It is possible to restate staff coping and responses (conceptualised as 'consequences' to behaviour) as TPPs in a similar way. For example, Hill and Dagnan (2002) described wishful thinking as a staff coping style associated with poor outcome.

Lloyd and Williams link studies on staff–client interactions to the concept of problem procedures that sustain challenging behaviour:

- withdrawing to avoid being hurt, resulting in client resorting to challenging behaviour to re-engage staff
- referring on to find a magic answer
- trying to be the friend and not challenging the client, leading to frustration
- cutting off from the pain and avoiding emotional responses, feeling you can cope with anything so leading to aggressive abusive responses to maintain this position
- bored carers overreact to small incidents, escalating situations that cause hurt, avoidance and boredom.

(Lloyd and Williams 2003)

The use of the CAT concepts of recognition and revision may also be useful for staff following the reformulation, and their progress and motivation to succeed may be sustained using this approach. See Table 10.4.

CAT-informed interventions
The letter
Writing a reformulation letter may transform a rather dry and impersonal behavioural model into an empathic narrative that is accessible and in line with person-centred and positive behavioural approaches. Sinason (1992) noted the importance of taking up the scribe function for those who can't think, remember, read or write. The reformulation and goodbye letters are a good tool for providing an empathic and hopeful narrative for the person around their behaviour, and also for their carers, in order to support a more traditional formulation. This use of contextual reformulation for staff teams is well developed in the CAT model (Ryle and Kerr 2002).

CASE STUDY: LETTERS – A TOOL FOR COLLABORATIVE REFORMULATION

Jenny, a lady in her late 40s was described as a 'real character' by her empathic, warm and valuing staff team. Despite being skilled and able, she lived in a large, specialist residential home due to episodes of challenging behaviour. During these episodes she would destroy her flat and hurt anyone who came near. The staff team found these episodes very difficult as they struggled to reach and understand the person they loved and to deal with their own fear and hurt.

Jenny had had a very difficult life, spending her early years rejected by her family and moving from place to place, including a number of secure forensic facilities, as she struggled to express her rage and loss. The staff marvelled at how far she had come and wanted her to progress with this able independent 'self'. A 16-session CAT therapy revealed that she was terrified of becoming the 'forensic' feared monster again and that she would be rejected. Therapy helped Jenny name her fear and some of the triggers (any 'mistake' meant that she 'failed' to maintain a competent and valued reciprocal role); she was also able to name parts of her TPPs – withdrawal and rejecting others before they rejected her – but Jenny struggled to integrate and make links between these discoveries and make use of the SDR to recognise and revise her procedures.

Jenny was very tearful during the reading of both the reformulation and goodbye letters and it was though the narrative function of the letter that she felt able to hold and accept the competent and feared selves. Together we decided to write another letter to the staff team from us both, with the therapist holding the scribe and integrating function and Jenny the emotional narrative and communication to staff. The letter to the team was a retelling of her (well known) story that enabled the staff team to understand the 'procedure' of the challenging behaviour, and also allowed Jenny to see that they could hold both her competent and feared selves in mind without rejecting her and without (her) shame. Slowly, as staff were able to name the emotional procedures 'in the moment', Jenny was able to cope with setbacks without withdrawing or rejecting and was able to be truly supported by staff. She experienced a new healthier reciprocal role of hearing and respecting – known and validated.

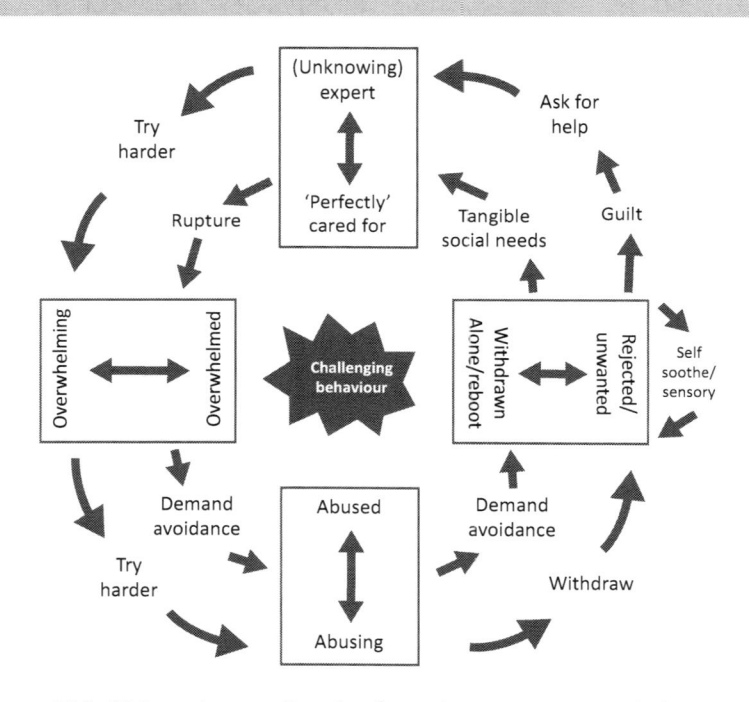

Figure 10.2: SDR: understanding the dance between carer and client (Parent problem procedures on outer circle, child problem procedures on inner circle)

The diagram

Recognition and revision of the client's behavioural TPP can be achieved using traditional functional assessment tools. However, by completing a relational assessment and using a 'map' of challenging behaviour, the reformulation makes the challenging behaviour more understandable/predictable to an often wary or frightened carer. It is also a helpful structure for naming, in a non-blaming way, the possibility that the carer or service may be inadvertently reinforcing the behaviour. It also aids recognition and supports the development of alternative interventions in an accessible way.

Working with carers

In their study of why parents find challenging behaviour support unhelpful, Wodehouse and McGill (2009) concluded that better partnership working and respectful collaboration increased behavioural change and that parent–professional conflict regarding formulation, particularly 'blaming formulation', made interventions less helpful. They proposed that staff training should also follow this model. CAT provides a model of enhancing work with parents and carers as equal partners in formulation.

Wanless and Jahoda (2002) recommend that carers' thoughts and emotions are important and that this assessment is vital in understanding their care responses to challenging behaviour. Their work also implies that discussing these 'hot' cognitions is more valid and useful an assessment than a cold appraisal of the events, in that it captures the reality of the care process.

A number of tools have been developed to look at appraisal of challenging behaviour (Hastings 1997b). Those wishing to explore a CAT-informed tool to gain insight into carer understandings of challenging behaviour might be supported in this by the helper's dance tool developed by Potter 2013 (see Chapter 6).

The CAT relational approach is important in creating an environment where staff can feel able to access their dreaded or warded off responses in a curious and non-blaming framework. The therapist should seek to explore these responses within a workshop so that they can be acknowledged, accepted and gently challenged within a therapeutic dialogue.

Conclusion

Challenging behaviour is defined by the powerful effect it has on others, and any understanding or intervention needs to be able to support carers to cope and overcome their difficulties. Farrell *et al.* (2010) observe that current training for staff focuses on knowledge and skill acquisition inviting an interactional approach looking at client and staff factors seeking for solutions. Carridice's (2004) and Lloyd and Williams's (2003) work to support staff teams to reformulate challenging behaviour using a CAT model, enabled them to develop less pathological formulations of challenging behaviour and derive exits that they can enact rather than expecting the client to change. In this way CAT may be used as a tool of service and system change in line with current guidance around creating capable environments (Royal College of Psychiatrists 2007).

Chapter 11

Heroic or Stoic

Why Do We Try So Hard, or Give Up So Easily, in Helping with Severe Autism?

Julie Lloyd and Steve Potter

Self, society and autism

In this chapter we explore how our understanding of work with people with autism is shaped by the helping relationships involved. We use Cognitive Analytic Therapy's (CAT) method of mapping patterns of interaction when helping. We use the concept of relational intelligence to think about the many-sided, multi-factored, many-layered nature of the interactions of establishing and maintaining help. The concept of relational intelligence (see Chapter 5), with its combination of intrapersonal, interpersonal, social and emotional intelligences, refocuses our attention on the system of relationships in any particular moment of help. We ask: to what extent are people with autism affected by relationships, whether in the early formative stages of their life as infants, children and teenagers or through their current relational environment that involves either care or neglect? We conclude by wondering whether a refocusing of our thinking on the process of helping, rather than the content or purpose, changes our understanding of autism.

The term 'autism' is used as a shorthand metaphor for a lack of social relatedness, with implications for a sense of self. It has even been used in some now discredited psychoanalytic literature to describe a normal stage of infant development (Klein 1987; Mahler 1949) when society doesn't seem to impinge on the infant. This early psychoanalytic idea has now been superseded by observational work, such as by Trevarthen (2001) and Reddy (2008) who demonstrate how new born infants are highly relational and aware of their immediate 'society'. They are active partners with an innate predisposition to work at relationships with increasing awareness and empathy, noticing when attunement is broken or misfires and seeking to restore it through joint activity. (Tronick gives a vivid example of this in his 'still face experiment' on YouTube.) Here lies one of the main conundrums when working with people with autism. Normally, when seeking to help someone who we can see is in a difficult position, we use empathy – our imagination about what it would be like to walk in their shoes, from our experience of walking in our own. This is a doubled-up process of feeling for the other and cross referencing with our own feelings, and also thinking about how we might act. Empathy is, in part, a call for action. In choosing how to respond we are working with immediate, raw feelings for the other person and our self, but also what we tend to conventionally call our 'second thoughts'. The story of the Good Samaritan is an excellent example. Previous passersby may have felt fellow feeling and a call to action to help but on second thoughts decided to go on their way. The Samaritan felt compassion and an inner sense of conscience decided to help, at risk to himself and against prevailing prejudices. Something important is involved in this process. This allows empathy and compassion; it involves projecting our feelings onto people and, as in Figure 11.1, some indecision to see how and whether they fit with our wider concerns and understanding. The projective identification is an intentional but not conscious process with which we must engage by thinking empathically; it is our relational intelligence. The risk or limitation is that, in seeking to understand, we project our material in a strong way onto other people without mediation.

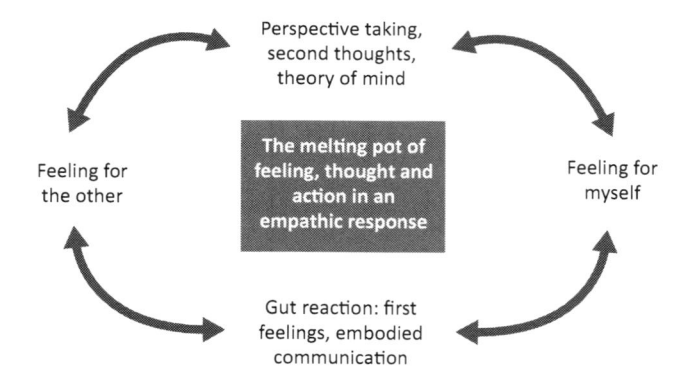

Figure 11.1: Empathy as a four-way interaction

This figure describes a four-way interaction combining feeling for the other with feeling for self, in relation to a gut reaction or immediate physical response (reacting out of hand), moderated by theory of mind-based perspective taking, or what we might more informally call 'second thoughts'. When a person with autism pushed into a queue at a fairground and was threatened by an outraged man, a member of the public attributing the first person's behaviour to autism, immediately approached him, protecting him by inviting him to go on the ride with her family. Both sets of behaviours were outside the norm; the man in the queue might not normally be outraged if someone pushed in, and the female member of the public might not normally approach a stranger to go on rides with her family. For the person who probably had autism, we can only guess how little sense it made to him to be on the receiving end of initial threatening anger and subsequently concerned welcoming (but perhaps unwanted by him) rescue and inclusion. So our imagination helps a bit, but we are not really able to merge, at least not for any length of time or sufficient accuracy, with an individual's experience of what it is to be autistic.

We try to balance altruism with self-interest, or the needs of the group with the needs of the individual. These, in turn, are thought of as not just individual abilities, but also abilities invested in our culture and society. Put in this way, the tasks of relationally intelligent interaction are complex and demanding. Empathy and our socialisation into a richly interactive group culture help us measure up to this and it is something we maintain through joint activity with others.

The experience of autism acts as a limit on how much of this complex of relationally intelligent interactions can be simultaneously held in mind. People with autism attempt to manage complexity by an extreme narrowing of their curiosity, resulting in them stultifying their repertoire. In autism this shutting out of wider intelligence and possibilities is a default setting that deals with fear through avoidance. People with autism may focus on one particular feature of the environment, such as water pipes or lampposts, excluding attending to anything else. As information floods in from societally intelligent sources, the person with autism may develop narrow areas of apparent felt control, but shut off or shut out much relational experience and chronically ward off intrusion by holding onto carved-out areas of some certainty. Some more able people on the autistic spectrum appear to cultivate an autistic identity and narrative. Cultivating identities is a task that faces people very intensely nowadays because society is so complex and there are so many choices available about how a person could be. Such a person may recognise that others consider some of their rituals to be eccentric, but assertively state that they do this because of their autism, insisting that onlookers accept that their behaviour is beyond their control.

There is a great deal of confusion regarding relationships in autism; opposing opinions are held passionately. Williams (1992) in her autobiography, *Nobody Nowhere*, describes how having autism protected her from being damaged when receiving maternal physical and emotional abuse. If a highly impaired theory of mind makes a person with autism less aware that another has intentions, they might be protected by not perceiving the tyranny of someone whose intentions are malign. It is possible that Williams' attributions of her emotional reaction are coloured by her expectation that someone with autism would be impervious.

However, just because a person with autism operates with seriously impaired social relatedness, this does not mean that they do not relate emotionally or do not feel pain inflicted by another person. From the point of view of relational intelligence, the person who shuts down from, numbs out or avoids a hurtful interaction has some degree of agency and is protecting themselves.

How we see our self, our personality and our general style in going about our life – what makes 'me' uniquely 'me' – develops through formative relationships, most strongly in childhood, although later relationships also change one's sense of one's self. This applies to people with autism as much as anyone else. Although autism is formed neurologically, people with autism are also influenced by what happens around them. A person internalises the social world and, in so doing, creates a two-way dialogue between them and society. This dialogic view works with an idea of internalisation of the social world, which is precisely what people with autism have difficulty engaging in. However, the social world does take a unique shape around and within the life space of people with autism, and the distinctive relational features of autism do play their part in the social construction of this in limiting or enabling ways. If staying open to several perspectives and responses at once is upsetting and overwhelming yet necessary to successful social interaction, it may be that where non-autistic people with sufficient healthy interactions will internalise an empathic and relationally intelligent stance towards self and others, people with autism will need much more of that work done for them. We might think of the unskilled, 'two left feet' kind of dancer being held and led along by the compassionate and experienced dancer. Of course, there is the easy possibility of the experienced dancer losing patience or not sensing their enabling role and being contemptuous, blaming or rejecting of the 'two left feet' dancer. Awareness of the supplementary and complementary relational work that the helper needs to do for the autistic person is our focus here. We think this requires additional levels of empathy and relational intelligence in the helper and to achieve this we make use of the relational mapping skills drawn from CAT. Our aim is not therapy but more relationally intelligent help where the empathic resources of the helper have a better chance of being appropriately channelled and expressed in line with the autistic client's needs.

For the person with autism, the ability to develop a sufficient level of astute social participation and control is severely compromised by:

- the simultaneous action of multiple deficits
- lack of theory of mind
- a level of attachment that is about seeking proximity to meet core biological needs rather than an inherent interest and curiosity in other people
- an inability to switch perspectives owing to weak central coherence
- a lack of a felt sense of what other's experience through deficits in mirror cell development.

Secondary deficits follow from this restriction. People with autism miss the accumulated relational wisdom gained from trying to relate, getting it wrong, working through the embarrassment, learning the lesson and gaining the skills. People with autism miss the fun, intrigue and curiosity that propel most people into unpredictably fascinating dialogues. This lack of curiosity is not merely passive, but insistent, definitive and final. They also lack the ability to dance out of the way by empathically reading the other's intentions. At times like this, being around someone with autism can feel very intrusive. Verbal exchanges with someone with autism are often more like consecutive monologues than conversations.

People with autism dread being overwhelmed, and others and the outside world are seen as overwhelming and impinging. Their way of gaining relief from this is to seek control in familiar, if narrow, ways. In stark contrast to what they dread, they desire control over emotional experiences and seek secure interaction with the world via highly rigid routines. In this situation, they often unwittingly push others away by restricting or attacking them. Helpers or therapists are likely to be routinely exposed to feeling dismissed, and hurt because of this.

The role of the helper

This lack of relational versatility is something that needs compassionate understanding by those in the helper role and, in turn, needs meeting by an added layer of relational skills in the helper as well as the focus and patience to give concrete shape to the helping relationship.

Autism has distinctive features that are challenging for people in the helper's role. Helpers can become frustrated, dismissive, heroic or numb. It is easy to become either too rigidly protocol adherent or dismissively sceptical in response to the autistic person's unique way of being in the world. For example, some staff said that an individual's refusal to go out was insurmountable, and were astonished when a new member of the team helped him to go out simply by distracting him with some chocolate.

Are there patterns of helping that, despite their best intentions or because of them, helpers and autistic people get pulled into (see Appendix 6)? Why do some people choose to become helpers? Common themes are about liking working with people, wanting to make the world a better place, relieve suffering and understanding the self and others. A common denominator is a wish to be in a relationship, though we shouldn't rule out the possibility that the attraction of the helper role is in keeping people controlled and at a distance.

There are many attractions to seeking relationships with people with intellectual disabilities, such as having more straightforward relationships – what you see is what you get. Feeling accepted and not judged badly, and working with people who function less well than ourselves, can help us feel better. When helping people whose lives are so impoverished, almost anything a helper offers could improve things (even if only in the present, as these moments are likely to be soon forgotten). Working with people with intellectual disabilities expresses sympathy with people who have a raw deal because their cognitive and social capacity to cope with the complexities of life is limited. However, for sociable and relationally minded helpers and therapists, this wish can be severely challenged by people with autism. The helper's own fears of being out of contact with the world and not being understood or held in mind might be triggered.

By mapping the helping relationship, we have both a tool for seeing what is possible with the autistic client and where things go wrong, and possibly a way of showing where we are and what behaviour we could employ.

The 'autistic' therapist

The therapist, who has chosen this line of work, may identify with some of their client's autism, recognising their own wish at times to be left to get on with life or to escape from being overwhelmed, hiding in detail and not having to try to see the bigger picture. Many therapists working with people with autism try to learn how to reduce the amount their own autism impacts on them, as is evidenced by the typical banter in Community Intellectual Disability Teams in which colleagues describe certain other colleagues or their specific behaviours as 'autistic', and perhaps by becoming vigilant at spotting when these tendencies occur in themselves.

The heroic therapist

Autistic clients may be experienced as hard to help and tend to evoke heroic attempts at empathic relating from helpers, carers and therapists wishing to fill the relational gap against all odds. Such heroic work may be a way of coping with the other possibility of feeling overwhelmed by the client or being dismissive, rejecting and abandoning towards them. Lots of people may have tried to help and failed, and the tempting narcissistic solution for the helper is to justify the struggle of help as special, go the extra mile and be the self-elected one who is going to succeed where others have failed. In autism, the push to be heroic comes from three sources: professional theory and aspirations, the client and ourselves. However, this push rebounds in unwanted ways, as the therapist is driven by three competing factors: professional demands, the client's needs and our own longings for connection. But getting caught up with these three issues can push the therapist into losing their therapeutic perspective. Psychological researchers view understanding autism as a chance to learn about why nurture and connection matter in human development and what happens when they go wrong. This huge responsibility placed on professionals' shoulders means that successes in therapy are also desperately sought to validate the accuracy of psychological explanation. However, in autism the therapist's dream to transcend such severe relational limitations is brought back to earth with a bump by interactions that preserve these limitations.

The longing therapist and the unwitting client create a relational environment that is dissociated. The need to treat the split team becomes pressing. The heroic therapist 'can see what is needed'. They are going to improve the system, run psycho-educational workshops for the staff who just need a bit of guidance and meanwhile be the client's caring, insightful, reliable, advocate and helper. Surprise and disappoint result when clients reject such overtures and therapists become unpopular with staff who discard the therapist's sensible advice. Similarly, referrals can be made from one agency to another or from families to agencies in which a catalogue of repeated failures are described and the demand is that 'they' get their act together and fix it. Receipt of such referrals can induce righteous indignation, guilt, determination to be the one to fix it, resentful concern or compassionate but stoic resignation.

When things fail to improve, therapists may feel their own inadequacy, blameworthiness and sense of being overwhelmed. Seeing a client's predicament from a position of a defeated therapeutic hero, therapists may try to keep their heads down. Statements about autism having a terrible behavioural phenotype for which little can be done lead to hopes the individual will be taken away to somewhere that is better resourced. A few referrals may be made, together with sympathy, helplessly disparaging 'care in the community' and 'inadequate resources' as bruised support workers are left to cope. A common response to such unresponsiveness in the client can be cast as a dilemma of either heroically striving to give care – in a way idealised by the therapist – which leads to disappointment or cold indifference so as not to be disappointed.

It is also easy to fall into a heroic therapist position by default. Trying to not play hero or vanquished, a therapist may seek to work as effectively and efficiently as possible by judicious selection of achievable goals, in a timed intervention, presented in carefully graded steps towards an integrated service. However, just as they begin to be effective, others bow out knowing the client is safe in their expert hands, expecting them to be able to manage each crisis so they steadily become isolated, ground down and resentful. People with autism may find themselves in an unpredictable and chaotic world as carers alternate between striving to give ideal care and then being abandoning or indifferent.

The stoic therapist

If we are not being heroic, we can struggle on in stoic ways denying our own feelings, distance ourselves from the person with whom we are working and end up feeling numb to ward off our own hurt. People with autism make powerful statements about themselves, which reach us and we respond. They often narrow down their range of connections to others to a single dimension, such as having their wants met. The response from the person with normal relational antennae looking for lots of hooks to connect is often to feel bewildered and then to cope in similarly restrictive ways.

Often when working with people with autism, nothing seems to change and daily care becomes tedious so bored workers or therapists can elaborate and 'beef up' their perception of what is happening in ways that might render the work more 'heroic'. A psychologist was asked to conduct a functional assessment on a non-verbal woman with severe intellectual disabilities who constantly and insistently sat on top of other people if they were sitting or lying down. Staff gave an elaborate account of the motives behind whom the client selected to sit on, but 16 hours of minute-by-minute detailed observation showed the woman's choice was entirely based on availability and no other distinguishing characteristic. Perhaps their elaboration had been an attempt to enrich the barren and empty reality of the relational experience.

When working with people with a personality disorder there is a notion of multiple transferences and highly charged enactments of the need to relate, whereas in working with autism there is only the real relationship, i.e., what the person with autism wants (Clarkson 1995). People like knowing where they truly are with others and hence may be particularly attracted by these relationships in which what you see, at face value, is how it is. There is no layering, illusions built out of projection or rehearsal of desires. However, there is physical violence and challenging behaviour, including behaviours that the therapist may find revolting, such as being alongside clients who spit or injure themselves. The therapist may feel helpless or furious when their attempt to soothe a self-injuring client does nothing. When walking into an autism unit, the helper or therapist may have that sinking feeling of being useless. Pushing out such disturbing feelings, staff may soldier on, throwing energy into areas that help them to be comfortable with being paid, such as focusing on the client's physical condition. However, this may feel preferable to being on the receiving end of someone else's transferences and projections.

Workers may dismiss the idea of breaking through to the client, as the person with autism remains relentlessly the same. On the one hand, non-reciprocation hurts and frustrates, but on the other hand, accepting the narcissistic wound of non-reciprocation in autism as replicating how life is, autism feels true, honest and based in reality. The helper's own characteristic transferences are highly exposed, as the person with autism does not dance to the helper's tunes. We are confronted with a dilemma: being hurt because we are invisible or being real because life (i.e., early infant wounding) is like that. In autism the worker may at best enjoy and at worst accept resignedly that autistic experiences confirm what their own early life has taught them.

Developing sensitivity to these patterns can be helped by peer supervision and reflective practice among helpers and carers using CAT's mapping methods. This has been done through teaching mapping skills to helpers and also taking a consultative role to teams of carers helping them map out the helping system.

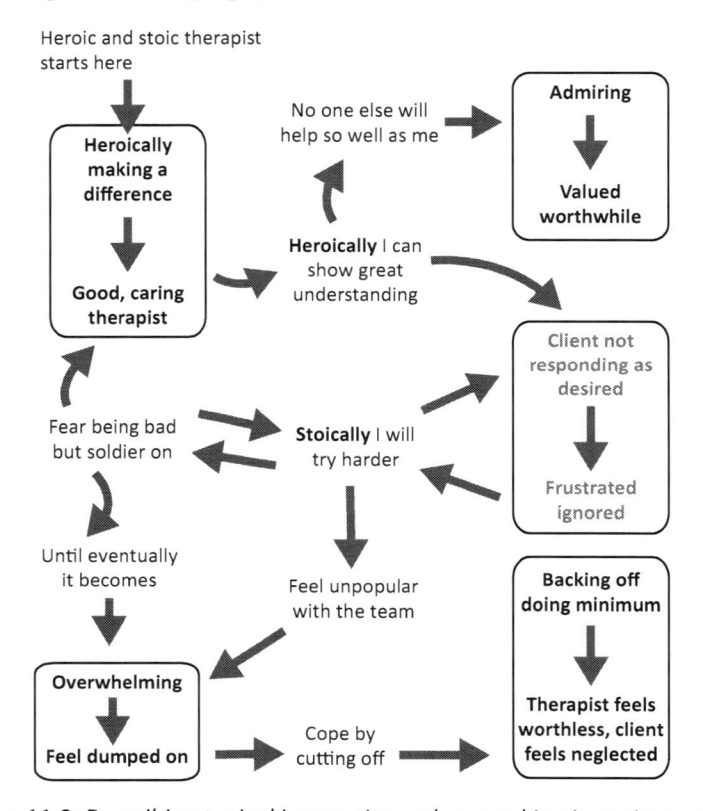

Figure 11.2: Describing typical interactions when working in autism services

Traditional understandings of autism fail to take full account of this complexity and how easy it is for any of us, despite our best intentions, to be drawn into heroic work with limited results. By searching for a breakthrough, the heroic therapist is faced with the gulf between their longing for a more mutually creative and expansive interaction and the timeless quality of stereotyped repetition. Autistically restricting behaviour depends on the therapist being untouched and unmoved, and does not acknowledge (indeed, an impaired theory of mind concludes, 'cannot acknowledge') that the therapist has their own unique, individual and unpredicted reactions that are different from how the client perceives them. The client with autism insists the only effect they have on the therapist is the only reaction that could exist and becomes demandingly outraged at variation, pushing away the existence of other options. Such restrictiveness by the client can reduce the therapist's sense of their own agency, leaving the therapist feeling anxiously stuck as their own ability to make a difference ebbs away. The autistic client or child tends to push the therapist or parent into behaving in an out-of-character way or more extremely than they would normally, testing patience and troubling the mind, as instead of being submissive or rebellious, they do not offer any reciprocation. Heroic therapists lose their capacity to be versatile.

Supporting the autistic person's social context using CAT

In response to autism, CAT offers a framework for working directly and indirectly to highlight ways of preventing and avoiding unhelpfulness, collusion or retaliation. CAT has a way of describing unhelpful patterns of interaction by using the idea of reciprocal role procedures as described in the introduction. From a CAT perspective reciprocal roles such as being caring in relation to feeling cared for, or being neglecting and hurting in relation to feeling neglected and hurt, are learnt and replayed repeatedly in one guise or another from early on in life. These reciprocal roles may be experienced in quite restrictive ways and elicit a powerfully fixed mood or state of mind. These then become familiar places or positions from which we experience and handle ourselves, and ultimately are how we come to know ourselves. Reciprocal roles can be used to describe different interactions between the various sources of relational intelligence. A lot of our interactions with ourselves and the world of people and things is coloured by trying to get out of dreaded positions or states of mind and get to more desirable or manageable ones.

If we focus not on the autistic person but on the caring and helping relationship, we come to see how the helper can compensate by doing all the relating. In training helpers and in learning from our own experience, we have identified a number of characteristic helping dances that we can fall into. Awareness of these and stepping out of them can help greatly with the quality of care and help. It is a reasonable assumption that in the absence of a full range of relational skills on the part of people with autism, the helpers involved may need to cultivate additional skills in noticing, orchestrating and negotiating the relational space making up the helping relationship. Given how hard it can be to work with people with autism, it is inevitable that many helpers end up either heroically seeking to make a familiar relationship but impinging on the autistic person or risking themselves becoming restricting, dismissive and attacking. By restricting others so as to gain control, people with autism miss out on a spontaneous important aspect of social and emotional knowledge, and some sense of this absence may keep perpetuating the heroic efforts of carers and helpers to connect in the way humans usually do. A vicious circle can be set up in which interactions are impoverished as others abandon trying to get into dialogue, because dialogue takes two playing whole heartedly and mutually together. The helper may then stoically struggle on, seeking a relationship but within these limiting and painful options. Such parents often learn how they must temper their expression, controlling and hiding it as they see how easily overwhelmed their autistic child can become. It is as if the child with autism has not been able to learn how to manage their parents' feelings.

As workers, because we are usually unable to tune in alongside autistic individuals, we tend to fill in the void through our own relationships. Conducting a functional assessment of a man with autism and very severe intellectual disability, the client approached the psychologist. She said and signalled 'hello' using an exaggerated waving arm movement. To her astonishment he copied the movement and so, for a split moment, delighted at having 'broken through', she joyfully repeated her arm movement. At the point when her arm was furthest away from her trunk, he grabbed and pulled off a button on her cardigan and put it in his mouth! The psychologist had wanted him to copy her movement, attributing relational intentions to him, whilst he saw his chance to grab the button he wanted. The psychologist was taking for granted this relationally rich mix of interactive awareness that wasn't being reciprocated.

The therapist may long to inculcate in the person with autism a sense of curiosity and a wish to be relational. This can lead to a sustaining fantasy for the therapist that at times they have broken through to the client with severe autism and for a tantalising moment there was true dialogue. Maybe the belief is that to be significant, dialogue has to be sustained. For example, Pat, who had no speech and spent all her time standing rooted to one spot at a distance from the group, responded to a brief game of 'Round and Round the Garden' on her hand (with no tickling) and, to her psychologist's surprise, made eye contact and then copied the game on the psychologist's hand (they are surprised because people with autism do not usually copy and also avoid eye contact).

However, the door was slammed shut when, after a tantalising glimpse at a meeting of minds and bodies, Pat physically pushed the psychologist away to get rid of her. The beginnings of dialogue were overwhelming and she could only stand a little contact. The psychologist refrained from chasing after Pat, who could tolerate a silent passive proximity, sitting side by side whilst the psychologist attended to others.

We know the world can be a wonderful place with interesting people; the distress for the therapist is seeing the client with autism not knowing this, and not wanting to find it out, as they do not want to relate to people or novel stimuli. At the level of direct intervention, if the person with autism is safely engaged in one of their rituals, the therapist is able to make a choice about whether to leave them alone, or join in and, by taking part in their rituals, trying to make it a relational moment.

People with autism may be portrayed as hiding their real self – a self that is lost, estranged or feral – with the hope that the passionately heroic therapist will break through, releasing the human being from their prison. The therapist may respond by searching heroically to lift the level of dialogue, hunting for delight and interpersonal curiosity, hoping to make an impact through a live relationship, only to be pushed out repeatedly.

There are a number of tools aimed at teaching a person who does not wish to communicate that dialogue results in rewards, emphasising Functional Communication. For example, the Picture Exchange Communication System (PECS) is a highly structured attempt to foster dialogue, using rewards to reinforce desired behaviours, errorless learning and formal techniques for extinguishing errors. Augmented Interaction, taking as its model infant–parent proto 'conversations', encourages the worker to join in with the client's stereotypes and bit by bit developing these routines playfully into more of a turn-taking interaction.

As it is, the behavioural learning that matters in autism, our theory of change, is associational. Applied Behavioural Analysis and specific applications such as PECS are criticised as reducing people with autism to the status of Pavlovian dogs, yet they remain the most effective approach in terms of teaching basic communication skills. But these behavioural techniques can work better when staff and parents can hold in mind the relational issues of working with people with autism, otherwise interventions can be dehumanised and lose a sense of authentic reality.

If capacity to relate is absent in the autistic person's interaction with the world then we, the authors, suggest the intervention of the therapist has to be to the system of care and support, with a view to reducing the risk of unhelpful helpfulness of trying to make the autistic person do relational dances that they are not capable of doing. The relational thinking available to individuals and teams working with autistic people helps in the following ways.

- It allows the workers space to think about the patterns they may be falling into.
- It can help formulate a plan of support, which is more relationally intelligent.
- It can soften and help adjust those tendencies to want to recast the autistic person's particular patterns into more empathic relating ones.

Thinking in terms of a limiting or narrow pattern of relational intelligence helps thinking about our dependency on its abundant, routine availability in daily interactions and the difficulty of helping someone without such a basic, shared human resource. It is an unfortunate temptation to blame and pathologise the client. We have explored how heroic work locates the gap in intelligence or its wilful absence in the person, and we suggest it is better understood as an absence that needs working on in the specific and changing context of the person's daily life. In the lives of people with autism, it is a systemic gap rather than an interpersonal or developmental one. The therapy 'client' in work with an autistic person should be seen as that person's social system. Accordingly, the focus of therapy is the integration of the system of support for the people with autism rather than the integration of their personality or temperament.

A care team consulted a psychologist following an outburst of challenging behaviour from a woman with severe autism who screamed at a bus driver and passengers because the bus was unexpectedly late (impinging, overwhelming). The client was initially given a brief break from going on buses (perhaps a communally and emotionally intelligent response; familiar and safe but limited), whilst a letter explaining autism was sent by the home manager to the bus company (socially intelligent). The home manager also boarded the bus at the time the client normally went on it in order to talk to a passenger who had burst into tears when the client had screamed abuse at her. The client rehearsed a Social Story™ script with the consultant to the team about why buses may be late and how to handle this tension, and staff now practise this with her whilst waiting together at the bus stop.

Since the person with autism cannot mediate or construct their states of mind in relationally intelligent ways, staff must hold such work. To the extent that the relational gap is genetically structured, it cannot be filled by the heroic longing of the therapist. Understanding our impulsive, heroic or rejecting reactions and determining how far, how fast and by what means dialogue may be established is the key professional skill. An indirect intervention is needed where the therapist, as consultant, creates a well-attuned compensatory and complementary, relationally intelligent environment. This work needs the therapist to establish an agreement on the possible and necessary limits of the work and agree role differentiations. In this way they can hold in dialogue people with severe autism, themselves and society.

The investment in the special education, welfare and treatment of autism needs to build this in. Similarly, although we are describing here experience of working with people on the severe autistic continuum, some of these observations may not be restricted to that and could apply more widely. In this respect, autism challenges us to think more about what it means to be human and connected with society in relationally intelligent ways. What CAT can offer us is how mapping this out enables us to see better what is going on.

Chapter 12

What is the 2005 Mental Capacity Act and How Can Cognitive Analytic Therapy Help Us to Make Sense of the Decision-making Process at its Heart?

Hilary Brown and Julie Lloyd

Introduction

The Mental Capacity Act (MCA) 2005 was introduced into law after much consultation and deliberation in the fields of intellectual disability, older people and people with mental health problems and, on the whole, is seen to be an enabling piece of legislation that struck a creative balance between the rights of an individual to self-determination and the responsibilities of those around them to step in when someone is not able to make decisions for themselves. The MCA was welcomed because it filled a vacuum. Before it was introduced only a few precepts of common law allowed one person to step in and act on behalf of someone who was not able to make their own decisions. People were deemed to lack capacity in all areas of their lives or to have it across the whole span of their activities, when clearly this dilemma shut out the many people who operate in the middle ground, managing some or all of their lives but requiring assistance at key times or around particularly difficult or painful issues.

As therapists, we sometimes have to use this legislation ourselves, especially if we work with people with intellectual disabilities whose ability to make decisions is often at issue, but also if we are working with people with serious mental health problems, dementia or addictions or when a person's instability cuts across their self-management. We may need to call upon its framework in relation to eating disorders or addictions or when working with people with autism; in these cases people can get stuck or their thinking can be seriously distorted so that they make decisions that cause harm to themselves, or refuse to make decisions that could help them. We may need to use this legislation when these matters are sufficiently serious and draw on the thinking behind the MCA in making our own judgements, but we also have much to offer to other professionals who are caught up in assessing or decision-making on behalf of our clients. Cognitive Analytic Therapy (CAT) takes a view about how fragmentary we all are and how our different self states might operate in relative isolation from each other. It has ways of understanding that trauma, neglect and abuse create extreme places in the mind that a person would be driven to avoid or to manage through familiar patterns of avoidance or disruption. It also has a clear sense of how 'others' can take control and override the wishes of a more vulnerable person who may then feel as if they have limited ways of protesting or asserting their own choices. So this is an area of practice that requires our attention and our input.

We need to understand it in case we need to invoke it in our own practice, but also our CAT understanding helps us to think about some of the tensions within the MCA, its principles and the model of decision-making at its core. In this chapter we begin by exploring the MCA and then move on to use a number of key psychological and CAT concepts to 'test' its model, suggesting why 'one size' does not necessarily 'fit all' when it comes to making decisions.

A wide range of decisions and circumstances

The MCA was designed to address one-off, serious decisions, specifically those relating to serious medical treatment and to changes of accommodation, but in intellectual disability services we find it necessary to apply the MCA in relation to a much broader range of decision-making that is more likely to be ongoing. For example, the framework within the MCA sits much more easily alongside a decision about cancer treatment than ongoing management of diabetes.

Both authors regularly receive referrals to make capacity assessments in relation to complex situations where an understanding of reciprocal roles is at least as important as an understanding of the person's cognitive processing abilities.

The kinds of cases and decisions that result in such referrals have included assessing issues around marriage, whether to stay in potentially abusive relationships, sexuality including when taking risks, staying in or leaving the parental home, signing over property or giving away money, setting up a power of attorney, working without pay in a context that could be seen as exploitative, eating a very restrictive diet, managing aggressive behaviour or acting to curtail stealing that might lead to prosecution. Often the subtext of a referral is quite punitive, and formulated as if the only options are to step in and be controlling or step back and let the person sink or swim, so we are asked: Is this person responsible for what they are doing? If not we will take over and if so we will back off and let them take the consequences. The Act that sought so assiduously to avoid an all-or-nothing approach ends up being wielded as a blunt instrument.

A decision may be needed at some point and this needs careful consideration, as there may be a shift from the collaborative to authoritarian position (role), which could manifest as a dilemma. This requires confidence borne out of reflective practice, and supervision is one of the tools practitioners utilise to navigate such switches.

Applying the MCA in complex cases

Moreover, the issues rarely present themselves in a clear order or package. Often, the proposed intervention comes at the end of a long road of difficulties and compromises, when options are limited and time is in danger of running out. At other times, decisions are front-loaded, such as those a diabetic person makes when considering today whether they should eat a bar of chocolate that might harm them in the distant future.

A recent study (Brown and Marchant 2011) of cases deemed complex by health and social care professionals identified the components of a case that made these matters problematical. The cases suggested that complexity could be inferred in the following circumstances.

- There was a spiralling set of inter-related concerns and no clear trigger that put a single, well-formulated and boundaried 'matter' on the table.
- The person's capacity was at issue in a number of ways, they may have been inconsistent but articulate in what they wanted, vociferous (especially in refusing services) but not informed, or they may have *reacted* rather than *decided* around important things suggesting to us that the person may have been triggered into different mental states from which contradictory decision-making could be expected and made sense of.

- A person's ability to separate out information from emotional responses, addiction or neurological drives was in question, for example, a woman would not let a carer into her house to change her incontinence pad because she had a fear of social workers dating back to 30 years ago when they had been involved in a more controlling role in relation to her children, so we saw her as being triggered into a controlling to controlled reciprocal role that took over from her need to get looked after in this most basic and immediate way. In another case, a person did not want to go into a home where they could receive the physical care that they undoubtedly needed, because they feared that their drinking would come under renewed scrutiny.
- The person's capacity for retaining pertinent facts and for *conceiving of alternatives* to their current situation was compromised – social workers spoke about people getting stuck on the '*mythical option*' and not even being able to think about the things that were possible: CAT therapists might see this in terms of where the idealised trumps the real and blocks compromises. Sometimes this means that someone will reiterate that they want to 'go home' or to be cared for by a loved relative, even when that person is saying they can't do what they are being asked to do. People with autism are particularly prone to getting stuck in a rut in these ways and in doing so test the patience and flexibility of those around them.
- In situations where the decisions were more like dilemmas than choices, and revolved around relationships and belonging, not information, risks and consequences. For example, they might present as family ultimatums of the 'you can choose your boyfriend or stay part of this family' kind.
- When the Court of Protection stepped in (often after large damages awards in respect of catastrophic injury), the money complicated rather than mediated family dynamics.

We should not be surprised about this primacy of emotion and relationship. Psychological research has long established the role of emotion and heuristics in decision-making (Brown 2011; Brown and Marchant 2013). Damasio's series of studies (2010) showed that where a person has brain lesions that block access to emotions, they are also unable to make decisions because emotion helps us to prioritise salient information and drives our intentionality and motivates us in acting on and implementing decisions we have made.

Moreover, as CAT therapists we can draw on a body of theory that describes how shifts in mental state occur – how our emotional states vary greatly, our cognitive processing is specific to those states and our recall of memory in those states is distinct and contradictory.

Kahneman (2011) sets out the evidence base for there being two distinct systems of thinking: 'fast' and 'slow' modes of operating. The former is intuitive, emotional and jumps to conclusions, taking what are usually helpful shortcuts. The latter is more computational, requires concentration and can inhibit or steer the more impulsive and driven qualities of the former. In CAT terms we might think of 'fast' thinking as the assumptions we make on the basis of habitual reciprocal roles and procedures that while absorbed from our experiences, can often escape rational scrutiny until we engage a more questioning, reflective stance. That is why in CAT we write a narrative in the form of a reformulation letter but also produce an overview via a map and work with enactments in the relationship as it is manifest 'in the room'.

What can CAT tell us about the limitations to this model?

CAT therapists expect to see people occupying different mental states with varying degrees of integration and organisation. We think of people as having sets of reciprocal roles and recognise/expect inconsistency as people move in and out of different, sometimes contradictory and/or intense self-states. For clients with very painful or un-worked-through procedures, decision-making is hampered in the ways we describe in CAT as dilemmas, traps and snags.

This suggests the need for assessments that contextualise decision-making in terms of history and relationship. It hints at other important measures of capacity such as how *stable* the person is, how open-minded the person is when canvassing options and how far they are able to act on their understanding to put options and choices into operation. It is interesting that in recent legal thinking about when to acknowledge a person's wish for assisted suicide, the phrase that is used is that the person should have a 'fixed and stable' wish to die, not a fleeting despair or depression. We also have to make an assessment of 'suggestibility' to describe the extent to which a person might be literally 'under the influence of' another person, especially if that person has a long history of abusing or controlling, or represents a previous abusive figure in the decision-maker's inner world.

People with intense emotions are more likely than other people to make decisions that are contradictory or that have the quality of knee-jerk reactions rather than thought-through deliberations. They may have powerful splits that are reflected in decisions that come to be labelled by exasperated others as manipulative. For example, a woman with intellectual disability and borderline personality disorder in one of our services spent much time involved in demanding a doctor because she had been struck off by local surgeries and she had been asked to attend a special scheme. She went to enormous lengths to seek perfect care, but as soon as a specific service was offered she would come up with endless reasons why the arrangement was not good enough – she refused to be seen by one man and she refused to be seen by another because he was older. Her objections made no sense in isolation, but when her history of abuse at the hands of her mother was known, her behaviour represented multiple fears that what she was asking for might turn out to be as toxic as the care her mother had given her. She was like Snow White being offered a *poisoned* apple when she craved a sweet and crisp apple like those offered to her siblings. This cycle cut across this client's mental capacity in relation to her health care, not because she did not 'understand' at a cognitive level that she needed medical treatment, but because, caught up in the intensity of this procedure, she was not able to *think* about her actual health-care needs at all.

The research on complexity also identified the difficulties posited by addiction and by self-states that are tightly bound up with and/or overridden by, physical and neurological triggers. For example, a person with Prader-Willi syndrome may understand nutrition but not be able to use this knowledge to manage their pressing need to eat, as Holland and Wong (1999, p.233) state, '*At its most basic it is not simply an issue of understanding, it is one of control.*' Acting on our decisions is therefore another step in an already complex chain reaction. A man with Down's syndrome and diabetes was able to differentiate healthy foods during an educational session with a community nurse, but on leaving the building, he always headed straight for the nearest sweet shop. This elicited punitive responses from staff who had taken his earlier compliance at face value. Frustrated and powerless, they assumed that he was acting defiantly and that he knew exactly what he was doing, rather than interpreting his behaviour as indicative of a state shift. They would then hide behind the notion that he has full capacity in relation to this arena of decision-making, even though *acting on* the nutritional information he had been given was way beyond his Zone of Proximal Development.

CAT's relational understanding might formulate this as a sequence of unhelpful reciprocal roles, starting with a compliant and pleasing role in response to a concerned, benevolently controlling one, moving into a more needy/abandoned position in which he seeks immediate comfort, which is perceived as him being defiant, which in turn meets with dismissive and punitive responses from staff. The client's shifting states are much more reflective of instant attempts to elicit or maintain relationship and to manage feelings than of planned or 'deliberate' choices. People with intellectual disabilities may be more likely than others to be operating with a restricted set of reciprocal roles, making these clumsy shifts more frequent and eliciting more punitive or negating responses from those around them.

Viewing decisions as traps, dilemmas and snags

When decisions are seen in a CAT context, habitual reciprocal roles and procedural sequences help us to understand the limits of a person's capacity to change and move on. We know that people without cognitive impairments also get caught in these nets and that thinking is not enough to scaffold change unless it is supported within a significant and often therapeutic relationship. As decision-makers, we all risk getting caught up in dilemmas, traps and snags.

At the stage of considering options, a person can become so bound up in polarised options that making choices becomes aversive as neither option is wanted. Often the service embeds these black and white positions in its policies and practice; for example, in relation to sexual options for people with intellectual disabilities it is as if the client can only have the sexual freedom to have sex with whomever she chooses doing whatever act, at whatever place, at whatever time, which leads her to being abused, *or* she is kept away from sex altogether, but experiences herself as not a real woman.

This then risks becoming a trap because the client is kept away from appropriate opportunities for learning and thereby made more vulnerable to being seduced or exploited so that the services lurch between these rival options without seeking good middle ground where she can feel confident, take manageable risks and yet remain somewhat protected.

Traps are thereby driven by these constraints on options. CAT dilemmas are often enacted as controlling (taking over) or neglecting (doing nothing) responses to service users who lack capacity. A typical decision maker's trap is shown in Figure 12.1.

A decision maker's trap

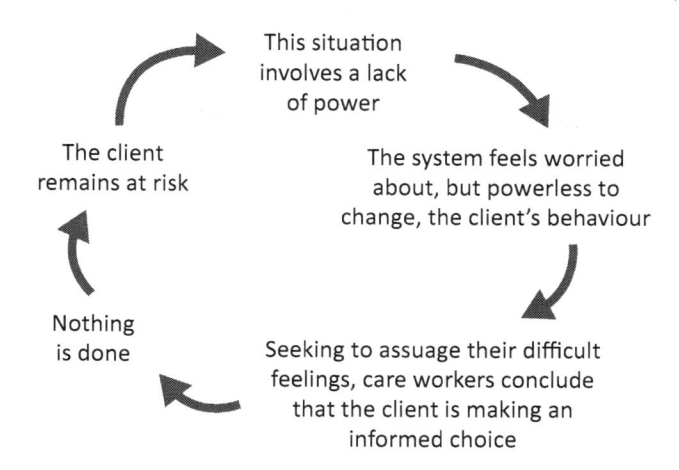

- This situation involves a lack of power
- The system feels worried about, but powerless to change, the client's behaviour
- Seeking to assuage their difficult feelings, care workers conclude that the client is making an informed choice
- Nothing is done
- The client remains at risk

Figure 12.1: A decision maker's trap

These inconsistencies get turned into 'be perfect' loops when the desire to be perfectly consistent and in control leads to systems-level enactments in which evermore elaborate policies and guidelines are developed to anticipate all eventualities that then become unworkable and are left on the shelf.

Snags occur when a person's behaviour is so much under the control of others that they have no freedom to move, and this is captured in the legal formulation of 'undue influence'. People who have capacity may find themselves 'incapacitated' by violence, fear or control to the point where they can no longer think of options or act to bring them about. Steven Hoskin (Flynn 2011)[1] stands as an example of this. He wanted friends; he got tormentors to whom he could not stand up. He was afraid that involvement with services would lead to old patterns of control and to him feeling different and isolated again, so he asked for help in a 'scatter-gun' way and did not reveal the scale of the horrors he was facing at home or the extent to which he was being abused. His case was extreme and he ended his short life by being murdered, but even 'caring' control can undermine the attempts many people with intellectual disabilities make to change.

Moreover, professionals can also be caught in snags when they adjudicate in contentious issues. The expectations of other agencies, or

---

[1] For full reports into, and discussion of, this case read Serious Case Review conducted by Dr Margaret Flynn which can be accessed at www.cornwall.gov.uk/Default.aspx?page=5609

the interpretations of fellow team members, can exert a powerful influence over the way issues are framed and the role of decision-maker, so within the MCA there is a clear tension between reaching a consensus and acting collaboratively with other professionals, and 'taking a stand' in ways that might go against them.

What does CAT's collaborative stance have to offer?

A case managed by Julie Lloyd involved a capacity assessment under the MCA and a subsequent best-interests decision that was submitted to a national research study (Mental Health Foundation 2012). It was selected as one of two cases demonstrating exemplary practice. The psychologist had previously worked with the client using a CAT framework and the researchers concluded that this intervention had kept the situation out of crisis over a period of many months. The researchers underlined the complexity of the case and that 'much depended on the particular sensitivity and skills of the psychologist, care manager and staff in the home. They felt that conflicts were avoided by this detailed level of partnership work over a period of years' (p.60).

The CAT therapist was asked to conduct a capacity assessment when, some time after the therapy had ended, the situation dramatically deteriorated to the extent that a police investigation had ensued. The client had repeated assessments of his capacity around important issues and the fact that strong attempts had been made to support his decision-making were framed as additional evidence that he did indeed lack capacity. Strategies had included using accessible information and pictures to enable him to understand the risks he was facing. Contextual work with the staff team had also been very positive, and there was a trusting partnership between agencies, but in the end the situation went beyond what was possible for the care providers if they were to keep this client safe.

When the case was deliberated on within the adult safeguarding process, the formal aspects of the chairperson's role lent objectivity to the best-interests meeting in which the parameters were carefully stated. The client was invited to attend the second part of the best-interests meeting with his advocate to give him the opportunity to work with the meeting, not against it. A large part of the resultant action plan involved careful planning and working with the client to support his safety. The researchers commented that 'the skill of that meeting was at least partly the skill of enabling (the client) to have a voice and express his concerns' (Mental Health Foundation 2012, p.73).

Nuanced judgements

In deciphering these issues, professionals need confidence to make nuanced judgements that are both decision-specific and that take into account the contours of the person's relationships and history. Capacity assessments that take emotional as well as cognitive processes into account can then be used to inform grounded approaches to clients and to scaffold professional networks that are robust enough not to split. CAT's model of collaborative working and of recruiting healthy self-states to make sense of complexity provides a way forward when 'thinking straight' has been put in jeopardy. By being aware of how capacity fluctuates across different self-states and of how dilemmas, traps and snags start to operate out of awareness, we can conduct capacity assessments that more closely approximate a holistic view of real life.

Part 3
Using Cognitive Analytic Therapy in Forensic Settings

Chapter 13

'Behind the Mask'
A Case Study
Michelle Anwyl and Pamela Mount

Using Cognitive Analytic Therapy (CAT) with a woman with an intellectual disability who suffered domestic violence

This is a case study about a woman with an intellectual disability who suffered domestic violence throughout her life. In this chapter we will explore how CAT and its tools can be used creatively in an intellectual disability setting.

Domestic violence

Domestic violence is defined by the Home Office as 'any violence between current and former partners in an intimate relationship, wherever the violence occurs. The violence may include physical, sexual, emotional and financial abuse' (Department of Health 2005, p.10).

Domestic violence occurs across society regardless of age, gender, culture, sexuality, wealth and geography. Statistics show that the majority of domestic violence occurs against women and is perpetrated by men: (*findings from the British Crime Survey*) 45 per cent of women and 26 per cent of men had experienced at least one incident of inter-personal violence in their lifetimes (Walby and Allen 2004).

In our experience, domestic violence is rarely referred to within the case files of forensic learning disabled clients and there is a scarcity in research around this issue for this population.

Using CAT in cases of domestic violence

Very few methods of abuse treatment for people with disabilities have been empirically evaluated (Lund 2011).

The integrative, time-limited nature of a CAT can help to model appropriate and healthy inter-personal relationships that are equal and shared in terms of respect. There is a natural start, middle and end phase that are reflected in the reformulation letter – a middle phase of developing change strategies and marking the end of the journey with a goodbye letter. Use of the Sequential Diagrammatic Reformulation (SDR) in highlighting traps, snags and dilemmas together with the reformulation letter helps validate experiences. It can provide solace in times of doubt about a future that is not focused on the needs of another; rather, it shifts the focus to self care and preservation.

If we can accept a view that domestic violence is a strategy to gain or maintain power and control over the victim, we can begin to map out reciprocal responses to this position – i.e., powerful to powerless and controlling to controlled with a whole host of behavioural and psychological consequences by way of problematic procedural enactments. The victim can come to believe that it is their own behaviour within the abusive relationship that provokes such responses from their abusive partners. CAT helps victims to look at all aspects of relationships – self to self, self to others and others to self – as well as the problematic procedures that play out.

CASE STUDY: JANE

Background information

Jane is a 52-year-old woman who is described as having a borderline intellectual disability (Full Scale IQ 70) and mental illness. She is the middle sibling of eight, having six brothers and a younger sister. One of her brothers died of cancer in 1991. Her parents are deceased, they were divorced but both died in 1984 when Jane was aged 34. Her mother remarried and her stepfather is also deceased.

Jane suffered early experiences of sexual, emotional and physical abuse and neglect. From the age of seven she was sexually abused by her father until the age of 11 when she was sent to boarding school. Her accounts of the sexual abuse that she suffered at the hands of her father were extremely graphic and disturbing. She described how she was often covered in bruises but felt that nobody cared enough to ask her what was happening. Her relationship with her mother was characterised by a lack of love and affection, for example, her mother told Jane at one time that she wished she had never had her and that she didn't love her, and she did not protect her from the abuse despite knowing about it.

When her mother remarried in Jane's teenage years, the sexual abuse continued at the hands of her stepfather. Jane's experience of sexual abuse occurred both as a young girl and also as a teenager. Jane began to feel as if it was her fault that she was being abused, almost as though she was inviting it. Jane is aware of two of her siblings who also experienced sexual abuse from her father. From her description of this period, they seemed unable to support each other as they were all struggling to survive the family experience of severe deprivation and neglect.

Jane was in mainstream education but because of the challenges she presented, she attended a special school for children with emotional and behavioural disturbances as a boarder at the age of 11. She returned to the family home with her mother and stepfather at the age of 16.

Jane left the family home as a young adult and there followed a period of unemployment whilst she was living in a flat on her own. She was identified as someone with mental health problems and received some supportive contact from the Community Mental Health Team. Between the ages of 20 and 42 she developed several relationships with men, all of which she described as abusive, and she eventually married. She described her husband as an abusive man who frequently humiliated her. For example, one day he made her strip off all her clothes then proceeded to push her out of the front door, locking the door behind her. He would not let her back in and she was forced to make her way to her friend's house without any clothes on. She divorced him but continued finding herself in abusive relationships with men.

This pattern continued for many years. Her last relationship with J was no different. He would shame and humiliate her by conducting relationships with other women, for all to see, leaving her feeling rejected and worthless. He would also persuade her to engage in sexual acts that she found degrading and that she experienced as abusive. Eventually, a series of events culminated in a violent and murderous attack on him, where she attempted to poison him. This attack was not reported to the police. Jane was in a distressed and angry state for several days and despite seeking help from friends and services she was unable to contain these feelings, which resulted in an arson attack on her elderly neighbour.

Assessment phase

Initially Jane's presentation was loud and brash; she used shocking sexual swear words and presented as very angry. This 'filthy' language perhaps represented the way she felt about herself – unlovable and not entitled to any care. She spoke of one female adult, Mrs B, who was a 'lovely lady' – the only adult who said she was a beautiful girl and allowed her to feel entitled to love and care. My counter transference response at this time was to feel overwhelmed by her neediness; I was a little fearful that if I became the perfectly caring adult that I too may eventually let her down.

Jane was eager to attend therapy and in the initial sessions she was almost out of control in terms of the amount of material she attempted to present. Jane's lifetime search for someone (an ideal mother) to pay attention to her needs, to love and adore her, was perhaps expressing itself in this pressured way of presenting her problems in this written form and alerted me to the idea that this may form part of a target problem procedure. These patterns of behaviour were also evident in her relationships with the staff team at this time. She described the team as reminding her of her neglectful mother. She appeared to be striving to get care from the nurses but she experienced them as pushing her away. Through her descriptions of her early experiences and her more current relationships with the staff team, I was also beginning to formulate some initial ideas about reciprocal roles, particularly rejecting/neglecting to rejected/neglected, abusing to abused.

I gave Jane the psychotherapy file to fill in at the second session. In the following sessions she brought along reams of written material, poems, diagrams and descriptions of events (as she had with her previous therapist), rather than the completed psychotherapy file. She presented this in a later session, but my feeling was that she had completed this in a somewhat perfunctory manner, having ticked all the boxes making it unusable, and that her written material was of more significance to her.

She wrote me a long letter after the first session, which began with:

Dear Michelle,

Thank you for our first meeting... I wish to continue discussing our plan about the family. Then in a few weeks, I will co-operate with you and move on to something different.

Issues of control were clearly apparent and this gave me another early indication that perhaps a reciprocal role of controlling to controlled was relevant.

Initially we tried to work with her written material, but it became overwhelming. In supervision we were able to see that all this information was in fact hindering the therapy and clouding the real issues. I made the decision that I would ask Jane not to bring any more material of this nature until we had decided on the problem areas that we wanted to focus on. This was difficult for Jane; she experienced this as a criticism and I was left feeling that I was enacting the above reciprocal role of controlling to controlled. However, it allowed us to think more clearly about her target problems. Jane wanted to be less angry and to learn how to deal with her angry responses. She also wanted to try to make sense of her fire setting behaviour, which she worried she may resort to again.

Reformulation

This was a crucial phase of therapy. During supervision the need for containment was identified and as such we decided that the SDR should be developed prior to the prose reformulation. I also wanted to create an opportunity to name the reciprocal roles in therapy; the SDR was a way that this could be done collaboratively and hence maintain the alliance. I felt that the presentation of the letter would be highly emotional and that having the diagram would in some way help to contain some of Jane's emotional responses within the session.

From session five we began mapping and developing the SDR (Appendix 7); Jane was able to focus on more specific issues and I noticed that this process allowed containment and managed some of the emotional outpouring. The collaborative nature of the development of the SDR also helped address some of the issues around the theme of control. A key element in the SDR referred to the two aspects of herself – the hurt, vulnerable child who sought love and care and the 'unmanageable', angry, furious aspect of her that led to explosive violent outbursts. She described a way of protecting herself from these aspects of self – hiding behind two masks: the 'happy smiling' mask and the 'I'm hard' mask. This was an important tool that we used throughout the therapy to understand current unhelpful ways of relating to others.

The containing function of the SDR enabled me to present the reformulation letter in session eight (Appendix 8). The letter contained some ideas about the tasks in therapy, i.e., to create some space to process the feelings that she had been left with and to find a way of accessing the pain and grief without having to act upon her feelings of fury. Additionally, the letter focused on the opportunity the therapy would provide her to begin to think about caring for herself, as opposed to feeling that this could only come from idealised others. With these issues in mind the following target problem procedures were identified.

Target problems procedures

- When I feel others are rejecting me, I feel unloved and vulnerable; I put on my 'happy, smiling' mask and try to please them. I expect in return to be cared for, when this doesn't happen I try harder but others feel overwhelmed and suffocated and end up rejecting me.

- *When I feel others are controlling/abusing me, I feel powerless and have a burning fury inside. I put on my 'I am hard' mask lashing out at others. I feel powerful and in control but end up abusing others.*
- *Jane had an emotional response to the letter but felt unable to cry, remembering her attempts as a child to hide this emotion from her parents for fear of reprisal.*

Therapy sessions 9–19

Jane and her care system

During the therapy, Jane was able to see how the pattern as depicted in the SDR was being enacted between her and the nursing team. This process helped Jane to learn about her patterns of coping and she presented other day-to-day ways of relating with the nursing team that we were able to track similarly on the diagram.

Jane frequently discussed events that had arisen with the staff team. For example, shortly after we looked at the reformulation letter she wrote a threatening letter to a nurse that said she was going to kill her. Understandably, the nursing team felt anxious about the threats; this resulted in Jane being placed on a high level of supervision. In the therapy we tried to understand this incident by using the SDR. Jane told me that the other women clients with whom she was living were getting more positive attention, and that the restrictions that the Mental Health Act placed upon her meant that she was unable to arrange outings whilst others were free to enjoy community outings and family visits. She described overwhelming feelings of jealousy; her longing for care increased along with the demands for nurses' attention. The nurses' responses to her neediness were to withdraw and dismiss her demands. Jane felt rejected, became furious and put on her 'I'm hard' mask. She wrote the letter and felt in control and powerful, however this was short lived and resulted in Jane then feeling more controlled due to the increased supervision levels.

Use of CAT tools for self-reflection/recognition

During this stage of therapy we could see that Jane could make good use of the SDR to look retrospectively at situations that had occurred. However, we began to wonder how she could start to recognise defeating patterns and prevent them occurring by using monitoring sheets to record when she was feeling needy. Jane found great difficulty in completing the monitoring sheets. We discussed these monitoring sheets in session; she expressed her willingness to complete them but never filled them in. On reflection, this may have been experienced by Jane as a demand from me and a repetition of the earlier dynamic in the assessment phase. We decided not to use them; repeated mapping of the SDR helped Jane to move away from retrospective analysis and she began to think about exits. We identified two ways in which this could work. Jane looked at her issues and, with her consent, I shared the reformulation letter and SDR with the nursing team in order to help them to identify when they were re-enacting the reciprocal roles.

Jane became good at recognising when she was becoming needy and/or angry and developed simple but effective strategies to deal with her feelings at these times; these included going to her room to listen to music or read. She also explored the idea of going to her room to cry.

My work with the nursing team paralleled some of Jane's reciprocal roles and necessitated some careful management. Team supervision sessions were crucial to process the complicated projections and transference issues that arose within the team.

Exits

Jane identified a healthy reciprocal role of respecting to respected. An important new insight for Jane was recognising that respecting others leads to respect from others and of oneself. Jane began to understand the importance of caring for herself and of being in control of her own life and how she feels about herself. To this end, we decided that it was important for her to begin to do things for herself and not expect that others do things for her. She found the prospect of implementing this exit quite daunting, stating that she was scared to be 'normal' as this meant that others would not take care of her or want to spend time with her. Even so, during this phase of therapy she took a risk and began to take care of her appearance. She came to the therapy with a new hairstyle; she wore makeup and told me that she felt attractive.

The second exit was recognising when she had been given enough by others and to be able to see their needs. She tested this with the staff; she spoke about how the staff had praised her without her seeking this out. This had felt good enough for her and she had not continued to ask for more. She was also able to think about the difficulties that her sister faced in bringing up a young family and in also visiting Jane regularly. Jane was able to recognise her previous demanding behaviour towards her sister and negotiate visits that paid attention to her sister's needs.

Index offence

Jane was admitted to the unit because of a serious arson incident. Once I felt more comfortable about the analysis of these reciprocal roles, it felt safe to address this issue using the SDR, which we were able to use to trace the sequence of events that lead up to the incident. Prior to the arson, Jane had been involved in a turbulent relationship with J. She contracted a sexually transmitted disease and it was clear that he had been having unprotected sex with other women. She felt powerless, unloved and extremely jealous, just as she had as a child. This sent her into a fury and in turn set off the sequence of the red loop in the SDR diagram (Appendix 7). In a desperate attempt to gain control, she gave him drinks that contained poison and suggested to him that she would have sex with him. She tied him to the bed and piled clothes in the corner of the room with the intention of setting a fire; in effect she became the controlling abuser. She then left the room, at which point he managed to escape and left the house.

Jane recognised the dangerousness of her actions. Feeling out of control, she attempted to get some help from the services who were involved with her care. She found herself in the blue loop of her SDR (Appendix 7) trying hard to get someone to listen to her, but presenting in a demanding and angry way. The day centre suspended her and the hospital felt that they were not in a position to help her. Again, she felt rejected, but also jealous, believing that others in the same position would receive help. On her return home she began to ruminate on her belief that others always got more than her. She thought about her neighbour's home that was neat and tidy with nice things in it, compared with her own squalid flat. It was at this that she decided to set fire to her neighbour's flat. After the arson attack she contacted the police and was charged with arson, having confessed to the crime.

Jane used the diagram frequently throughout the therapy to map current problems in her life and as such seemed more able to identify and understand the intense feelings behind the masks. Using the same diagram to trace the sequence of events that led up to and took place during the offence enabled Jane to be clearer about where this extremely dangerous and destructive behaviour came from.

Ending

As the end of therapy approached Jane resorted to earlier ways of coping with stress. She became more demanding with the staff, and earlier patterns of demanding and controlling emerged between her and the nurses. She wrote another threatening letter but this was dealt with by using the shared reformulation and nursing staff were less anxious and threatened, and able to understand some of the dynamics of the reciprocal roles that were potentially being enacted.

During the ending phase themes of loss emerged including:
- her feelings of a wasted life
- the brother who died
- therapist
- wish for an ideal mother

- 'I'm hard' mask.

Jane was able to weep about these losses, which was possibly the first time in her life that she was able to experience the pain and sadness of loss in this way. She began to empathise with her mother's life, exploring the idea that maybe her mother had also been treated badly and that she hadn't been able to be a good mum because she had not had a good experience with her own mother. She was able to say that she had more positive loving feelings towards her mother and no longer just anger.

My goodbye letter (Appendix 9) incorporated these issues. Jane's goodbye letter that she wrote to me showed some evidence that we had managed to develop and sustain a relationship based on new reciprocal roles including helping/interested/listening to heard and responded to, which she appeared able to internalise.

Follow up
With Jane
The follow-up session took place six weeks after the final session. During this session Jane spoke of the difficulties she was having in using the exits that we had developed during therapy. In the first weeks following the end of therapy there was evidence that there had been a return to her old ways of coping and the relationships with the nurses had become problematic again. My thought at the end of the session was that the therapy had been a container for anxiety within the system and I wondered why it could not be maintained; both Jane and the nurses were asking for more therapy.

With the team
I encouraged the nursing team to look more systematically at the SDR and hold this in mind in their interactions with Jane. This continues to be an issue but with support, both Jane and the nurses are able to use the SDR as a tool to process Jane's difficulties in relationships.

Next steps
At the end of therapy, even though I had recommended group therapy for Jane, everybody including myself was left with a feeling of wanting our work together to continue – I wanted to provide her with more therapy, but perhaps this was a counter transference manifestation in response to Jane's neediness rather than that she genuinely had not had enough. I felt that this was reflected in her patterns; again she was placing pressure on others to give her more, and people were struggling to say no. It seemed important to find a way for the service to contain this, we therefore held to the therapeutic

decision to refer Jane to group therapy where she could build on the gains she had made in individual therapy. In this way we allowed her an ending and an opportunity for a shared experience where she may begin to think through some of her issues around jealousy and rivalry.

Discussion

This case raised several issues about the use of CAT with individuals with complex needs and histories of domestic abuse who often present as chaotic and out of control. The structured nature of the approach lends itself to working with this client group and the use of the tools, particularly the SDR helped contain anxiety within the client, the therapist and the wider team. This tool was particularly helpful when reciprocal role enactments occurred within the therapy session, namely controlling to powerless and rejecting to rejected.

Jane was unable or unwilling to use the monitoring forms to support recognition of target problems. This is not uncommon when working with individuals who have an intellectual disability. On reflection, for monitoring to be useful, owing to the memory limitations of many individuals with intellectual disabilities, they need to be given the monitoring forms most days, rather than just weekly.

CAT provides a shared language to understand the distress that our clients experience. The shared reformulation with nursing teams helps to disrupt the enactments of reciprocal roles within the client's everyday living environment. It enables staff and professionals supporting chaotic and distressed individuals to hear their story and to place themselves within the SDR. In doing so, this provides a shared understanding and capacity to develop interventions that are collaborative and relationally driven.

Chapter 14

Cognitive Analytic Therapy Integrated into a Therapeutic Community Approach

Philip Clayton and Simon Crowther

Introduction

This chapter will describe the utility of Cognitive Analytic Therapy (CAT) as a relational understanding in the treatment of individuals with a diagnosis of Intellectual Disability and Personality Disorder, within a forensic context informed by Therapeutic Community principles. The aim of this chapter is to show how CAT has utility within such settings in helping clients and staff teams work together, deal with overwhelming feelings and address offending behaviour. Whilst the chapter focuses on a forensic context, there are aspects of this approach that have utility beyond this setting, including: the reformulation of offending behaviour, the sharing of Reformulations to promote systemic working and the importance of recognising relational enactments as they occur within systems.

It should be noted here that the term Personality Disorder is used to describe the presentation by individuals characterised by significant difficulties in relating to others (Livesley 2003; Ryle 1997). The CAT model, as outlined here, proposes that these relational difficulties have emerged as part of a life narrative. The broad conceptualisation is that traumatic early life experiences, and other forms of adversity, have led to the development of restrictive and damaging reciprocal roles that are enacted intra-personally, inter-personally and across systems.

Background

Historically, people with a diagnosis of Personality Disorder struggled to access appropriate treatment, with the diagnosis leading to stigma and exclusion (National Institute for Mental Health in England 2003). However, in recent years there has been a surge of interest and research in this area, which has led to improvements in service provision. In the field of CAT there is longstanding recognition of the usefulness of this approach in working with people who have a diagnosis of Personality Disorder. The clinical practice in this area has led to the development of models for Borderline and Narcissistic presentations (Ryle and Kerr 2002). Much of the evidence base for CAT had been drawn from the publication of the case studies, describing the way in which CAT has been conducted (Clayton 2010; Kellet 2005; Withers 2008). However, Clarke, Thomas and James (2013) have recently published a randomised controlled trial using CAT for people with Personality Disorder and reported evidence that 24 sessions of CAT was more effective than standard treatment received in public health-care settings for a range of Personality Disorders. However, the study exclusion criteria included those with an intellectual Disability. For people with Intellectual disabilities and a diagnosis of Personality Disorder the evidence base for treatment is still emerging. However, the continuing demonstration that interventions initially developed for people without Intellectual disabilities have applicability for people with Intellectual disabilities suggests that there are likely to be a range of therapeutic options available. The current clinical consensus for working with offenders with Personality Disorder is that treatment needs to have multiple focuses in order to improve functioning across a range of areas, whilst being co-ordinated in order to facilitate personality integration (Livesley 2003, Figure 1). This framework suggests that different interventions will be needed at different times, depending upon where an individual is in their treatment pathway, with each stage of the pathway building upon the previous.

One intervention that lends itself to this framework is the Therapeutic Community (TC) approach. TCs have an established place in the treatment of offenders with a diagnosis of Personality Disorder in the Prison Service, and there has been recent interest in this approach for people with Intellectual Disabilities. This provision now exists within the National High Secure Intellectual disability Service and the initial evidence is promising (Morrissey, Taylor and Bennett 2012; Taylor *et al.* 2012). Indeed, the interest in this approach is starting to gather momentum, with other examples of Intellectual Disability TCs emerging in the literature (Cappleman 2013), and there are currently plans to Develop an Intellectual Disability TC in the Prison Service.

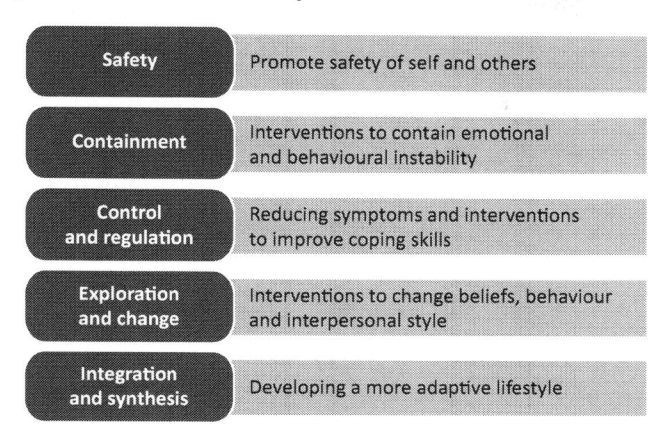

Safety	Promote safety of self and others
Containment	Interventions to contain emotional and behavioural instability
Control and regulation	Reducing symptoms and interventions to improve coping skills
Exploration and change	Interventions to change beliefs, behaviour and interpersonal style
Integration and synthesis	Developing a more adaptive lifestyle

Figure 14.1: Proposed treatment pathway for offenders with Personality Disorder

In a TC an emphasis is placed on how community members (clients and staff members) work together to promote well-being and change. Therefore, the development of helpful and supportive relationships is crucial to the functioning of a TC. All community members are encouraged to work together, support each other and provide constructive feedback to each other. A number of principles underpin the ethos of a TC and they are:

- democracy of decision-making
- permissiveness of behaviour in order for it to be explored by others
- collaborative working by all members of the community
- a curiosity about the behaviour of others
- the process of providing constructive feedback to others.

The environment is organised around structured occupational activities, community meetings and therapy groups.

A CAT TC approach

With its focus on relationships, dialogue and patterns of behaviour, CAT is well placed to compliment the TC model. Through the Reformulation process a client and therapist construct an understanding of how the client relates to themselves and others. An aim of this process is to validate the difficulties the client experiences and consider how change is possible. If shared with others in the form of a Sequential Diagrammatic Reformulation (SDR) or 'map', community members are provided with an empathic understanding of the difficulties the client experiences, and the map highlights the relationship patterns that others are invited to reciprocate. Therefore, an alternative, non-pejorative understanding is promoted and it is one that locates difficulties within relationship patterns, rather than conceptualising clients as 'manipulative', 'unmotivated' or 'controlling'. That is not to deny that at times clients can be experienced as like this by others, but the Reformulation/SDR conceptualises these experiences as relational enactments, which encourages others to consider their roles in these enactments and opens up the possibility for 'exits' into more adaptive relationship patterns. Indeed, without this understanding there is a risk that community members will be invited into reciprocating unhelpful relational patterns, which can have a destabilising effect on the group as a whole.

Within a traditional TC environment there has been a tendency to see difficulties with engagement as an indication that clients are unable to benefit from the TC approach (Kerr and Gopfert 2006). Whilst it is important to assess an individual's ability to benefit from an approach that relies on a level of social ability and reflective capacity, for clients who struggle in the TC process, rather than this being considered grounds for exclusion, it may be grounds for extra support from community members. Within the traditional TC model, traits such as 'insight' and 'motivation' are considered key to a client's ability to engage in the TC process. From a CAT perspective this could be reformulated relationally, perhaps as either 'unmotivated/given up (client) – controlling (other)' or 'unknown/confused (client) – overwhelming (other)'. The inter-personal restatement of these traits allows an opportunity to consider how such positions are being maintained within systems and whether alternative relational patterns would lead to a shift in position or understanding. Furthermore, CAT emphasises the importance of providing therapeutic interventions within an individual's Zone of Proximal Development (ZPD) (Vygotsky 1978) so that learning opportunities are accessible and successful. Difficulties engaging with the TC may reflect areas where clients may need a greater consideration from others of their needs. For example, conceptualising difficulties with emotional regulation relationally would allow members of the community to alter their expectations or provide extra support, rather than seeking to remove the individual from the community.

The TC CAT model outlined in this chapter has a multifaceted approach. There are five elements that are considered necessary in the process of helping clients who live in the community.

1. The TC informed environment itself, based upon principles of democratisation, permissiveness, curiosity, communalism and reality orientation. These values underpin the approach. Structurally, the TC is organised around occupational activities and group meetings.

2. The model of CAT, which provides a 'core' relational understanding in the form of a Reformulation of the client's problems, with 'exits' to enable the client to relate differently and more effectively. Clients' ability to relate differently may be problematic, as they may not necessarily agree with staff and peer perceptions. Consequently there may be the enactments of unhelpful relationship patterns. The focus is on how the community manages these enactments and offers opportunities for reflection (recognition) and exits into more helpful patterns (revision).

3. The resilience of the staff team and how the system is enabled to help the client recognise patterns of relating that are a replication of problematic behaviours. This requires education, consistent reflective practice and supervision.

4. An assessment of risk in relation to offending behaviour and Offence Parallel Behaviour (Shine 2011) is crucial to public safety and relapse prevention. CAT Reformulations are used to describe how offending behaviour developed, including the setting conditions likely to be necessary for reoffending and parallel behaviours that can be addressed within the community.

5. Occupational Therapy is considered to have a central role in providing structured activities to promote collaborative, supportive, healthy relationships with others. The monitoring of enactments or parallel offending behaviour within this setting also provides an opportunity to assess whether the client is consistent in the development of pro-social behaviours, and whether the skills being learned in community meetings are generalising to others settings.

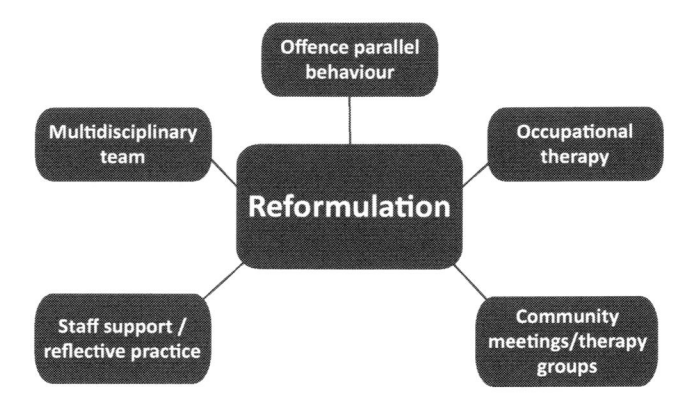

Figure 14.2: Therapeutic Community-informed environment

The use of CAT within the TC

Reformulation is central to the TC process and as such each client receives a CAT therapy following admission to the TC. Within the team it is important that all staff members have supervision and some training in CAT in order to promote a relational understanding.

The therapeutic action of TC is a relational one with the community itself considered to be the primary mechanism of change (Taylor 2011). The underlying TC principles aim to foster relationships that are supportive and validating, but also challenging. Supportive and collaborative relationships are promoted through occupational therapy sessions, shared tasks on the ward and group trips off the ward. The CAT understanding aims to augment this way of thinking by making the Reformulation (written, pictorial, aural, diagrammatic) available to the client and to the staff team. Reciprocal role enactments can be perplexing and confusing. A clear and formulated CAT Reformulation/SDR aims to alleviate potentially distressing interactions between clients and staff. Opportunities for therapeutic interactions can happen at any point, during informal conversations on the ward, or in the formalised therapy groups and community meetings.

Staff and clients are considered to be equal members of the community, although given the forensic nature of the context there is a clear power differential as the ultimate authority rests with the staff team. Attempts are taken to reduce the impact of this by 'flattening' the hierarchy amongst the staff team with all members of staff contributing equally to decision-making, regardless of job role. Furthermore, and when possible, clients are involved in the decision-making process and the setting of rules within the community. Where this is not possible and members of staff have to make a decision, perhaps due to an issue of risk, the reasons for the decision are explained clearly and transparently to the community through the community meeting.

Clients contribute to the treatment of other clients through their participation in the community. This is explained to the clients when they join the TC and they are encouraged to think about how events affect not only themselves but also others. In terms of reciprocal roles, this is the self-self, self-other and other-self analogy; clients are encouraged to think about how they relate to themselves, how they relate others and the patterns that they invite others into reciprocating.

Community meetings are often the forum where matters related to community functioning are discussed. In traditional TC models community meetings happen daily, sometimes twice a day. Given that such meetings may be unfamiliar and anxiety provoking for staff and clients alike, some preparation is needed about the roles people are expected to take and the rules of the meeting. Often, community meetings have a client elected chairperson, and this is a role that is rotated after a period of time. There is often an agenda to focus discussion and any issue related to community functioning can be placed on the agenda. The chairperson facilitates discussion of the issues raised by the agenda and items not covered are carried over to the next meeting. Taylor (2011) identifies a number of functions for community meetings, including:

- the development of cohesion
- transparency of decision-making
- providing feedback to others
- challenging others
- exploration of rule breaking or inappropriate behaviour.

Community meetings are also a place where positive behaviour should be acknowledged, pro-social responses modelled and support offered. Without this there is a risk that community meetings can be viewed as a place where community members are criticised or attacked, which has the potential to replicate aversive early life experiences and destabilise the community. Within the traditional TC model, therapy groups also happen once or twice a week and focus on lifestyle and offending behaviour (Taylor 2011). Within the current service provision, therapy groups are not provided for clients due to difficulties resourcing this. Alongside their involvement in the TC, a number of clients access other offence-related therapies such as the sex offender treatment programme or anger management. The CAT Reformulation provides an overarching framework for this, as these other interventions are seen as providing 'exits' from unhelpful and harmful patterns of relating.

With therapeutic approaches in forensic settings there is an explicit power hierarchy, which has the potential to replicate damaging or abusive early life relationships (Kerr and Gopfert 2006). The reciprocal role relationships invited by the environmental context need to be considered as part of the Reformulation. Therefore, reciprocal role enactments can be conceptualised as being influenced by the client, the other person in the relationship and the context the relationship is embedded in (see Chapter 6). In a forensic setting the focus on risk and offending can lead to particular types of reciprocal roles. Examples of this at a systems level include: concerns about risk leading to controlling-controlled patterns, experiences of feeling overwhelmed leading to blaming/criticising-attacked/blamed and unmanageable feelings, particularly anger, leading to abusing-abused or withholding-neglected patterns. The Reformulation process, and particularly the SDR, can map out these patterns and help multi-disciplinary teams (MDTs) think about what is happening in their relationship with clients, and where 'exits' are possible.

CAT and Offence Parallel Behaviour in the TC

In conceptualising offending behaviour CAT seeks to understand the states that have led to patterns of offending behaviour. In understanding patterns of offending behaviour often the starting point is to consider what the individual's aim or intention was (Pollock and Stowell-Smith 2006). Often the aim is benign and reflects an intolerable state from which the individual wants to find a solution, for example, to escape pain, to prevent harm or to feel close to someone (Shannon 2009). Using case material, Shannon (2009) describes that when offending behaviour is pervasive, there are often very few non-offending, healthy reciprocal roles and little behavioural flexibility. Offending behaviour therefore becomes the primary solution for relational conflict. For others who possess some healthy reciprocal roles, offending behaviour may not be an intentional act at the start of the procedure, but may occur because the individual has no other solution (or has exhausted all other solutions) for the management of intolerable feelings.

It is at the point of Reformulation that the concept of Offence Parallel Behaviour (OPB) will be introduced to enable the client to understand that offending may prevent them from living their life to the full. OPB has been defined as 'any form of offence related behavioural (or fantasised behaviour) pattern that emerges at any point before or after an offence'. It does not have to result in an offence; it simply needs to resemble, in some significant respect, the sequence of behaviours leading up to the offence (Jones 2004). The CAT conceptualisation of offending behaviour is that it represents a type of target problem procedure (TPP) and follows the sequence of: aim, belief, behaviour and consequence. This conceptualisation overlaps with the OPB framework and, considered in this manner, any aspect of a TPP that led to offending behaviour can be considered to be 'offence parallel', and is therefore open to the process of Recognition and Revision.

The CAT model incorporates three stages: Reformulation, Recognition and Revision. It is only at the point at which the client understands their Reformulation that it can be used for the purposes of Recognition and Revision. For some clients, the notion of collaboration, trust and openness might be dimensions of relatedness that are alien, uncomfortable or actively rebuffed. This has implications for their ability to engage in the Reformulation process. Consideration therefore needs to be given to a client's ZPD, in terms of what is tolerable, what is possible and how steps can be taken towards change. If clients have significant difficulties developing trusting relationships it may be that other, potentially less exposing, interventions are offered first. There may also be difficulties engaging in the therapeutic process due to difficulties related to communication or level of intellectual ability. Collaborative work with a Speech and Language or Art Therapist may assist with offering other forms of communication or ascertaining how best to communicate with a client.

The TC environment attempts to model socially acceptable behaviour, demonstrate constructive problem solving and offer healthy relationships. The process of Recognition and Revision occurs within this context, as unhelpful interactions are discussed and 'unpicked' to enable greater understanding both at an individual level and within the MDT. Considerable work is done in collaboration with each nursing case manager and their client, with a view to aiding reflection and revision. Wherever possible, the CAT formulation is used to think through patterns of relating. Clients need to consent to their SDR being shared with the community, but the aim is for them to be as open as they feel comfortable about the nature of their problems in relationships with others. Often, the process of disclosing aspects of the SDR with the community is a validating one, as they learn that others have similar difficulties, which provides an opportunity for discussion about potential 'exits' from these patterns.

Staff supervision and reflective practice

The TC approach can involve a shift in roles for staff from a role of supporting activities, carrying out tasks and upholding the rules, to that of a 'pseudo therapist', facilitating meetings, repairing relationships, promoting insight and offering supportive feedback. The team members are given access to training, which helps to provide them with the tools they need to work as efficiently, empathically and resiliently as possible. Crucial to the model is that staff are provided with regular and consistently available supervision (Jacob and MacAllister 2010). Through supervision, staff are supported to freely express how the work affects them and understand the tasks they are undertaking. Reflecting on transference and counter-transference processes can be unsettling for the team, particularly if one member of staff is unwittingly in receipt of projections from the client, or 'hooked' into a reciprocal role. 'Burn out' or 'Splitting' can be the result of such interactions, and it is the territory of the CAT therapist to survey and think through these interactions, in order to find a way of enabling the staff team to manage difficult enactments. When given a safe context, staff members will often disclose uncomfortable and difficult feelings such as anger, disappointment or disgust. This is rich and useful material to explore, particularly in relation to the SDR. Indeed, SDRs are often extremely useful tools in exploring where the staff member might be on a map or where they might be on the map in relation to other team members.

CASE STUDY: CAT AND OFFENCE-RELATED BEHAVIOUR

G has a history of serious neglect that has been known to social services since he was eight years of age. There were reports of him being frequently chastised, taunted and treated as the 'odd one out' in the family. He had been assessed from a very early age as having significant problems with learning, and his behaviour in school was challenging to the teachers. The behaviours he exhibited were oppositional and aggressive. As he progressed through the school system it appeared that he worked very hard to make sure that he was in control of potential conflict situations. There was a clear behavioural repertoire of challenging any authority and an increase in the intensity of what seemed to be a denigration of others, including sexual touching and hostile verbal attacks in an attempt to put other people down.

As G grew into adolescence his behaviour became of great concern. His ability to relate to others became such that he was ostracised and felt alone. On an occasion when he used public transport he assaulted a bus driver who asked him to step off the bus. The driver had asked him to hurry up paying for his ticket and this was experienced as an act of controlling humiliation (an enactment from home life) as he was at the front of the queue and there were many people waiting to board the bus. A court appearance followed when G sexually assaulted a woman who had told him off for jumping the queue in a local shop. Following an assessment G was referred to the local intellectual disability medium secure unit as he was constantly challenging authority whilst on remand and threatening to escape.

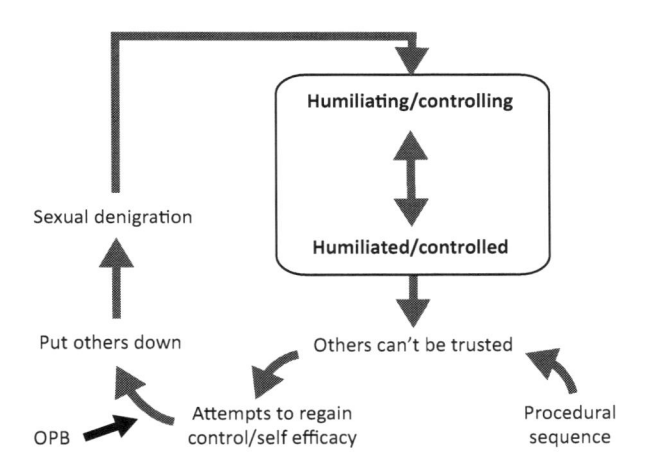

Figure 14.3: An example of a procedural sequence and a related OPB

G's offence-related behaviour was also evident within his relationship with community members and when others challenged him about his behaviour in community meetings. He would struggle to hear feedback from others and in anticipation of this he would verbally attack anyone who put him on the agenda. Within the community he was often derogatory towards others and would make disparaging remarks when passing people in the corridors, which led to aggressive conflicts with peers. Within his Occupational Therapy sessions he challenged the running of the sessions and attempted to subvert rules whenever possible. This led to conflict with the staff team who felt that he was attempting to tell them what to do and struggling to engage with what was being offered to him.

The starting point for intervention for G was to use the Reformulation to help him understand how and why he developed this way of relating to others. In the Reformulation process G explained that he attempted to humiliate or control others in order to feel safe. G was able to recognise that his ways of relating to others were leading to conflict and he saw this as a barrier *to his progress. Positively, G expressed an interest in developing healthier relationships with others. Therefore, in the Recognition phase G was helped to recognise the triggers for the enactment of the humiliating and controlling patterns and he started to assess whether at the times he felt vulnerable he was really under threat from others. This process served to increase his awareness of the procedural process that follows from this state. G was able to start to revise some of these patterns by taking steps to 'exit' the procedures of humiliating and controlling responses. Work was also undertaken with the staff team members about the signs that G was attempting to draw them into controlling or attacking relational patterns. Consideration was given to how they could respond at this time in order to neutralise potential conflict situations and offer alternative relational interactions. Over time, G has gradually been able to develop more trusting relationships with others, which has lessened the need to 'control' others and promoted collaboration and negotiation.*

Conclusion

The TC-informed model outlined in this chapter provides a structure and therapeutic environment that many of the clients who live within it have rarely experienced. The model described here is still in its infancy and the Intellectual Disability TCs are a relatively new treatment approach. Over time further outcome data will reveal the utility of this approach. The intervention is also resource intensive and there will be some clients for whom this intervention is not the most appropriate. However, for individuals with complex presentations who reside in systems, supported by staff teams, it seems clinically useful to have a formulation to guide treatment and understand difficulties. Clients bring with them many experiences of their lives that are overwhelming to them and others. They find it difficult to explain these experiences in words because of an Intellectual Disability and because they have internalised reciprocal roles that are damaging and destructive. The active CAT relational approach brings to the fore, clearly and visually, relational difficulties in the shape of patterns of relating that can be wrestled with by the client and all members of the community in a way that is understandable and transparent. Through this process the aim is to develop healthy reciprocal roles that promote independent functioning, pro-social behaviour and an improved quality of life.

We would like to thank Jon Taylor and colleagues at Rampton High Secure Service for their support and assistance in setting up a TC approach.

Chapter 15

A Group Approach
The Brooklands Offender Relationship Treatment Programme
Nicola Murphy

In this chapter I will describe a new offender treatment group that is based on the theoretical underpinnings of Cognitive Analytic Therapy (CAT) and the Good Lives model, both of which have a similar ethos and similar aims. To put the group in context, I will first describe the service in which it is embedded and the rationale for the group. I will then describe the content of the group, including some of the creative methods to explain the concepts of CAT to the learning-disabled group members.

Brooklands Specialist Secure Service for Adults with an Intellectual Disability

Brooklands is an intellectual disability hospital. On site are specialist services: the Young Person Unit, the Adolescent Service, the Specialist Assessment and Treatment Service and the Secure Service in which I work.

There are 57 beds within the Secure Service. These include capacity for 42 male patients and 15 females from the age of eighteen onwards. Patients have a mild–moderate intellectual disability and all have a forensic history. Most of the patients also have complex needs, for instance they have additional diagnoses of Autism/Asperger's Syndrome and Personality Disorder. Other complexities include the ongoing risk they present to others in terms of their offending behaviour, as well as some presenting a high risk of absconding, self-harm or suicide. All the patients are detained on secure units under a section of the Mental Health

Act. One of the units is medium secure; the other five units are low secure, locked.

Background to the development of the Brooklands Offender Relationship Treatment Programme (BORTP)

The Lead Psychologist of the Secure Service conducted an audit of all the male patients who had been detained in the service between 2007 and 2011. From this it was deemed that 66 per cent of those men would benefit from some work around relationships/interactional difficulties, as this linked directly with their offending behaviour (e.g., sexual offending, arson, violence).

Thus, in 2012, the Brooklands Offender Relationship Treatment Programme (BORTP) was developed by a multidisciplinary team including myself (Senior Clinical Psychologist/Cognitive Analytic Therapist), qualified nurses and an Advanced Occupational Therapist. The group was then embedded within the already existing treatment pathway.

Background literature

I was interested to see if the audit of our patients was paralleled within the literature, and so conducted a review of the literature on relationship/attachment difficulties of adults with intellectual disabilities, and in offender populations.

ATTACHMENT THEORY

Attachment Theory is the study of how we attach to people in the early stages of their development and its impact on how we view ourselves and develop relationships throughout our lives (Golding 2008). John Bowlby proposed the view that early experiences in childhood have an important influence on development and behaviour in later life. Forming secure attachments leads to the development of self-esteem, positive affect, good peer relationships, good relationships with adults and a strong personal autonomy (Carr 2003). Creating and maintaining relationships are vital parts of our lives and help to support our social and emotional well-being.

Attachments difficulties arise when secure attachments are not made and maintained within the early years of life. Champion (2010) states that evidence indicates that prematurity and extended periods in intensive care can lead to disrupted attachments. This is because normal bonding between parent and infant is difficult, often due to a lack of contact as the infant is in an incubator and cannot be held and fed in the normal way and/or normal contact is reduced due to fear of infection. This is often the case for infants with intellectual disabilities. The rejection (whether consciously, or sub-consciously) of an infant/child who has an intellectual disability is also very common and can lead to attachments being disrupted or not forming. Attachments can also be disrupted due to people with intellectual disabilities being in the care system/residential care where there is a high number of staff providing care, often resulting in inconsistent and instrumental care being given; thereby reducing the opportunity to form meaningful, consistent attachments to another. Attachments can also be disrupted when the person with an intellectual disability has experienced abuse or been raised in an abusive environment.

Thus, on the basis of early attachments the child develops expectations about their own role in relationships. At the same time they also develop expectations about the role of the other person in the attachment relationship (e.g., expectation that all relationships will end in rejection or abuse). This then affects how they relate to others and their attachment style.

THE ROLE OF ATTACHMENT PROBLEMS AND SEXUAL OFFENDING

In a review of the literature, Maniglio (2012) states that there is evidence that an insecure attachment style developed in response to dysfunctional parenting practices may generate feelings of inadequacy and inferiority to others, as well as a lack of the self-confidence and social skills to initiate or maintain consensual intimate relationships with appropriate others. Maniglio (2012) hypothesised that such problems may, in turn, promote low levels of intimacy and satisfaction in romantic relationships and serious chronic emotional loneliness, withdrawal and negative attitudes towards potential partners leading to deviant sexual fantasies in order to achieve the power or control absent from reality. All these factors may thus predispose to sexual offending.

Similarly, Marshall states that attachment deficits:

> make the transition at puberty to peer relationships more difficult, and make attractive those social messages that objectify others, portray people as instruments of sexual pleasure, emphasise power and control over others, and deny the needs for social skills and compassion for others. (2010, p.73)

Poor attachments also lead to low self-confidence, poor social skills, a lack of empathy for others and loneliness. Marshall (2010) concludes that there is a connection between these factors, resulting in a propensity to sexually offend.

THE ROLE OF ATTACHMENT PROBLEMS AND OFFENDING

Research by McCormack, Hudson and Ward (2002) investigated whether there was a link between offenders' early attachment experience and offending. Interviews with 147 male prisoners were conducted. The prisoners had either sexually offended against children (n = 55), adult women (n = 30), had violent offences (n = 32) or were imprisoned for neither sexual nor violent offences (n = 30). The findings were that the majority of offenders (over 75%) reported insecure attachment styles as adults. This was in contrast to normative samples where 55–65 per cent were securely attached.

Other findings were that 'adult rapist' and violent offenders had:

1. less responsive fathers
2. looser boundaries from both parents
3. experienced more physical abuse
4. felt less safe.

The child offenders had experienced significantly more sexual abuse themselves. They, and the violent offenders, were said to evaluate themselves more negatively.

All offenders were found to manage their emotions in a defensive or avoidant way, rather than seeking support from others.

TREATMENT RATIONALE

As the literature consistently states that sexual offenders experience significant loneliness, a lack of intimacy in their lives and a lack of skills to make and maintain relationships, treatment needs to focus on equipping patients with skills necessary to establish appropriate adult relationships and thus meet their needs pro-socially.

Theoretical models

It is important to base any treatment programme on a theoretical model (or models) in order to both maintain and enhance its integrity.

As CAT is a therapeutic approach that is used for interactional difficulties, the BORTP has been partly developed based on a CAT model. The other theoretical model underpinning the BORTP is the Good Lives Model-Comprehensive, as this is a rehabilitation model guiding treatment practice.

CAT

In addition to CAT being identified as the therapeutic model of choice to address such difficulties, CAT had already been used successfully with a number of patients within the Secure Service, so much so that members of the multidisciplinary team refer patients specifically for CAT. In addition, the patients share their formulation with their nursing staff and other professionals. This has then led to a shared understanding of their difficulties and further enabled the staff in being able to work effectively with hard-to-engage and very difficult patients, often those with personality disorder who are splitting the staff teams.

GOOD LIVES MODEL-COMPREHENSIVE (GLM-C)

The Good Lives Model-Comprehensive (GLM-C) is a new, integrated, systematic and comprehensive model for the treatment of sexual offenders. It is based on two types of theoretical resources: the original Good Lives Model of offender rehabilitation (GLM-O) (Ward and Stewart 2003) and the Integrated Theory of Sexual Offending (ITSO) (Ward and Beech 2005).

The GLM-C assumes that as human beings, offenders are naturally predisposed to seek certain goals, or primary human goods. In this context there are ten human goods:

1. life
2. knowledge
3. excellence in play and work
4. excellence in agency
5. inner peace
6. friendship
7. community
8. spirituality
9. happiness
10. creativity.

It is assumed that offending reflects socially unacceptable and often personally frustrating attempts to pursue primary human goods.

The primary aim of treatment of offenders is to instal in them the knowledge, skills and competencies to gain primary human goods in an acceptable manner once 'released' into the community. The focus is on the core ideas of agency, psychological well-being and the opportunity to live a different type of life: one that is likely to provide a viable alternative to a criminal lifestyle.

By focusing on providing offenders with the necessary internal and external conditions (e.g., skills, values, opportunities and social supports) for meeting their human needs in more adaptive ways, the assumption is that they will be less likely to harm others or themselves. In the model the primary goal is to help offenders to live better kinds of lives and thereby reduce their likelihood of committing further offences.

The GLM-C places important emphasis on the construct of personal identity and its relationship to offenders' understanding of what constitutes a good life. People acquire a sense of who they are and what really matters from what they do. So, for therapists it is not enough to simply equip individuals with skills to control their risk, it is imperative that they are also given the opportunity to fashion a more adaptive personal identity: one that bestows a sense of meaning and fulfilment.

Furthermore, according to the overarching principles of the GLM-C, when developing treatment plans clinicians ought to explicitly consider the nature of the environments offenders will be discharged to. Early exposure to adverse environmental factors will compromise the basic internal strategies and resources individuals acquire as they develop, making it less likely that they will be able to secure the primary goods needed for a good life, or secure these goods in an appropriate manner. So treatment is partially about helping offenders to secure human goods that are important to them, but to do so in ways that are socially acceptable and also more personally satisfying.

The Brooklands Offender Relationship Treatment Programme

Men who fulfil the inclusion and exclusion criteria meet the facilitators for a consent session. Once this has been granted, pre-group assessments are completed.

The current group consists of five men: four in-patients and one out-patient. There are three facilitators (one male and two females). It is run on a weekly basis for four hours a week. Facilitators meet for a planning session prior to group and then meet with me for supervision immediately after the group. Supervision not only ensures adherence to the group aims and content, but also provides an opportunity for the facilitators to reflect on any transference/counter transference that has arisen with the group, both with patients and amongst the facilitator team.

The aims of the programme are to enable the men to gain insight into their interactional difficulties and link these to their offending behaviour; then to enable them to identify more appropriate and non-offending ways to interact with others in order to get their needs/desires met.

There are ten blocks within the programme.

BLOCK 1: RULES AND ICE-BREAKER

To adhere to the CAT model, the group facilitators emphasise the running theme of how the group members are in a relationship with each other, by the very nature of the group process. Thus, a set of rules is developed that not only enables the group to run efficiently, but also enables the men to think reciprocally. They are therefore asked to base rules on how they would expect others to behave in the group room and how others would expect them to behave. In addition, the group members are asked how they would feel if the rules were broken. How would others feel? How might that affect their relationships with one another?

The ice-breaker also emphasises the reciprocal nature of relationships, as the group members work in pairs and ask three questions of their peer:

1. 'What is your name?'
2. 'Where do you live?'
3. 'What is your favourite food?'

Each group member then feeds the information about their fellow group member back to the rest of the group; the purpose being to emphasise the importance of listening to one another and other skills needed for reciprocal communication.

BLOCK 2: 'DIFFERENT TYPES OF RELATIONSHIPS', 'EXPECTATIONS WITHIN RELATIONSHIPS' AND 'DIFFERENCES BETWEEN RELATIONSHIPS'

The aims of this block are for group members to:

1. categorise and distinguish between different types of relationships
2. explore their expectations of the different relationships, and where those expectations have come from
3. enhance their understanding that there are different types of conversations that can be had with different groups of people
4. understand that there are differing degrees of intimacy/physicality in relationships and how this impacts on their behaviour and others' reactions.

As in the previous block, the running theme is the reciprocity of relationships; thus it is emphasised how relationships are a two-way interaction – they are about both giving and receiving (and, for example, not all about being 'cared for').

Various creative methods are used, such as role plays, DVD/TV material of interactions and card-sorting tasks. An example of the latter is a card that says 'sex' is shown to the group and patients discuss the card in relation to different people (e.g. stranger, friend, family, professional) and say whether or not they can have sex with that person.

BLOCK 3: 'RELATIONSHIPS AND THE LAW' AND 'CONSENT'

The aim of this block is for patients to understand the law and sexual relationships. This includes who they can and cannot have sexual relationships with according to the law, as well as where they can and cannot engage in sexual activity (the difference between public and private places is emphasised).

To relate both topics to the theoretical underpinnings of the programme, it is imperative for patients to understand that consent is also a two-way process, as it has been emphasised that all relationships are two-way. Specific to the Good lives model it is emphasised how adhering to the law relates to patients' life goals.

BLOCK 4: 'BUILDING AND MAINTAINING A RELATIONSHIP'

As the literature states that offenders experience significant loneliness, a lack of intimacy in their lives and a lack of skills to make and maintain relationships, it is imperative that treatment equips the patients with skills necessary to establish and maintain appropriate adult relationships.

Therefore, in this block patients participate in a range of role-plays and exercises that teach them skills in how to approach somebody and how to recognise when is not a good/appropriate time. The block also looks at skills in how to start, maintain and end a conversation, how to recognise when somebody wants to speak to them and the rules of conversation (e.g. turn taking, maintaining eye contact, listening, nodding). Group members not only practise this in the group, but also practise these tasks with their nursing teams, so that the skills are generalised.

BLOCK 5: 'EQUALITY IN RELATIONSHIPS' AND
'POWER DYNAMICS IN RELATIONSHIPS'

The aims of this block are for the patients to be able to identify what constitutes a healthy relationship and what factors result in an unhealthy relationship. It also helps them to understand the concept of power and recognise when there is an imbalance of power in relationships. To start with, the patients think about general interactions between people, before relating the concepts directly to themselves and others in their lives.

In terms of the CAT model, there is consideration of both self-self, as well as self-other. For example, it is promoted that one aspect of a healthy relationship is having one's own interests, as well as getting to know and listening to others' interests. Another example is that one aspect of an unhealthy relationship would be to neglect one's self in order to please the other person.

In general, the men are asked to consider why it is important to share. Is it to be equal? Is it to have appropriate relationships? Facilitators bear in mind the theoretical underpinnings of both models and so get the men to think about what treating people equally might achieve for them. Why might that be a healthy way to relate to others? How does it make them feel to be treated equally? How might others feel?

Facilitators then work individually with the men and get them to identify significant people in their lives and whether they have an equal or unequal relationship with them. They are asked to identify a difficult/unhealthy personal relationship and to identify related thoughts, feelings, actions and consequences, in particular those related to offending behaviour. Within this they are asked to consider future relationships, and how this relates to their life plan in line with the Good Lives model.

A creative way of explaining these complex concepts is the introduction of traditional weighing scales that have been designed to tip in both directions, or are straight, to illustrate the concepts of power, healthy/unhealthy and sharing/equality. For example, when the patients are describing the factors that make an unhealthy relationship (e.g., constant arguing, physical violence, sexual assault, being critical, not allowing the other person personal time or space, not spending time together) these factors are put on one side of the scales to show there is an imbalance. Likewise when the patients are describing healthy attributes (e.g., commitment, open communication, accepting people for who they are, emotional support) these are placed on the scales to show sharing and equality within the relationship.

With the concept of power there is the recognition that there is an imbalance of power within a staff–patient relationship and that the patients have lost some of their power through their detention. With this in mind, the men are asked to consider the professional relationships they have and the powers those professionals hold, and then how they can go about sharing some of that power. They are also asked to consider their personal relationships in which they have felt powerful, and powerless, and to tip the scales back and forth to illustrate this.

Facilitators also demonstrate role-plays in which there are imbalances (one person does all the talking) or balances in conversation or interaction whilst the scales are tipped, or balanced, accordingly.

In order to then generalise the work, patients are set homework tasks to identify unhealthy/equal and healthy/unequal relationships on the television, or units in which they live.

BLOCK 6: 'ROLES IN RELATIONSHIPS'

The aim of this block is to introduce the concept of reciprocal roles (RRs) used in CAT.

Research conducted at Brooklands by Psaila and Crowley (2006) looked at the records of 16 learning-disabled patients who had received CAT. There were 11 male participants: five living in the community and six in the Secure Service. There were five female participants: four in the community and one in the Secure Service. Out of all 16 patients, the study found that the most common RRs were Rejecting-Rejected, Damaging-Damaged and Abandoning-Abandoned.

Out of the seven Forensic patients 86 per cent had the RR Abusing/Bully to Abused/Victim. In the Forensic patient group 86 per cent also identified the ideal RR Rescuing/Caring to Rescued/Cared for. An ideal RR reflects a fantasy or idealised projection of a relationship. As dependency is a common issue in a learning disabled population, this ideal RR may be a reflection of this. It may also be a reflection of a disrupted attachment process. As stated in the literature review, many offenders have an insecure attachment style, so being rescued/ideally cared for may also be a fantasy reaction to disrupted attachment processes.

In the Forensic patient group the other main RR identified (57%) was Controlling-Controlled.

In order to get the patients thinking about roles in general, they are first asked to consider what roles people have in life (staff, patient, friend, teacher, actor). They are then asked to define their roles and others in relation to them (e.g., 'boyfriend' in relation to a 'girlfriend', 'mother' in response to 'son'). In order to follow on from the theme of the previous blocks, the roles are considered in terms of equality and sharing of power.

Once the patients have the concept of different roles, the concept of RRs is introduced. This is done creatively by a spinning wheel. So, the five main (not the ideal) RRs identified above are symbolised on laminated cards (e.g. Rejecting) and the patient picks out what other role they think matches (Rejected). Then, taking one role (e.g. Controlling) at a time the patients are asked to think about a situation or occasion when they have felt others have been controlling of them (thus, they are in the opposite role of feeling controlled). They are also asked to describe a situation or occasion when they have been controlling of others (which may include their Victim) and so the other person has felt controlled. The spinning wheel is used to illustrate both poles and how these can change according to the situation. The aim is also to conceptualise that the patient can play both roles. Some patients only like to see themselves in one role, for example, they are comfortable in the 'Victim' role, but do not like to see themselves as a 'Bully', so it is important to try and acknowledge both parts of the role.

Other significant RRs are discussed if identified by the patients, the facilitators, or through the weekly supervision.

BLOCK 7: 'DIFFICULTIES IN RELATIONSHIPS'

The aim of this block is for men to create their own 'maps' that clearly delineate their RRs and the procedural sequence of thoughts, feelings and actions and how these result in them going around a 'vicious circle'/trap. As this is an offender relationship group, the difficulties identified are those relationships that have led to offending behaviour, such as violence, arson or sexual offending.

BLOCK 8: 'REPAIRING RELATIONSHIPS'

In this block, difficulties in relationships are emphasised further. Pictures of roller coasters are used to a illustrate that relationships can be up and down (and to a certain extent that this is normal), or you can feel you are going round in circles with the same problem reoccurring or you can feel you are in a 'black hole' with one feeling, as if there is no way out. A road map is also used to illustrate that there are often bumps or obstacles along the way.

The men are then asked to think about how they can repair relationships, if they want to, and whether this would have a 'healthy' outcome.

BLOCK 9: 'ENDING RELATIONSHIPS "WELL"'

In this block, the men are asked to think about significant relationships (teacher, foster parent) that have ended. They are then asked to consider the positive (abuse stopped) and negative things as a result of the relationship ending.

With regards to those relationships, or ones ending due to their offending, the facilitators help them to consider how else the relationship could have ended, what might have been more helpful and what actions may have led to different outcomes.

In this block, the issues of safety and being abused and manipulated are also discussed, in order for patients to recognise when they may have been in these positions, and how to seek help in order to move to a more healthy position.

The men are also asked to think about the group ending and what factors they feel would facilitate a 'good' ending that balances any negative feelings they might have about the group ending with what they have gained.

BLOCK 10: FUTURE 'SELF-IDENTITY'
As in other blocks, the CAT and Good Lives model work in conjunction with one another.

Taking their main RRs (e.g., Bully) the men are supported to identify the costs and gains of relating in that way. They are then asked to identify more 'healthy' RRs and the costs and gains of these. In order to aid this process they consider people they admire (e.g., David Beckham) and what traits/qualities they admire. They look at how those qualities fit with themselves and what they might need to change in order to achieve positive qualities; for example, famous/successful role models (footballers, actors) have rarely achieved their success through crime or violence.

The patients are given a large wooden jigsaw, with 12 red and 12 green pieces. On the red pieces (to illustrate 'Stop') the men attach symbolised cards of all the things they have learned in the group about what has not worked well for them (e.g., offending in order to feel powerful). They then replace this with a green ('Go') piece with an alternative way of achieving the same outcome (power) through non-offending means. In offender treatment it is not enough to just expect the offender to stop what they are doing without replacing it with a meaningful alternative. The Good Life model emphasises the importance of achieving human good and aims in more adaptive ways, as well as having a sense of self-worth. The green jigsaw pieces therefore emphasise activities/achievements/goals that will enable them to feel good about themselves and that boost their self-esteem.

Outcome

At the time of writing, the group is not yet complete, so there is no outcome data from the post-group assessments. However, at the end of each block we have an 'End of block quiz' and these scores demonstrate that the men are retaining the material covered. Their ability to draw on and use material from previous blocks also demonstrates that the men have internalised the work, have gained insight into their difficulties and are making positive changes in their lives. This is consistent with reports from the nursing teams.

There seem to be numerous benefits from this group treatment. As the group is long-term (15 months), it is enabling the men to build up trusting relationships with one another and the facilitators and meaningful attachments can be built. The group approach enables the patients to get feedback from their peers and facilitators on their unhelpful beliefs, interactions and behaviours. It also means that the men can practise their interactional skills in real life and with the nursing team, meaning that the skills are more likely to be internalised and generalised outside of the group setting into everyday life.

The group approach means that the facilitators are able to model appropriate interactions. Having both male and female facilitators means that the concepts being taught, such as equality and sharing of power, can be seen in practice.

Acknowledgements

I want to gratefully acknowledge the contributions of Dr Su Thrift (Lead Psychologist, Secure Service) for the original idea and framework for the group. I also wish to acknowledge Sioux Cosgrove and James Preston (Registered Nurses) and Sam Bicker (Advanced Occupational Therapist) for their valuable input and consistent motivation when developing the content of the group. I also want to thank the group facilitators Rani Dhaliwal (Forensic Trainee Psychologist), Bill Evans and Linda Soderlund (Health Care Assistants) for their hard work running the group on a weekly basis and for their for ongoing development and bringing creative flair in order to explain the concepts to the patients. Many thanks to Ann Bancroft for her support, input and constructive feedback on an earlier draft of this chapter.

Chapter 16

The Application of Cognitive Analytic Therapy Used Therapeutically for Personality Disorder and Offending Behaviour and Contextually Within a Secure Service

Nicola Murphy

CASE STUDY: ROY

Roy (a pseudonym), a 33-year-old man, with multiple convictions against property and persons is detained in a Secure Service for adults with intellectual disabilities (LD). He has a mild LD (FSIQ-65, VIQ-68, PIQ-64) and can read and write, with good numeracy skills.

Pre-CAT assessment

As a female psychologist I found reading Roy's history an alarming experience. In addition to his lengthy history of offences, reports highlighted extreme violence to staff members in previous forensic units (e.g., an attack on a psychologist resulting in serious neurological problems for that psychologist). There were also engagement difficulties with female staff, as he either subjected them to verbal and/or physical abuse or made unwanted demands beyond the boundaries of their professional relationships with him (including one sexual one for which the female health care assistant was subsequently imprisoned).

Against this backdrop, Roy's presentation as a vulnerable and confused 'boy', trying to put on a confident face, but barely concealing his desperate need to be cared for and nurtured was both surprising and rather a relief! Despite initially fearing I would not be good enough to face the challenges that Roy would pose, his presentation enabled me to feel more confident that I would be able to work with him therapeutically.

During this pre-assessment period the main focus was to establish a therapeutic relationship, where we could work together and orient Roy to the Cognitive Analytic Therapy (CAT) model.

On reflection I can now see that we were both testing each other out; Roy by first making excessive demands on me, for example, by airing his grievances about staff members and pressurising me to meet with the unit manager to 'tell her' to call a staff meeting to resolve difficulties (incidentally, the nursing team mirrored this behaviour, wanting me to 'do something' to alleviate the difficulties they encountered with him). Second, Roy demonstrated his difficulties trusting others by seeking corroboration from nursing staff on things that I said to him; to test whether or not I had been truthful. Finally, Roy would talk to other patients and staff members about me, asking questions about what I was like and what I did; putting me to the test. Not surprisingly, I felt unsure of myself and my skills. I kept myself on 'red-alert' as I noticed my actions might feed into my own concerns about not being good enough.

In response, I too tested Roy out by attempting to set clear boundaries with him (and the nursing team) about what could, and could not, be achieved. I was checking that he would accept these boundaries.

By the end of the pre-assessment sessions, it seemed clear that relational issues were central to Roy's difficulties and, as we had established the beginning of a therapeutic relationship, we agreed to work together on a 16-session CAT. On reflection, 16 sessions was too short a therapy given the complexity of his difficulties but, at that time, I judged this was as much as Roy (and possibly I!) could tolerate and was within his (and possibly my) level of proximal development (Vygotsky 1978). Using Vygotsky's idea meant checking that he was capable of learning a better way to relate to other people and to himself and not setting him up to fail at something that was beyond him.

CAT assessment

Use of Psychotherapy File

During the first two CAT sessions, Roy and I collaboratively completed the Psychotherapy File adapted for people with LD (Bancroft 2010). Roy engaged well with this process, adding his own examples to illustrate some of the patterns of actions, or 'procedures' as these are called in CAT. He highlighted antagonistic interactions with others, which mirrored my experience of Roy.

Roy's early experience

Roy gave a factual account of his family structure, his schooling and the hospitals in which he had been detained. His description was devoid of emotion and felt very impersonal. The way in which he described his childhood, as being unremarkable, did not fit his presentation, as he fulfilled the criteria for several Personality Disorders. Despite specifically asking him about any abuse, violence, alcohol and drug use within his family he denied it all, stating that he had a 'very happy childhood'. When I probed this further he responded in one of two ways. He brought in photographs of family holidays and events, eagerly pointing out how everybody was smiling. This seemed to be his way of trying to prove to me that he was telling the truth. The alternative was that he would respond angrily, raising his voice and saying things like 'You don't believe me' and 'Are you calling me a liar?' From the development of his map (Appendix 10) in later sessions, this fits with one of his idealised states of wanting to be completely trusted. His responses, however, resulted in me finding it very difficult to challenge or question him further, in case I was conveying that he was not telling the truth and thus could not be trusted.

On reflection, his denial of difficulties was probably a self-protective function of avoiding painful feelings. Although he claimed a good relationship with his mother, she never telephoned him during her long trips abroad or visited him when back home. With other patients I would usually, gently, question things like this. Yet, with Roy, I felt unable to do this because of how he responded and my anxiety about how he might perceive that I did not trust him. I was thus trapped into colluding with his denial. Trying to understand this within the context of his (later) map, I can see that I feared that I would be punishing him, saying hurtful things, which would have 'taken things too far' and upset/hurt him and risked him disengaging from therapy.

CAT formulation

Consideration of his history, early enactments, style of relating with others and me and the Psychotherapy File highlighted two pertinent procedures. One was how Roy set himself up to be rejected, as he perceived that others would reject him and so wanted to 'get in there first'. The second was how he interacted with others in a hostile way, based on his mistrust of them.

Prose reformulation

Given the still tentative nature of our relationship, Roy's reformulation letter was difficult to write. My aim was to achieve a balance between naming his difficulties and possible enactments between us, yet being respectful of his vulnerabilities. I also wanted to be mindful that if it was experienced as too 'exposing', he may reject therapy, as a way of protecting himself.

In my uncertainty, I took the letter to my supervision group. Interestingly, their feedback was that my letter was very 'boundaried' and, as a result, 'lacked my usual warmth and empathy'. On reflection, I saw that this was the case. However, given Roy's history of unboundaried relationships with female professionals, and his attempts to make excessive demands upon me and my role, it did not seem appropriate to make changes to 'soften' this aspect of the letter.

I felt unable to refer to Roy's early history, as I felt unable to challenge his idyllic account, for fear of further conveying that I did not believe/trust him.

It was with some trepidation that I read the letter to Roy, but this lessened somewhat when I got to the bottom of the first page and Roy remarked 'F***ing hell, you have got me down to a T.' At the end of the reading he commented on how 'well I knew him', but he thought he may have 'talked too much' and should 'say less'. We thus discussed what it was like to hear the letter and our reflections on the development of our therapeutic relationship. It was encouraging that Roy was able to say that he was not entirely happy when I said 'I think there are times that you are still cautious of me and test me out', as he felt that he had 'let his guard down' with me, now trusted me and thus did not feel the need to 'test me out'. He said my honesty (even when I said things I knew he would not like), and listening to him, had aided this process.

Map (also called in CAT a Sequential Diagrammatic Reformulation (SDR))

The development of the map began during early pre-assessment sessions where we started with two simple diagrams, highlighting one procedure at a time: the 'rejection trap', and 'hostile trap', as described above. From this, Roy began to talk to members of staff about his 'cycles' when he recognised his unhelpful patterns with them.

As therapy continued, and Roy demonstrated that he could understand the sequential nature of procedures, we were able to integrate the previously developed simple diagrams into a more complex pattern. Both within sessions and outside of sessions with staff, Roy actively used his map, demonstrating where he and others were (in relation to him). In addition, he had internalised it to the extent that he could talk about it with others, without having to refer to it (Appendix 10).

Without prompting, Roy brought written information into our sessions identifying how he was getting into these patterns with others. Although this was true in itself, I also began to wonder whether this was his way of communicating how he felt about me because he could not tell me directly. An interesting reflection is that this was paralleled, as I also struggled to tell him *things directly, by me being unable to challenge him.*

Indeed, the map became a useful tool for us managing difficulties in sessions. I would always ask Roy how he felt the procedures were being enacted between us. He could point to the diagram to communicate his difficulties, whilst I used it to contain the sessions. One example was that Roy requested that I bring a member of staff into the session to 'tell them' how he was having difficulties with other staff on his unit. When I would not do this, he got angry and said that I was there to 'support him' and that not doing as he requested showed that I did not care, and he thus felt that I was rejecting him. I was able to reflect that I often felt in a 'no-win' situation with him, because if I had brought the member of staff in, I would have been doing something for him that he was capable of doing himself, which could have reinforced his beliefs that he was 'not good enough'. Yet, when I did not do as he demanded, he perceived it as a rejection. I was also able to reflect that this often left me feeling frustrated by the situation he seemed to place me in. I wondered with him whether him putting me in 'no-win' situations was his way of setting me up, so that he then had, in his words, 'ammunition' to punish and reject me?

Target Problems (TPs)
Roy and I agreed that the focus of the sessions would be on the following areas of difficulty.

MISTRUST OF OTHERS
Roy perceived that people were going to take advantage of him and that even when they appeared to have good intentions, this was false and really they were out to 'get him'. Owing to these underlying beliefs, he misinterpreted others' interactions with him as being unfriendly and hostile. He also perceived that others were talking about him in a negative way. As a result, he interacted with others in a hostile way. At times he was aware he was being aggressive but did not know how to change that. Others were then more likely to be aggressive and hostile to him, which confirmed his beliefs that others could not be trusted and were out to 'get him'.

FEAR OF REJECTION
Roy also had the underlying belief that others would reject him. He was hypervigilent to any sign that this was about to happen. Sometimes he was hostile to others, in his words 'to get in there first', as he perceived they were about to reject him. However, he then felt lonely and isolated and so sought interaction with others again.

'MACHO' IMAGE

As Roy often felt invisible to others, he attempted to portray a 'macho' image of himself, as this style of interaction got him noticed. However, it seemed to sabotage any positive interaction with others, as they did not see the positive aspects of him but rather somebody who was being arrogant and offensive. They were therefore more likely to avoid him or become hostile towards him. That served only to reinforce his view that others rejected and ignored him.

I also suspected that behaving in a 'macho' way was a way of hiding his true feelings and vulnerabilities, as he believed that others would 'use it' against him, take advantage of him or make fun of him. Thus it was a psychological defence at keeping people distant from him by giving the message not to 'mess with' him.

Target Problem Procedures (TPPs): the patterns of unhelpful action that we agreed to work on

By pulling together information from the reformulation, Roy and I were able to agree the TPPs.

1. *Snag: I want to get along with others. But I believe that people will try and 'f*** me over'. I therefore test people out, and do not believe what they say. By acting in a suspicious and hostile way I never learn that people are genuine and can be trusted.*

2. *Trap: I believe that people do not like or love me, and that I am a bad person/not good enough. Therefore, relationships will never last and I will eventually be rejected. I therefore either keep myself isolated to avoid rejection or reject the other person first. Either way I end up lonely and isolated. This then takes me back to the start of the cycle of thinking people do not like/love me/I am a bad person.*

CAT recognition and revision

During this intensive stage of therapy we used the map to contain the sessions, and me. Using Roy's language (including swear words!) on his map, and for the TPPs, ensured it made sense to him, so he could relate to it. Roy said that he would sit with his map and then write down how he got into these procedures with others. We then incorporated this information onto the rating sheets, to further aid the process of recognition.

In the sessions we also used the map as a tool to be able to talk about how he got into the procedures with me. This enabled Roy to be honest.

As therapy progressed, difficulties escalated and sessions eight and ten marked a series of ruptures. For example, although it was Roy's usual practice to bring independently into sessions written information identifying his procedures with other professionals, he told them I had asked him to do this for 'homework'. I immediately felt angry with Roy and had to work hard to monitor the tone of my voice, fearing that he may interpret my anger as me rejecting him, based on his procedure. I was, however, honest with him, saying that I felt he was creating splits in teams, because telling them I had asked for that information could potentially make them feel as if they were being evaluated/judged. It also put me in a position of power, which I did not hold. We used the map to see what was being played out: for instance was he 'punishing' me, as he perceived I had rejected/was about to reject him? Was he seeking revenge? Was he trying to maintain a 'top dog'/controlling position, as he was feeling vulnerable/weak/scared? Or was he trying to align himself with me and split us off from the rest of the team? However, when highly emotive Roy became more rigid and less able to reflect. As on occasions described previously, this resulted in me finding it even more difficult to question or challenge him further. Although Roy is very able, I realised that this was outside the range of problematic actions that he could change through therapy. Instead we used his map to determine how the discussion had left him feeling.

It was only towards the end of therapy that he began to discuss the impact of how his learning disability and stammer had led to him feeling 'not good enough' (underlying belief on his map) in comparison to his non learning-disabled siblings. We also discussed how the only way he felt he was noticed in the family was if he behaved badly. We then understood this in terms of why he had numerous offences, as this got him noticed. We also considered how that explained why he was often in conflict with others, as he felt that he would otherwise be overlooked.

Once he had a good understanding of his procedures we then identified Exits, for example, challenging the negative views that he had about others' perceptions of him and identifying the particulars of an interaction that had resulted in a more positive outcome. We also modelled and practised these in sessions (Appendix 11).

Staff awareness sessions
As part of the recognition and revision stage, Roy shared his map with his treatment team (seven professionals), with me in a supportive role. Although, Roy was very motivated to do this, I was mindful of how potentially exposing this could be, so Roy and I discussed how we would manage the session. Despite this leading to a rupture (see review and reflection), the session went well and was a turning point in the therapy. The main factor was that Roy cried when describing the beliefs he has about himself. This led to a shift in

his belief that crying was shameful, as he learned that despite him showing his vulnerabilities, people did not 'use this against him', but rather supported him and were very empathic. It also led to a significant shift for some of the staff team. Many of them had been 'punished' by Roy in his attempt to reject them. They had found it difficult to work with him and had strong emotional reactions towards him. However, when they saw his vulnerabilities, rather than the 'macho' image he tried to portray, they were moved by his tears and got more of a sense of the whole of him. It was also the first time I had seen him cry and was genuinely moved by his tears. I considered reaching out and touching his arm but did not do so in case it gave him the wrong impression of our relationship.

The session also challenged Roy's beliefs that people did not care about him, as others could now have a conversation with him about his procedures and be part of helping him to recognise where he was on his diagram. It also enabled them not to be drawn into collusive procedures with him.

A second staff awareness session took place to share his map with Exits, in order to aid revision. Feedback from the team at this was that he was taking more responsibility for his actions, being more open and honest with others about his difficulties, checking things out before making assumptions or rejecting others and showing more of the 'real' Roy.

These sessions were instrumental to change occurring, as not only were others informed about his procedures, but he could begin to relate differently to other members of the team and generalise this outside of the sessions. They also helped to challenge his view of others.

CAT ending phase

Broaching the end of therapy was another difficult issue for us both. Given his issues with rejection, we discussed the ending of therapy from session 12 onwards. Roy had mixed feelings. Positive emotions were him being happy that he had completed a further treatment, and so saw it as one step closer to being discharged from hospital. He was able to acknowledge the positives of what he had achieved. He named these as:

- *challenging his beliefs that others are rejecting him, and looking for alternative evidence*
- *being noticed for positive interaction, rather than for being in conflict with others*
- *not rejecting/punishing others*
- *allowing others to see more of the 'real' Roy.*

Thus, he was working hard to implement the Exits that were incorporated onto his diagram.

I agreed that Roy was relating to others in a more reciprocal way, for example, seeking clarification and advice from others, rather than making assumptions about their intentions and then getting into an unhelpful procedure of rejecting others or relating to them in a conflicting way resulting in hostility and arguments. I also thought he had more realistic relational expectations of what could be achieved.

An indication that our therapeutic relationship was stronger was that, as well as identifying positives, he was able to present himself as more vulnerable. He found it increasingly difficult to talk about the ending without getting tearful. Him wanting to avoid the painful feelings and showing his vulnerabilities by not talking about the ending made it difficult for me to keep raising the ending.

He was able to name that he was sad the sessions were ending and that he would miss me. As is common with in-patient work, Roy said that it did not feel like a 'proper goodbye', as he would see me around site, and I would be attending his meetings. I therefore felt it was important to name this in my goodbye letter to him.

I had mixed feelings about therapy ending. I felt sad, as we did have a therapeutic rapport, but there was also a huge sense of relief given how difficult he had, at times, been to work with. In contrast with the reformulation letter, the goodbye letter was much easier to write, as I felt that I was more able to be honest, whilst being less worried about his response. As a result of being more able to express feelings than at the initial formulation stage, I think the letter has more warmth and empathy.

When it came to reading our letters, Roy wanted me to read mine first. Roy began to cry when I described how it was nice to see more of the 'real' Roy and my view of him. He said that it was difficult to hear positive things about himself and for him to believe that people saw positive aspects, as this was the opposite of his view of himself, as named on his map. He then cried again when I read 'the time has now come for us to say goodbye' because, despite him having mixed feelings about therapy ending, we had a genuine emotional connection. We discussed how he had avoided the pain of ending by reassuring himself that he would still see me.

Roy then read his letter to me. Interestingly, he perceived that I had actually touched his arm in the staff awareness session, when I had wanted to but did not! This reflects the strength of that therapeutic moment between us; it reflected his need to be comforted and my desire to comfort, so it was so poignant that he perceived I had touched him when I had not. I was very moved by his letter to me, particularly the part in which he referred to finding a good person in me.

Follow-up

At his follow-up session Roy said that he was still able to recognise his procedures, but he was having difficulty implementing his Exits. The staff's view was that there had been a significant deterioration since the end of therapy, stating that he needed more sessions. Again, I felt under pressure from all to 'fix' the problems. We agreed a further follow-up session, in order not to:

1. collude with the pressure
2. de-skill Roy
3. stop Roy from working through an ending.

As difficulties ensued, we had a further eight sessions to work on his Exits.

Review and reflection

All of the work with Roy had been challenging. Throughout he had been constantly testing me: to see whether he could trust me and to test whether or not I would reject him. Prior to sessions I felt apprehensive, as I never quite knew what to expect. I would wonder to myself if he would be calm and engaged. Or would he greet me in a conflictual manner, and try to provoke a reaction from me so that I would reject him. In the challenging sessions I would experience strong emotions: mainly frustration and irritation. When he was engaged, however, I would experience a major sense of achievement and satisfaction. Both clearly link with my own sense of striving, and whether or not I am achieving what I hope for and my perception of others' evaluation of that. Following sessions I would always feel quite drained, because regardless of how the session went, it was always very 'active' in terms of the amount of material covered and how I felt I had to always 'second guess' him. I was also drained by the effort it took for me to remain calm when challenged by him, particularly if he was behaving in a conflictual manner. I was always so aware of my own body language and what I said, as he was so hypervigilent to any signs of rejection.

The CAT tools, such as the map and naming the procedures that were being enacted between us, enabled us to deal with conflict and be able to have honest conversations when difficulties did occur. Rather than him then disengaging as a way of rejecting me, it helped us to work through the difficulties and maintain a therapeutic alliance. It also demonstrated that 'conflict' with others could be worked through, without him resorting to violence.

From his map, we also understood that he liked to maintain control in order to avoid feeling vulnerable. Thus, his avoidance of discussing painful childhood *experiences was also probably a way of him maintaining control. Although it is important to share power and control in any therapeutic relationship, it is particularly so with offenders, as much of their offending is based on the desire to maintain power and control over situations and people. As Roy responded in such a hostile way when I questioned him, I was more tentative with him than I would usually be, because I felt that if I were to challenge him further I would be taking control and that this may lead to him feeling vulnerable/weak/scared. Based on his history and map, he often then responded with violence. Thus, it seemed as if we were both protecting ourselves in some way: he from painful feelings and me from his potential violence.*

On reflection, I can now see that I did not challenge when I would have done ordinarily. I am now aware of how much my own procedures were activated. There was also the pressure from Roy to want to 'get better', as engaging in and completing treatment is a way to be discharged from hospital. Thus there was the combination of my own striving and pressure from the team to 'fix him', as well as Roy's desire to complete treatment. I was aware of the strong impact on me of Roy wanting me to nurture him and 'make everything better' combined with his own procedures of wanting perfect trust and care.

A 16-session therapy was not long enough, given the complexity of his difficulties. Yet in other respects it was enough time, given the intensity of his interaction and the dynamics being 'played out'. Nevertheless, Roy had a further eight sessions with the specific focus on his Exits, and eight months later a further block of sessions was agreed due to a reoccurrence of difficulties directly linked with his procedures.

Owing to the complexities of Roy's presentation, and the emotions that could be evoked when working with him, sharing the formulation with the staff was instrumental in enabling the team to understand his interactional difficulties and thus be able to work empathically with him, despite the challenges. Is also helped them to try and share the responsibility, to reduce the pressure for all. Involving Roy was vital in order for change to occur.

Chapter 17

Cognitive Analytic Therapy in Forensic Intellectual Disability Settings

Perry Morrison

This chapter considers the applicability and usefulness of Cognitive Analytic Therapy (CAT) for offenders with an intellectual disability and for men with an intellectual disability deemed to be at risk of offending. The CAT described within this chapter is provided within the context of a forensic intellectual disability setting. There are significant challenges as well as rewards when working within forensic intellectual disability settings, and several different cases are reflected on, which include: outpatient CAT for a community forensic client; CAT for a man detained in a medium secure unit; CAT with a treated sex offender stepping down out of a secure service; and sharing CAT formulations with a staff team. A primary focus of the intellectual disability forensic service is on progression through the forensic pathway quickly and safely, which is underpinned by effective treatment combined with meaningful risk assessment, management and formulation.

CASE STUDY: A 24-SESSION CAT FOR A COMMUNITY FORENSIC OUTPATIENT

Jack, a 33-year-old man with a mild to borderline intellectual disability, was referred for CAT due to concerns about his potential risk of offending. Jack was referred to the clinical psychologist, also a CAT practitioner, for outpatient psychotherapy. At the time of referral Jack was an informal patient in an assessment and treatment unit for people with an intellectual disability.

The psychologist saw Jack for several assessment sessions prior to beginning the CAT. These early sessions focused on orientating Jack to the CAT approach, establishing a therapeutic relationship and completing the adapted psychotherapy file and additional baseline assessments. After several sessions, Jack and the psychologist agreed to contract to a 24-session CAT to work on the difficulties that had been named in the referral letter; Jack also stated that he was attending therapy to please his parents.

Jack's parents had been very involved in his care historically and took responsibility for transporting him to sessions, which were held at the secure unit. Jack's parents had previously transported Jack to a voluntary agency for weekly psychotherapy over a period of ten years; this agency is well known for working with people with an intellectual disability who have been sexually abused and/or who sexually offend. The local authority, the assessment and treatment unit, Jack's family and Jack, each had a slightly different perspective and expectation regarding the outcome of treatment, which contributed to a challenging yet interesting context, which confused who the customer for treatment actually was.

There was a degree of idealising associated with referring Jack for CAT, given that Jack was only concluding his open-ended, long-term psychotherapy in exchange for undertaking time-limited CAT; the inference being that CAT would deliver results that so far had not materialised and within a relatively short space of time. There was an expectation that CAT would make a difference, or else would be time-limited at the least.

The reason for Jack's referral for therapy was due to a longstanding history of sexually deviant fantasies; the violent nature of the fantasies and the degree to which he attached to them caused considerable anxiety in those around Jack and there was a large measure of uncertainty as to the levels of risk that were posed as a result. Jack's sexual fantasies involved the torturing and murdering of young attractive women; his fantasies included tying women up, gagging them and then punching or kicking them until they bled before shooting, stabbing and/or dismembering his victims. His fantasies would also involve eating his victims' body parts, which he would make into 'cow' soup or pie.

Jack presented as a tall, quiet and shy man who is the older of two brothers. Jack had cerebral palsy from birth, resulting in poor motor co-ordination and speech that could be difficult to understand. Jack attended special school from the age of five and was transferred to a mainstream school within a special educational unit at age 11. Several years ago he was diagnosed with osteoporosis and coeliac disease. Jack had a history of depression with some suicidal ideation and had self-reported auditory hallucinations.

Regarding Jack's sexual development, he reported developing a fetish for women's shoes around the age of seven and at age 11 decided that he would remain single. As a teenager he would behave rudely to young, attractive, female teachers, trying to touch them and steal their shoes. Jack would write hostile angry letters to his teachers and this had continued, with female members of staff being the current target for his letter writing. Jack also had a history of making nuisance telephone calls to girls and young women. Jack had never had a girlfriend. Jack stated that he enjoyed the reaction he obtained from scaring or verbally abusing women.

In the beginning (Reformulation stage)

The early stage of therapy focused on developing the relationship and on processing and making sense of a vast amount of information that was being presented. This stage involved mapping patterns of relating to and/ or of experiencing others, as well as to self, and describing experiences and relationships and the associated affect or else absence of feelings in response to them. As thoughts and feelings were being mapped the learning and meaning taken from life experiences was similarly being clarified and mapped. Potter (2010) describes the power of words with arrows, referring to when thoughts and patterns are drawn out on paper and how they can then be easily linked or held in the process of the therapy.

It was important to draw conclusions tentatively, for example, when Jack smiled, were these smiles of recognition or of something else? It was often difficult to tell and enquiring would often not help to clarify the quality(ies) of such non-verbal communications. This stage of therapy culminated with the reading aloud of the reformulation letter to Jack. The letter sought to describe the process so far, whilst naming patterns of relating to others and to self, whilst also anticipating potential obstacles to achieving solutions and exits to recognising and revising familiar patterns. The reformulation letter can be seen in Appendix 12.

The map or sequential diagrammatic reformulation (SDR) that was generated within session, was developed incrementally, which began with the words and arrows on a page. I used the term 'map' with Jack, to refer to the SDR, which seemed to fit for him.

The middle (Recognition stage)
Ruminations, rupture and reparations
Identifying Jack's reciprocal roles or patterns of relating to and of experiencing the world was not always straightforward, particularly as his responses would often be tangential, unclear or else possibly avoidant. Statements indicative of reciprocal roles included:

- 'I'd like them to see the pain I had'
- 'They are less powerful with their shoes off' (referring to young, attractive women)
- 'bullies don't have a high IQ...they are weak themselves...they are hurting themselves'.

This last comment provided an opportunity for Jack to consider being the bully and the bullied, given his experiences of being bullied at school. However, even with referring to the map to help link the flipping between these poles of this one reciprocal role, it was difficult to gauge whether recognition had occurred.

Similarly, ascertaining Jack's goal(s) for therapy could be difficult as it felt that he was often unspecific. Pleasing others and bottling up feelings are examples of traps that interfered with divulging and considering his own needs, let alone beginning to meet them. Jack's notion of a life worth living seemed to be more about the absence of a problem rather than about goals for living, although he did want to plan a big cruise with a friend and to eventually live in his own flat and to be more independent.

Less than ideal communication with external agencies represented some challenges, as did the invitation to be assessor and therapist simultaneously. The psychologist attempted to stay in the psychologist position for the duration of the therapy, and only on conclusion of the therapy, and with Jack's agreement, did the psychologist share views with the wider support network as to what might be helpful next steps. Managing expectations of other parties during the CAT added another dimension to the task, which was often present during the sessions; others' agendas felt tangible.

Towards the end (Revision stage)

As the 24-session CAT was drawing towards its end, the focus became more centred on the exploration, appreciation and reinforcement of exits from unhelpful over-learned patterns. Self-efficacy and self-mastery was recognised and reinforced wherever possible, and to whatever degree was possible, whilst making reference and linking this back to the map whenever any such opportunity occurred, for example, occasionally Jack would describe how he had employed helpful exit strategies or would be thinking or talking in a way more indicative of an achieving or caring-orientated reciprocal role. The co-constructed SDR is shown in Appendix 13.

Goodbyes (Ending and reflections)

A pie chart was used from early on to provide a visual indicator of the end of therapy getting nearer as each session progressed. This was particularly important given the previous importance and dependence on weekly psychotherapy; preparation for ending therefore required very careful attention, even by CAT standards. The goodbye letters to one another were read out in the penultimate session; the therapist's goodbye letter to Jack can be seen in Appendix 14. Due attention to ending from the beginning was particularly relevant for Jack as was the time-limited structure, which helped to focus the tasks relating to the stage of the therapy.

As the therapy concluded, future options required consideration. Jack was invited to a six-month Good Thinking Group, a cognitive behaviour therapy-based psycho-educational group for those thought to be at risk of offending. The group aimed to promote problem-solving skills and to reinforce the interactions between thoughts, feelings and behaviours. Additionally, I attended Jack's care programme approach (CPA), where we jointly shared some of the work that had been undertaken. It was also recommended that a monthly meeting with a psychologist would be necessary to support and monitor Jack's progress going forward.

Useful adaptations

Animal metaphors were usefully employed to help illustrate the reciprocal role qualities that had been identified and to convey the associated feelings in a creative way that made sense to Jack. Jack is a keen naturalist and the animal characters were meaningful to him; using and thinking about the cheetah, lion and shark and their different modes of being, moved the therapy relationship along considerably and onto a different platform.

Jack and I also incorporated pictures of women in order to convey those women who would pose emotional challenges; Jack cut out pictures of some women, or just their legs, and brought them to session. The pictures helped to elicit the arising thoughts and feelings that could be explored and worked on within session. In one session I brought a pair of women's shoes into the room for the same purpose as outlined above. However, Jack perceived this as a direct challenge to begin with, and a potential rupture ensued that required careful reparation. This seemed to remind Jack of other situations in which he had been 'put to the test' and so had unpleasant overtones for him. However, the anger and frustration that was generated provided us with energy with which to move forward and to uncover another layer of thinking that had not surfaced until this point.

A three-dimensional model head, used for group work, was also used in two of Jack's CAT sessions. The head contained different coloured balls to represent helpful or unhelpful thoughts, or the pictures of women that Jack had cut out. Thoughts that were elicited were then linked to the SDR that was being generated.

The 'Draw On Your Emotions' images by Sunderland and Engleheart (1993) were used in order to explore whether these would convey any additional meaning for Jack. It was interesting that the one picture that Jack related to was able to be interpreted more literally i.e., a picture of one person holding on to another person's leg (Jack was reminded of attempting to take off a female teacher's boots). Although this provided useful material for discussion, Jack did not particularly relate to any of the other images and remarked that it reminded him of Makaton; it seemed as if Jack felt that using these particular images was demeaning.

Jack's parents joined for one session at around the midpoint of the CAT in order to link theirs and Jack's perspectives. This required Jack's consent and careful negotiation. I was aware of the potential fragility of Jack's voice in this scenario, and whether or not it needed to be amplified and/or noticed in the event that it was turned down.

Pacing the therapy was critical, as was active listening throughout to attempt to successfully judge when to stay with the 'here and now' and when to focus on the 'there and then' of the past. Stern (2004) describes not rushing the moving-along process, and I believe this is particularly important with intellectual disability issues; this idea fits well with the concept of working within a person's zone of proximal development (ZPD) (Vygotsky 1978) i.e., the ZPD is the distance between actual developmental level (determined by individual problem-solving) and the level of potential development (determined through problem-solving with more capable peers). There were questions as to whether progress was sometimes affected by Jack's level of motivation to change or by ZPD matching issues; both of these hypotheses were held lightly throughout and strategies were altered in order to attempt to ascertain the most likely explanation, or to establish the degree to which either might have played a part.

On reflection, it would have been more helpful to have explored other creative methods sooner in the therapy. Sharing the reformulation earlier in the therapy or extending the therapy might also have been useful. A mind map or other form of pictorial representation of patterns and thoughts might have worked equally as well as the SDR that was actually generated.

Measures employed

The Psychotherapy file for People with Intellectual disabilities (Bancroft et al. 2008); CIRCLE; Personality Structure Questionnaire (PSQ).

Other examples of CAT within a forensic setting

CASE STUDY: INPATIENT PSYCHOTHERAPY

A 16-session CAT was used with a 39-year-old man with a mild to borderline intellectual disability. Andrew was detained in the regional medium secure unit for treatment for sexual offences. In this case, CAT was used to help make sense of the individual's anger, prior to him attending a sex offender treatment programme. This CAT experience was explained to Andrew as helping to lead to in-depth work that would increasingly focus on very personal issues, i.e., his index offence. One particularly powerful reciprocal role for this man was ignoring to ignored; Andrew would often expect to be ignored by others sooner or later and could often be seen to provoke this response in those around him. Andrew could quickly flip from feeling ignored by others to actively ignoring those around him. This pattern of relating to others and of experiencing others could be linked to his feelings of anger, which would typically escalate if active efforts to escape this cycle were not actively sought. Successful completion of this individual therapy was probably a first for Andrew as he had typically sabotaged his efforts prior to nearing completion.

CASE STUDY: STEP DOWN PSYCHOTHERAPY

A 24-session CAT was provided for a 33-year-old man with mild intellectual disability following completion of a sexual offender treatment programme. The funding authority would only agree to place the individual in the step down unit if CAT was provided. Sebastian had been requesting an opportunity to discuss his own experiences of sexual abuse, given that the treatment focus had previously been on the risks that he presented to others as well as to self. In this case, the 24-session CAT presented the chance to explore both poles of the abusing and bullying to bullied and abused reciprocal role in some detail and also afforded an opportunity to discuss Sebastian's sexuality, which was clearly a central issue for him and the source of many mixed messages.

Working with staff teams

With clients' prior agreement, reflections of therapy and SDRs have been utilised with staff teams and systems of support, to help to map the relations and patterns that are typical for an individual; wherever possible this has been done with the client present and actively contributing to the process. Helping the system to identify and recognise some of its own processes and how these might meet with clients' own processes is an interesting practice, which is potentially helpful for the wider network supporting the client and, ultimately, the client.

Conclusions

The spirit of CAT is creative and flexible and allows for exploration of depth within a given structure. CAT is a unique, time-limited, integrative and relational therapy that is increasingly being adapted for different populations. This exploratory chapter has indicated how CAT has been utilised with offenders with an intellectual disability at various stages along an individual's pathway of treatment and care. Stern (2004, p.198) discusses the importance of providing 'a present remembering context' with which to clarify patterns, experiences and learning; work of this nature, which attends carefully to the flow and to the process of therapy, is particularly valuable with offenders with an intellectual disability or those at risk of offending. Helping the client to name and/or to become more aware of their own processes, and highlighting where and how risks might be heightened whilst exploring pro-social and non-harming alternatives, fits well with the aims of rehabilitation with this population. CAT has also proved to be an engaging process that has held clients' interest, and all of the three clients described here sought to extend the therapy.

I would suggest that CAT has many potential applications within a forensic intellectual disability setting and that modes of delivery are still to be explored in this context for a variety of presenting issues and stages of treatment.

Afterword

In the early days in the development of Cognitive Analytic Therapy (CAT), the idea of offering the approach to people with an intellectual disability was little thought about. The Association of Cognitive Analytic Therapy had not suggested that CAT could not be done with people with an intellectual disability but, as it had started in adult mental health, it was a while before anyone thought it might be useful. Many other psychotherapies are not recommended for use with people with a learning disability.

Perhaps this began to change when people who knew about CAT and others who knew about intellectual disability started working more dialogically. The central idea of CAT as a relational therapy chimed with the understanding that relationships and relational intelligence are not based on IQ. Our position is that intelligence is relational in that it is the intelligence that lies between us that counts. Furthermore, CAT integrates approaches based on skills work and relationships whereas many other approaches do only one of these. We can describe relationships through reciprocal roles and encompass a behavioural skills approach in the development of new, healthier procedures.

When the CAT Intellectual Disability Special Interest Group began, an early concern was the predominantly verbal approach with the letters and rating sheets, so we set about devising adaptations generally involving stick figures, which seemed to work well enough. The fact that most of us are not skilled artists possibly helped to lessen the differences between our clients and ourselves! One of our jobs as CAT therapists in intellectual disability services is to become the scribe or person drawing to describe the relationship that others have been unable to describe.

In writing this book we hope we have demonstrated how we have moved beyond the concerns outlined in Mike Bender's 1993 paper entitled 'The Unoffered Chair' in which he described the therapeutic disdain of therapists towards people with an intellectual disability. We have found that not only does CAT offer a chair, but it can also offer a voice. In describing CAT's utility and usefulness, perhaps we have helped psychotherapy to become less 'handicapped' (after Linnington 2002). We no longer have to ask whether people with an intellectual disability and other cognitive deficits can benefit from psychotherapy; we are focusing on how to do it.

This book has been put together by various people and is thus not a single voice but a polyphony (see Bakhtin's ideas on polyphony). We hope, therefore, that many other practitioners will be encouraged to join in and develop their practice to include people with an intellectual disability and those who work with or live alongside them.

Appendix 1
The Psychotherapy File I

This is to help with understanding ourselves better so that we can begin to sort out our difficulties.

We all have one life, which is ours to live.

What has happened to us in our lives helps to make us the way we are now. What we have been through sets up ways of thinking, feeling and doing which we do over and over again as a sort of pattern in our lives.

Sometimes difficult things in our lives start up patterns of thinking, feeling and behaving which help at the time but later may become hurtful to us. We can get on better with our lives if we can break the patterns and learn to do something different.

This can be hard because we have had the patterns for so long.

The first step in sorting out your difficulties is to work out the hurtful patterns which you have in your life.

The second step is to see when they happen in your life.

The third step is to work at trying to do things in another way.

In this way you can begin to have more control or say in your life and more happiness.

Remember

- The patterns come because of what has happened to us in our lives.
- They are how we got by in difficult times.
- It is not because we are bad or stupid.
- We don't have to keep doing them if we learn to see what is happening.
- By changing the way we do things, we can learn to control our behaviour.
- When we change, the way other people behave towards us may also change.
- It is possible for things to change.

Keeping a diary of the way you feel and what you do

We can begin to sort out our horrible moods and difficult behaviour by learning to see when they come and what starts them off.

It would be good to start keeping a diary, everyday if possible about when:

....
....
....
....

Think about when it happened.

Try to write it down what you were *feeling* and *thinking* and what was *happening* at the time.

We can talk about this in our time together.

You can also talk about it with ....
and anyone else you would like to.

Thinking about patterns

This page will help us to work out your patterns. These questions will help us work out traps you can get into which go round and round in a hurtful way. Mark yes or no.

Are you afraid of hurting other people's feelings?	Yes	No
If yes – do you hide your feelings and needs inside when you are with other people?	Yes	No
Do you feel fed up about yourself?	Yes	No
If yes – do you think you can't do things very well?	Yes	No
Are you worried that you may not be good enough for other people?	Yes	No
If yes – do you try to please people who you are with?	Yes	No
Do you get worried when you go out?	Yes	No
If yes – does this make you stop going out?	Yes	No
Do you feel worried that you are not very good at being with people?	Yes	No
If yes – does this sometimes make it hard for you to be friendly?	Yes	No
Do you sometimes feel you are no good as a person?	Yes	No
If yes – do you think that you will not be able to get what you need or want?	Yes	No

If yes – do you think you can't have what you need or want?
Because if you do (tick which are like you):

- you will be told off ☐
- people close to you will go away ☐
- people will not like you ☐
- it won't last ☐
- you think you are weak and so you must not let yourself have what you want. ☐

More questions about patterns

Sometimes the way we have come to see things means that we live as if there is not much choice in what we can do. In this way we make things harder for ourselves than they need to be.

If we can work out how this happens in your life, we can try to find other ways of doing things which will give you more choices and give you more say in your life.

Do you have any of these patterns?

I must keep my feelings inside me. If I don't other people will not like me.	Yes	No
I must keep my feelings inside or I will hurt other people.	Yes	No
If I am told I must do something then I don't want to do it.	Yes	No
If I am told I must not do something then I want to do it.	Yes	No
If I get what I want I feel as if I have done something wrong.	Yes	No
If I don't get what I want I feel cross and unhappy.	Yes	No
I have to keep things very, very neat and tidy. If I don't I am scared there will be a terrible mess.	Yes	No
With other people either I get very close but feel scared I will be hurt: or I keep well away and feel lonely.	Yes	No
With other people either I stick up for myself and nobody likes me or I give in and get put on by others and feel cross and hurt.	Yes	No
With other people, either I feel very, very safe and very, very happy or I am being very, very cross with them and wanting to be in a fight with them.	Yes	No
I think I am better than other people or else I feel they are better than me.	Yes	No
With other people, either I am very close but feel taken over or I stay in charge but feel far away and feel lonely.	Yes	No
When I'm close to someone, either I have to do what they say or they have to do what I say.	Yes	No

More patterns

Sometimes we say: 'I want to have a better life or I want to change the way I behave *but*...' Maybe this is because other people in our lives have stopped us from having good things for ourselves. Sometimes it seems that we stop ourselves from having good things.

It is helpful to learn to see how this pattern may be stopping you from getting on with your life, so that you can begin to get a better life and keep it. The questions will help us to work it out.

Do you ever feel that you are stopped from doing good things or having good things because you are afraid of what other people might say or do?	Yes	No
Do you ever feel that you are stopped from doing good things or having good things by something inside yourself telling you that you are not good enough to have them?	Yes	No

Remember

- All these patterns come because of what has happened to us in our lives.
- They are how we got by in difficult times.
- It is not because we are bad or stupid.
- We don't have to keep on doing them now we are learning to see what is happening.
- By changing the way we do things, we are learning to see what is happening.
- By changing the way we do things, we can learn to control our behaviour.
- When we change, the way other people behave to us also changes.
- It is possible for things to change.

Difficult moods that come in a rush

Some people find it very difficult to keep control over their behaviour because of times when things feel very difficult and different from usual.

We can see if this is a problem for you. Is any of this like you?

How I feel about myself and others can change suddenly, in a rush.	Yes	No
Sometimes I get in a mood when I have very, very strong feelings which I can't control.	Yes	No

Sometimes I get in a mood when I feel muddled and I have no feelings.	Yes	No
Sometimes I can be in a mood when I feel very, very cross and angry with myself and want to hurt myself.	Yes	No
Sometimes I get in a mood when I feel that others are going to let me down or hurt me.	Yes	No
I can get in a mood when I feel very, very angry and hurtful to others.	Yes	No
Sometimes the only way to cope with confusing feelings is to blank them off, rub them out, and feel lost/far away from others.	Yes	No

More questions about very strong upsetting moods that may come in a rush

Do you ever feel strongly like this? Put in more words or cross out words if you want to:

No feelings, far away.	Yes	No
Out of control very, very cross, rage.	Yes	No
Very, very special, looking down on.	Yes	No
Let down by life and other people.	Yes	No
Playing others up.	Yes	No
Clinging to others, afraid of being left alone.	Yes	No
Very, very busy, can't think or feel.	Yes	No
Upset, all in a muddle, feeling scared.	Yes	No
Feeling wonderfully cared for, very, very happily close to another.	Yes	No
Not liked, not wanted, left alone.	Yes	No
Very cross with myself, thinking I'm no good.	Yes	No
Helpless and needy, waiting for others to make it alright for me.	Yes	No
Wanting what other people have, wanting to hurt and upset them.	Yes	No
Looking after myself and others.	Yes	No

Hurting myself and hurting other people.	Yes	No
Feeling cross about doing what other people say I must do.	Yes	No
Hurt and made to feel small by others.	Yes	No
Safe in myself and able to be close to others.	Yes	No
Very, very cross with others for things they can't do or mistakes they make.	Yes	No
Very scared of others.	Yes	No
Do you get any other very strong moods?	Yes	No

Write them below:

....
....
....
....
....
....
....
....
....
....
....
....
....

Appendix 2
The Psychotherapy File II

This is to help with understanding ourselves better so that we can begin to sort out our difficulties.

We all have one life, which is ours to live.

What has happened to us in our lives helps to make us the way we are now.

What we have been through sets up ways of...

thinking   feeling   and doing

...which we do over and over again as a sort of pattern in our lives.

Sometimes difficult things in our lives start up patterns of thinking, feeling and behaving which help at the time but later may become hurtful to us.

We can get on better with our lives if we can break the patterns and learn to do something different.

This can be hard because we have had the patterns for so long.

The first step in sorting out your difficulties is to work out the hurtful patterns which you have in your life.

The second step is to see when they happen in your life.

The third step is to work at trying to do things in another way.

In this way you can begin to have more control or say in your life and more happiness.

Remember...
- The patterns come because of what has happened to us in our lives.
- They are how we got by in difficult times. It is not because we are bad or stupid.
- We don't have to keep doing them if we learn to see what is happening.
- By changing the way we do things, we can learn to control our behaviour.
- When we change, the way other people behave towards us may also change. It is possible for things to change.

Keeping a diary of the way you feel and what you do

We can begin to sort out our horrible moods and difficult behaviour by learning to see when they come and what starts them off.

It would be good to start keeping a diary, every day if possible, about when these things happen.

Think about when it happens.

Try to write down what you were feeling and thinking and what was happening at the time.

………………………………………………………………………………………………
………………………………………………………………………………………………
………………………………………………………………………………………………
………………………………………………………………………………………………
………………………………………………………………………………………………
………………………………………………………………………………………………
………………………………………………………………………………………………
………………………………………………………………………………………………
………………………………………………………………………………………………
………………………………………………………………………………………………
………………………………………………………………………………………………

We can talk about this in our time together.

You can also talk about it with ……………………………………………………
and anyone else you would like to.

Thinking about patterns

This page will help us to work out your patterns. These questions will help us work out patterns of behaviour you can get into which go round and round in a hurtful way.

Mark yes (✓) or no (✗).

	Are you afraid of hurting other people's feelings?	Yes ✓	No ✗
	If yes – do you hide your feelings and needs inside when you are with other people?	Yes ✓	No ✗
	Do you feel fed up about yourself?	Yes ✓	No ✗
	If yes – do you think you can't do things very well?	Yes ✓	No ✗
	Are you worried that you may not be good enough for other people?	Yes ✓	No ✗
	If yes – do you try to please people who you are with?	Yes ✓	No ✗
	Do you get worried when you go out?	Yes ✓	No ✗
	If yes – does this make you stop going out?	Yes ✓	No ✗
	Do you feel worried that you are not very good at being with people?	Yes ✓	No ✗
	If yes – does this sometimes make it hard for you to be friendly?	Yes ✓	No ✗

Do you sometimes feel you are no good as a person?	Yes ✓	No ✗
If yes – do you think that you will not be able to get what you need or want?	Yes ✓	No ✗

If yes – do you think you can't have what you need or want because if you do (tick which are like you):

you will be told off	☐
people close to you will go away	☐
people will not like you	☐
it won't last	☐
you think you are weak and so you must not let yourself have what you want.	☐

More questions about patterns

Sometimes the way we see things means that we live as if there is not much choice in what we can do.

In this way we make things harder for ourselves than they need to be.

If we can work out how this happens in your life we can try to find other ways of doing things. This will give you more choices and give you more say in your life.

Do you have any of these patterns?

I must keep my feelings inside me. If I don't other people will not like me.   Yes ✓   No ✗

I must keep my feelings inside or I will hurt other people.   Yes ✓   No ✗

If I am told I must do something then I don't want to do it.   Yes ✓   No ✗

If I am told I must not do something then I want to do it.   Yes ✓   No ✗

If I get what I want, I feel as if I have done something wrong.   Yes ✓   No ✗

I have to keep things very, very neat and tidy. If I don't I am scared there will be a terrible mess.   Yes ✓   No ✗

With other people, either I get very close but feel scared I will be hurt, or I keep well away and feel lonely.   Yes ✓   No ✗

With other people, either I stick up for myself and nobody likes me, or I give in and get put on by others and feel cross and hurt. Yes ✓ No ✗

With other people, either I feel very, very safe and very, very happy or I am being very, very cross with them and wanting to be in a fight with them. Yes ✓ No ✗

I either think I am better than other people or I feel they are better than me. Yes ✓ No ✗

With other people, either I am very close but feel taken over, or I stay in charge but feel far away and lonely. Yes ✓ No ✗

When I'm close to someone, either I have to do what they say, or they have to do what I say. Yes ✓ No ✗

More patterns

Sometimes we say 'I want to have a better life or I want to change the way I behave *but*...' Maybe this is because other people in our lives have stopped us from having good things for ourselves.

Sometimes it seems that we stop ourselves from having good things.

It is helpful to learn to see how this pattern may be stopping you from getting on with your life, so that you can begin to get a better life and keep it.

The questions will help us work it out.

Do you ever feel that you are stopped from doing good things or having good things because you are afraid of what other people might say or do?   Yes ✓   No ✗

Do you ever feel that you are stopped from doing good things or having good things by something inside yourself telling you that you are not good enough to have them?   Yes ✓   No ✗

Remember...

- All these patterns come because of what has happened to us in our lives.
- They are how we got by in difficult times.
- It is not because we are bad or stupid.
- We don't have to keep on doing them now we are learning to see what is happening.
- By changing the way we do things, we can learn to control our behaviour.
- When we change, the way other people behave to us also changes.
- It is possible for things to change.

Difficult moods that come in a rush

Some people find it very difficult to keep control over their behaviour because of times when things felt very difficult and different from usual.

We can see if this is a problem for you. Is any of this like you?

How I feel about myself and others can change suddenly, in a rush.   Yes ✓   No ✗

Sometimes I get in a mood when I have very, very strong feelings which I can't control.   Yes ✓   No ✗

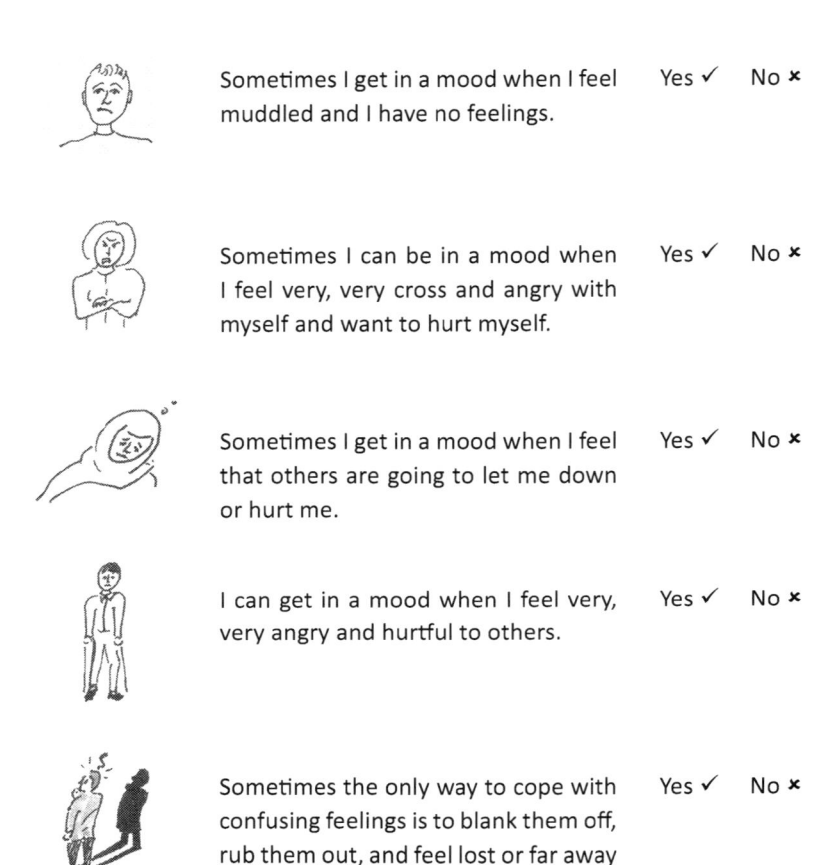

Sometimes I get in a mood when I feel muddled and I have no feelings.	Yes ✓	No ✗
Sometimes I can be in a mood when I feel very, very cross and angry with myself and want to hurt myself.	Yes ✓	No ✗
Sometimes I get in a mood when I feel that others are going to let me down or hurt me.	Yes ✓	No ✗
I can get in a mood when I feel very, very angry and hurtful to others.	Yes ✓	No ✗
Sometimes the only way to cope with confusing feelings is to blank them off, rub them out, and feel lost or far away from others.	Yes ✓	No ✗

More questions about very strong upsetting moods that may come in a rush

Do you ever feel strongly like this? Put in more words or cross out words if you want to.

No feelings, far away.	Yes ✓	No ✗

Appendix 2

	Out of control very, very cross, rage.	Yes ✓	No ✗
	Very, very special, looking down on others.	Yes ✓	No ✗
	Let down by life and other people.	Yes ✓	No ✗
	Winding others up.	Yes ✓	No ✗
	Clinging to others, afraid of being left alone.	Yes ✓	No ✗
	Very, very busy, can't think or feel.	Yes ✓	No ✗
	Upset, all in a muddle, feeling scared.	Yes ✓	No ✗
	Feeling wonderfully cared for, very, very happily close to another.	Yes ✓	No ✗

Not liked, not wanted, left alone.	Yes ✓	No ✗
Very cross with myself, thinking I'm no good.	Yes ✓	No ✗
Helpless and needy, waiting for others to make it all right for me.	Yes ✓	No ✗
Wanting what other people have, wanting to hurt and upset them.	Yes ✓	No ✗
Looking after myself and others.	Yes ✓	No ✗
Hurting myself and hurting other people.	Yes ✓	No ✗
Feeling cross about doing what other people say I must do.	Yes ✓	No ✗

Appendix 2

Hurt and made to feel small by others.   Yes ✓   No ✗

Safe in myself and able to be close to others.   Yes ✓   No ✗

Very, very cross with others for things they can't do or mistakes they make.   Yes ✓   No ✗

Very scared of others.   Yes ✓   No ✗

Do you get any other very strong moods? Please write them below:

....
....
....
....
....
....
....
....
....
....
....
....
....
....
....
....

Appendix 3
The Psychotherapy File Adapted for People with Intellectual Disabilities

This file is to help with understanding ourselves better. It can help us to think about how the things that have happened to us have affected the way we understand ourselves and others. Our experiences can lead us to develop patterns of thinking, feeling and doing which we repeat over and over again. Sometimes patterns that we have learned that were helpful in the beginning stop being helpful and end up in us making things worse for ourselves. Because we have done them so often we can find ourselves stuck and it is difficult to stop them and learn new, more helpful patterns. This is not because we are no good or stupid but because, at first, they were ways that got us through some difficult times. We do not have to keep doing them, though, once we realise that they are not the most helpful now.

The first thing we can do to help ourselves is to work out what our unhelpful patterns are. Then we can learn to recognise when we are doing them in our lives now. It is then that we can work out how to do things differently and learn more helpful patterns. In this way, we can feel more in control of our lives and feel happier with ourselves.

It is important to remember that it is possible for us to change, and that if we change the way we are with other people the way they are with us can change too.

A good way to start looking for our unhelpful patterns is to notice when we feel bad about ourselves or others and then think about:

- what we were feeling about ourselves, others and the world before the problem started
- what happened that started the problem off
- what we were feeling when the problem was happening
- what we were feeling about ourselves, others and the world after it was all over.

Keeping a diary every day can help you to do this.

Through our work with lots and lots of people we have worked out three different types of patterns. As you work through the psychotherapy file you can see if any of these patterns are like ones you have learned.

The first type of pattern is called *traps*.

Traps are like 'vicious circles'. Once we get into them they just go round and round and it is hard to stop them.

Do you have any of these patterns?

1: 'Keeping my feelings to myself' trap

I don't tell people how I feel or what I need because I worry that I will upset them

This means that sometimes people ignore me or hurt me

This makes me angry or upset

I think it's bad to be angry or upset, and that I'd better keep my feelings and needs to myself

Yes / Sometimes / No

2: 'Thinking I'm no good' trap

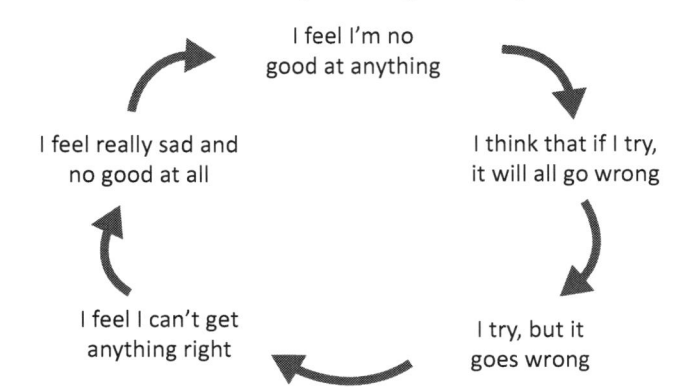

I feel I'm no good at anything

I think that if I try, it will all go wrong

I try, but it goes wrong

I feel I can't get anything right

I feel really sad and no good at all

Yes / Sometimes / No

3a: 'Trying to please' trap

I feel that I don't matter and that I'm not worth much

↓

I want other people to like me so I do what they want

↓

They take advantage of me. I feel hurt and angry

↓

I lose confidence in myself

↑ (back to start)

Yes / Sometimes / No

3b: 'Trying to please' trap

I don't feel confident about myself

↓

I want others to like me so I agree to do whatever they want even when I don't really want to

↓

I don't do all that they want and they get angry or disappointed with me

↓

I feel guilty and bad about myself

↑ (back to start)

Yes / Sometimes / No

4: 'Worrying about doing things' trap

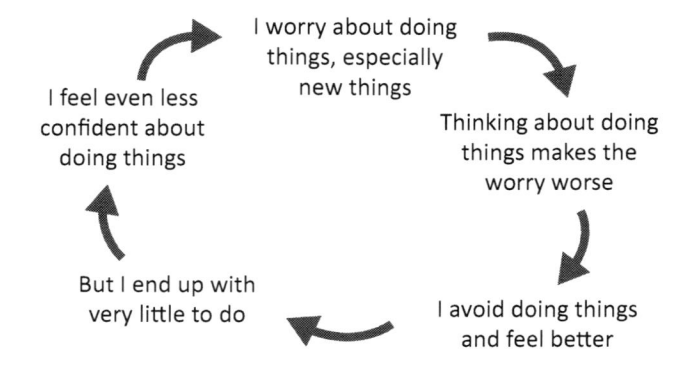

I worry about doing things, especially new things

↓

Thinking about doing things makes the worry worse

↓

I avoid doing things and feel better

↓

But I end up with very little to do

↓

I feel even less confident about doing things

↑ (back to start)

Yes / Sometimes / No

5: 'Worrying about being with people' trap

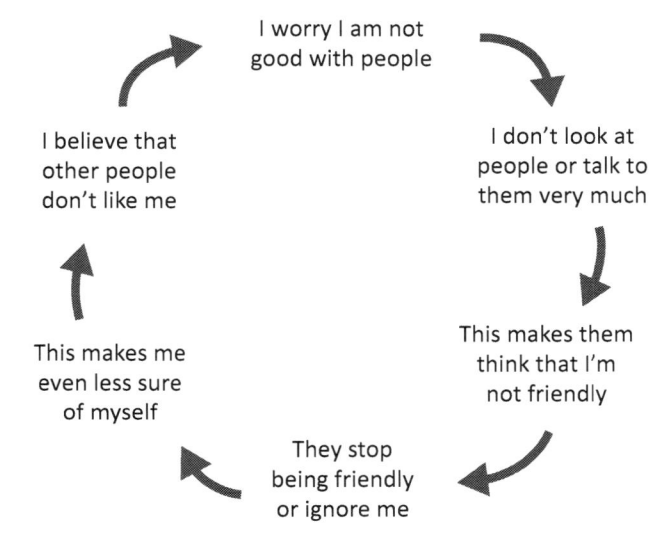

I worry I am not good with people
→ I don't look at people or talk to them very much
→ This makes them think that I'm not friendly
→ They stop being friendly or ignore me
→ This makes me even less sure of myself
→ I believe that other people don't like me
→ (back to start)

Yes / Sometimes / No

6a: 'Feeling I am not important' trap

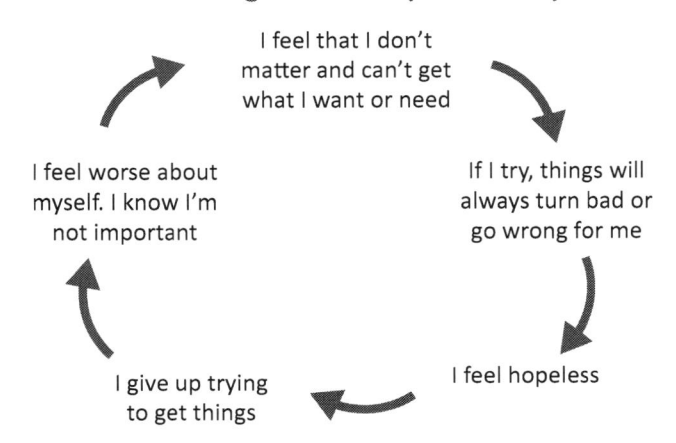

I feel that I don't matter and can't get what I want or need
→ If I try, things will always turn bad or go wrong for me
→ I feel hopeless
→ I give up trying to get things
→ I feel worse about myself. I know I'm not important
→ (back to start)

Yes / Sometimes / No

6b: 'Feeling I am not important' trap

I feel that I am not important and what I want or need doesn't matter very much

If I try to get what I want or need other people will tell me off or punish me
or
not like me or like being with me
or
will go away and leave me

I feel hopeless

I give up trying to get things

I feel worse about myself. I know I'm not important

Yes / Sometimes / No

The second type of pattern is called *dilemmas*.

Dilemmas are patterns where it seems that there are only two options open to us, for example, where we assume *if I do…then…will happen* and where we think *either…or….* It's a bit like 'black and white thinking' where only two choices seem possible. By thinking this way we can make things harder for ourselves by living as if there is not much choice in what we do.

Do you have any of these patterns?

First, in choices about myself:

Appendix 3

1: 'Upset feelings' dilemma

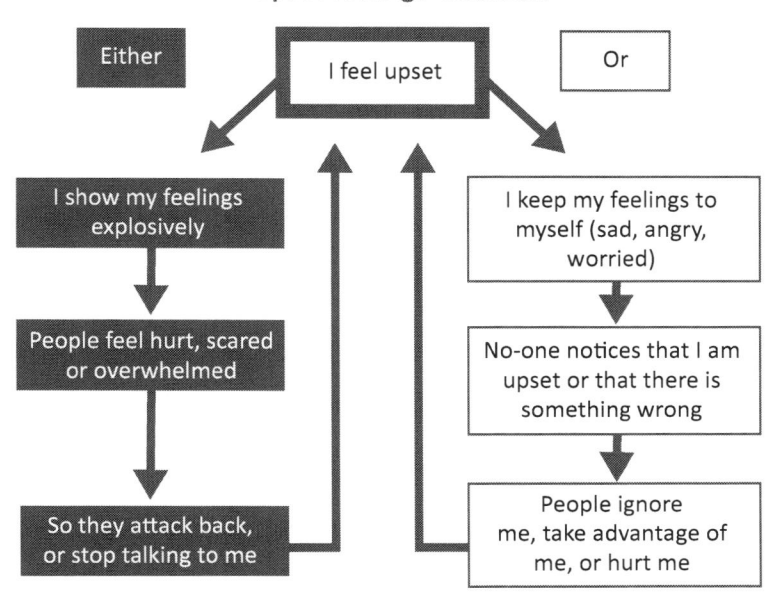

Either → I feel upset ← **Or**

Either branch:
- I show my feelings explosively
- People feel hurt, scared or overwhelmed
- So they attack back, or stop talking to me

Or branch:
- I keep my feelings to myself (sad, angry, worried)
- No-one notices that I am upset or that there is something wrong
- People ignore me, take advantage of me, or hurt me

Yes / Sometimes / No

2: 'Wanting things' dilemma

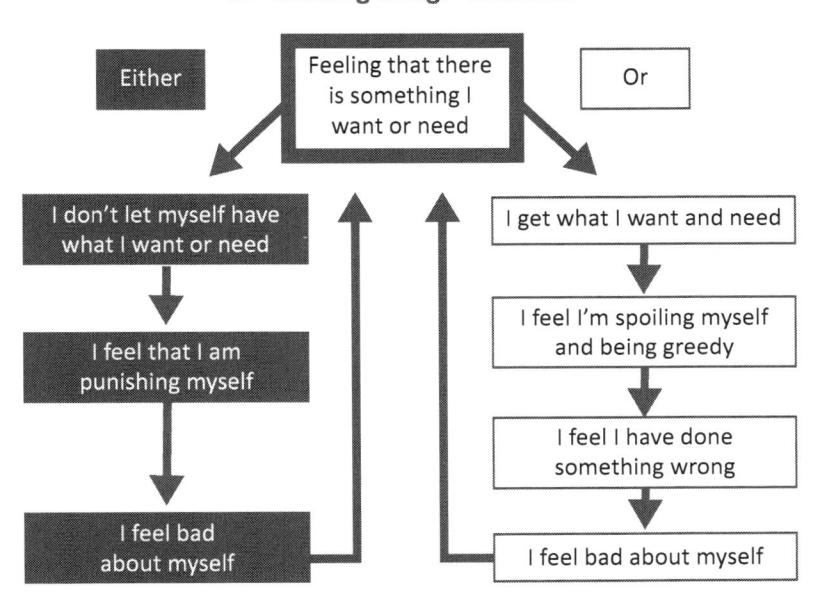

Either → Feeling that there is something I want or need ← **Or**

Either branch:
- I don't let myself have what I want or need
- I feel that I am punishing myself
- I feel bad about myself

Or branch:
- I get what I want and need
- I feel I'm spoiling myself and being greedy
- I feel I have done something wrong
- I feel bad about myself

Yes / Sometimes / No

3: 'Feeling no good' dilemma

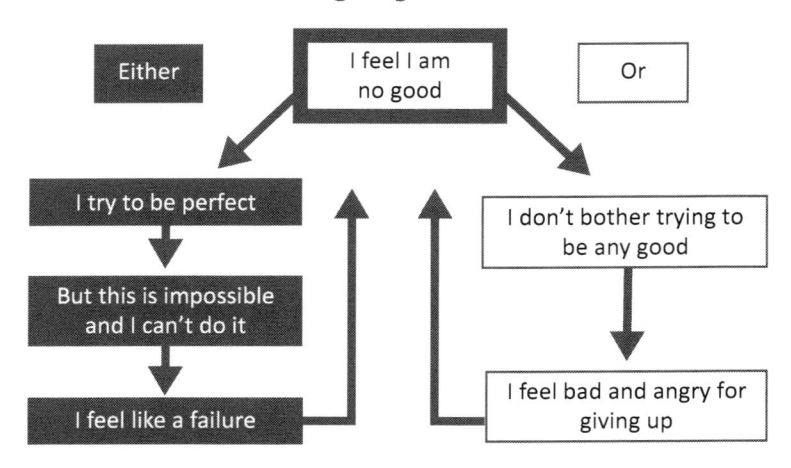

Either → I feel I am no good ← **Or**

- I try to be perfect
- But this is impossible and I can't do it
- I feel like a failure

- I don't bother trying to be any good
- I feel bad and angry for giving up

Yes / Sometimes / No

4: 'People telling me what to do' dilemma

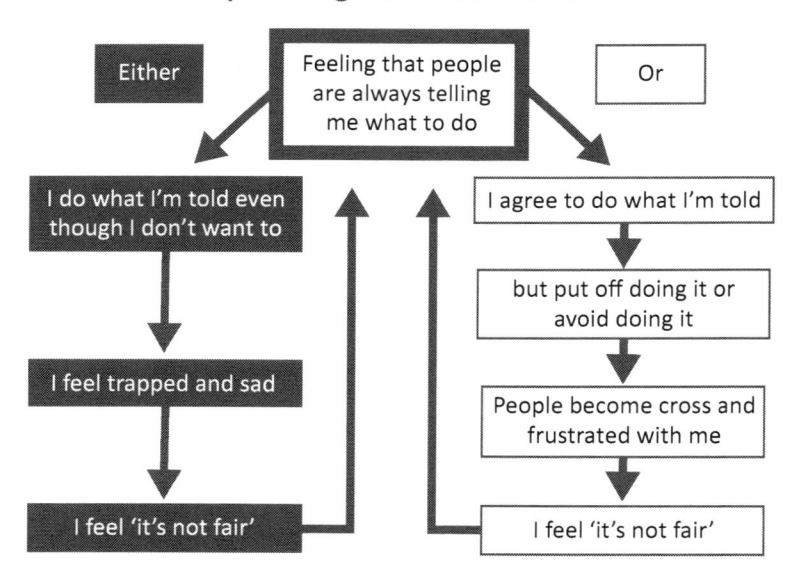

Either → Feeling that people are always telling me what to do ← **Or**

- I do what I'm told even though I don't want to
- I feel trapped and sad
- I feel 'it's not fair'

- I agree to do what I'm told
- but put off doing it or avoid doing it
- People become cross and frustrated with me
- I feel 'it's not fair'

Yes / Sometimes / No

5: 'People telling me what *not* to do' dilemma

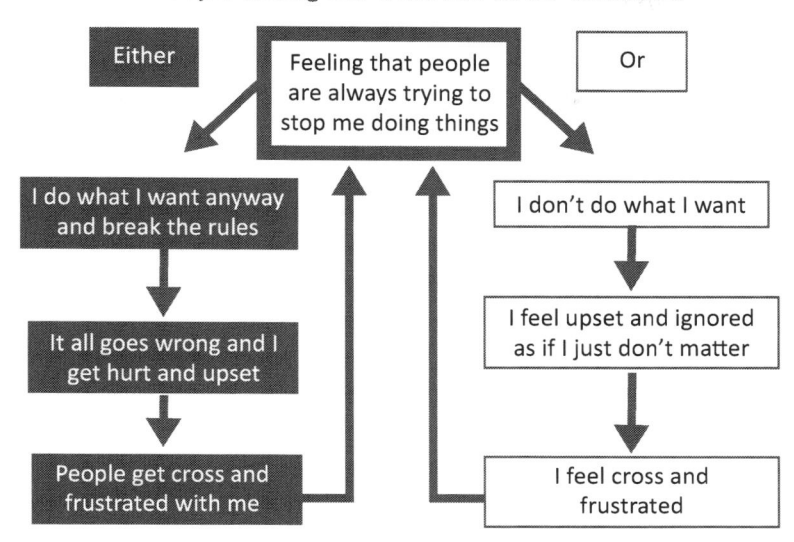

Either — Feeling that people are always trying to stop me doing things — **Or**

- I do what I want anyway and break the rules
  - It all goes wrong and I get hurt and upset
  - People get cross and frustrated with me

- I don't do what I want
  - I feel upset and ignored as if I just don't matter
  - I feel cross and frustrated

Yes / Sometimes / No

6: 'Responsibility' dilemma

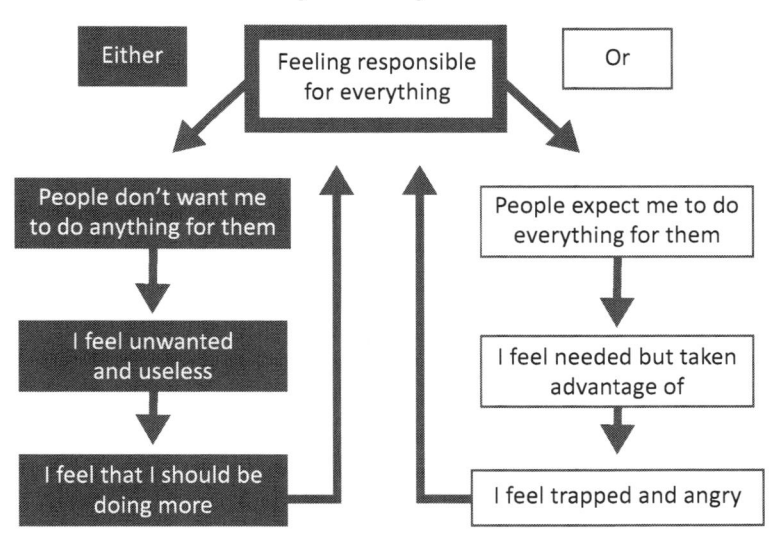

Either — Feeling responsible for everything — **Or**

- People don't want me to do anything for them
  - I feel unwanted and useless
  - I feel that I should be doing more

- People expect me to do everything for them
  - I feel needed but taken advantage of
  - I feel trapped and angry

Yes / Sometimes / No

7: 'Rebellion or sabotage' dilemma

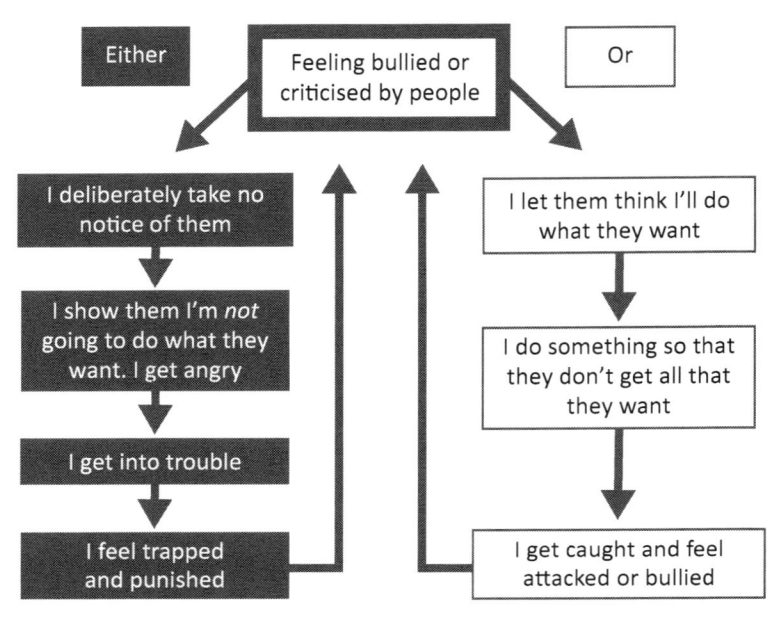

Either — Feeling bullied or criticised by people — **Or**

Either branch:
- I deliberately take no notice of them
- I show them I'm *not* going to do what they want. I get angry
- I get into trouble
- I feel trapped and punished

Or branch:
- I let them think I'll do what they want
- I do something so that they don't get all that they want
- I get caught and feel attacked or bullied

Yes / Sometimes / No

8: 'Looking after myself' dilemma

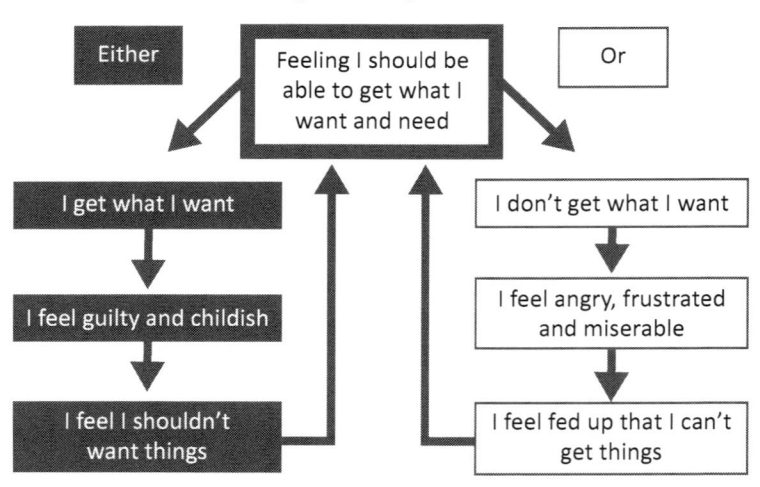

Either — Feeling I should be able to get what I want and need — **Or**

Either branch:
- I get what I want
- I feel guilty and childish
- I feel I shouldn't want things

Or branch:
- I don't get what I want
- I feel angry, frustrated and miserable
- I feel fed up that I can't get things

Yes / Sometimes / No

9: 'Anxious control' dilemma

Feeling anxious about what might happen

Either:
- I let things go, try not to worry
- I feel things are out of control and in a mess
- I feel more anxious

Or:
- I have to keep everything in perfect control
- I wear myself out trying to keep everything perfect
- This is impossible, so I feel more anxious

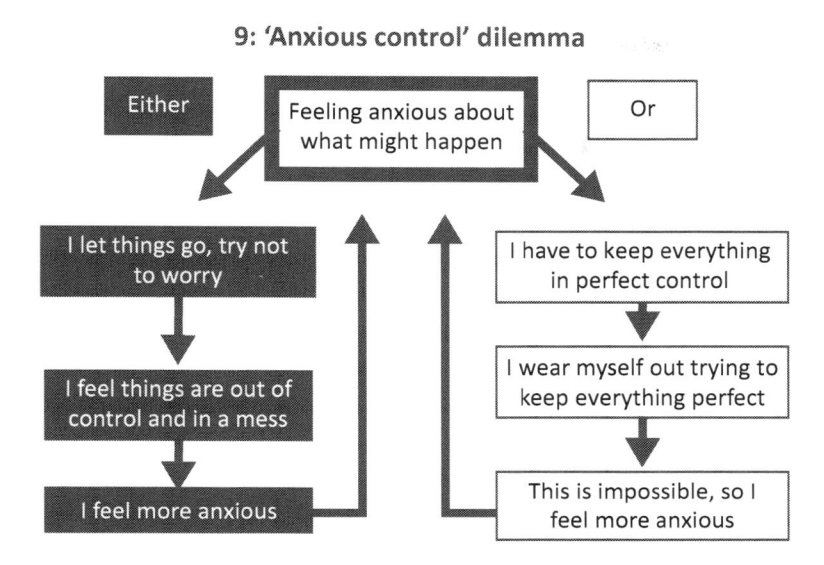

Yes / Sometimes / No

Second, in choices about how we behave with others:

1: 'Feeling unsure about relationships with people' dilemma

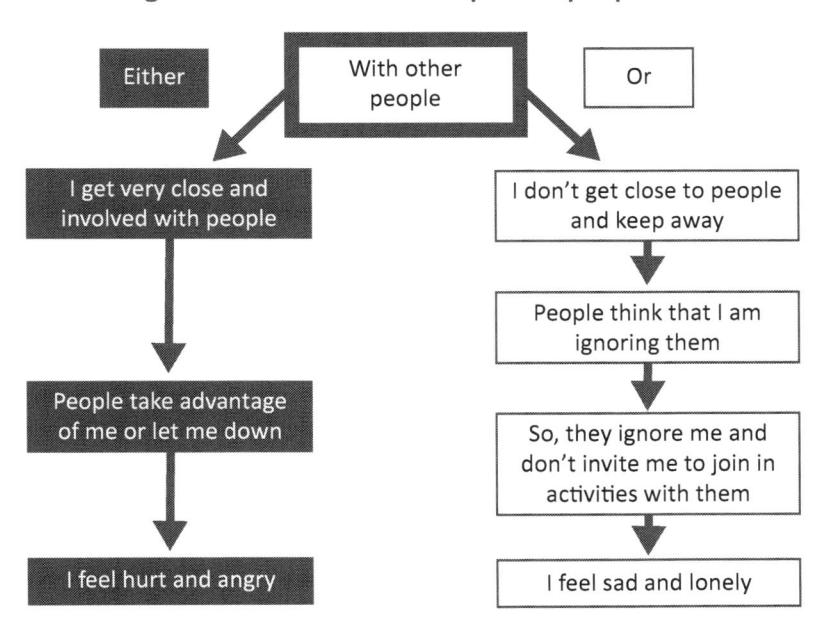

With other people

Either:
- I get very close and involved with people
- People take advantage of me or let me down
- I feel hurt and angry

Or:
- I don't get close to people and keep away
- People think that I am ignoring them
- So, they ignore me and don't invite me to join in activities with them
- I feel sad and lonely

Yes / Sometimes / No

2: 'Feeling unsure how to get what I want' dilemma

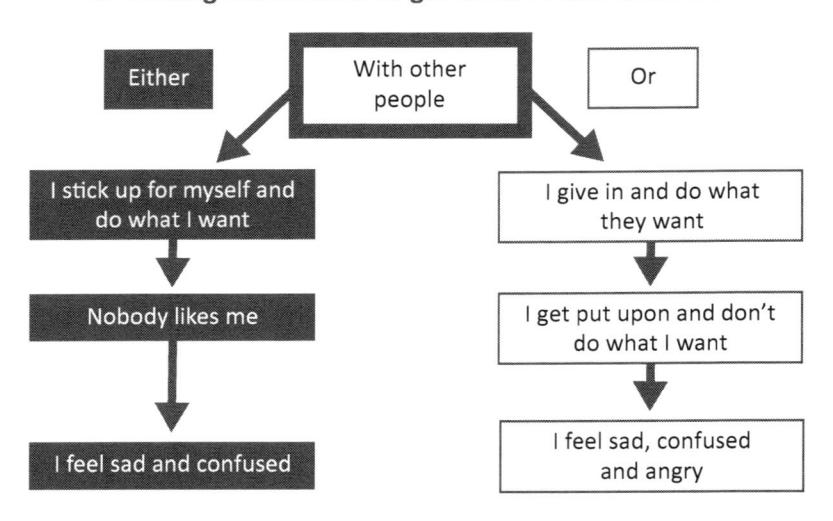

With other people

Either:
- I stick up for myself and do what I want
- Nobody likes me
- I feel sad and confused

Or:
- I give in and do what they want
- I get put upon and don't do what I want
- I feel sad, confused and angry

Yes / Sometimes / No

3: 'Dealing with others' dilemma

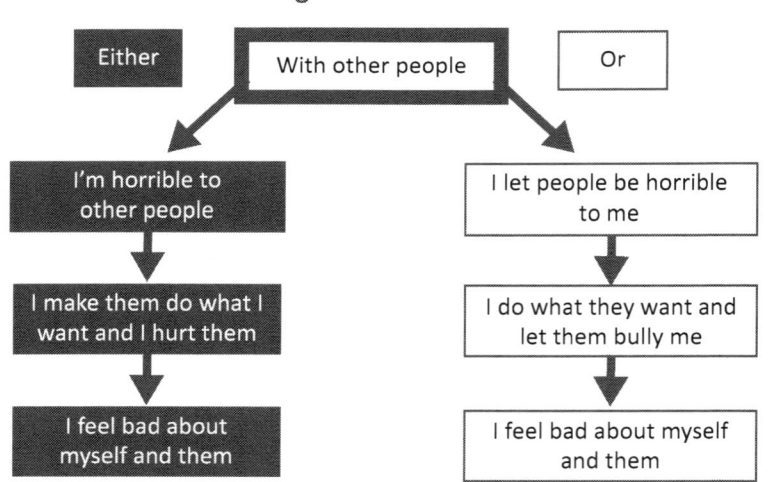

With other people

Either:
- I'm horrible to other people
- I make them do what I want and I hurt them
- I feel bad about myself and them

Or:
- I let people be horrible to me
- I do what they want and let them bully me
- I feel bad about myself and them

Yes / Sometimes / No

Appendix 3

4: 'Getting all I need or nothing I need' dilemma

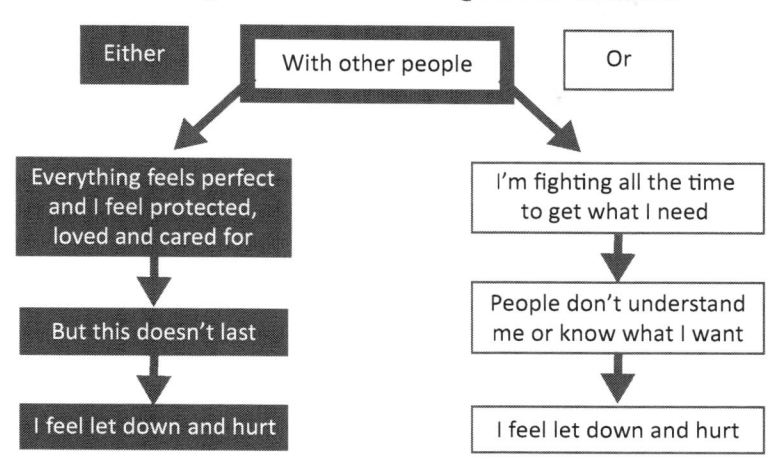

Either — With other people — **Or**

- Everything feels perfect and I feel protected, loved and cared for
  - But this doesn't last
  - I feel let down and hurt

- I'm fighting all the time to get what I need
  - People don't understand me or know what I want
  - I feel let down and hurt

Yes / Sometimes / No

5: 'Respecting people' dilemma

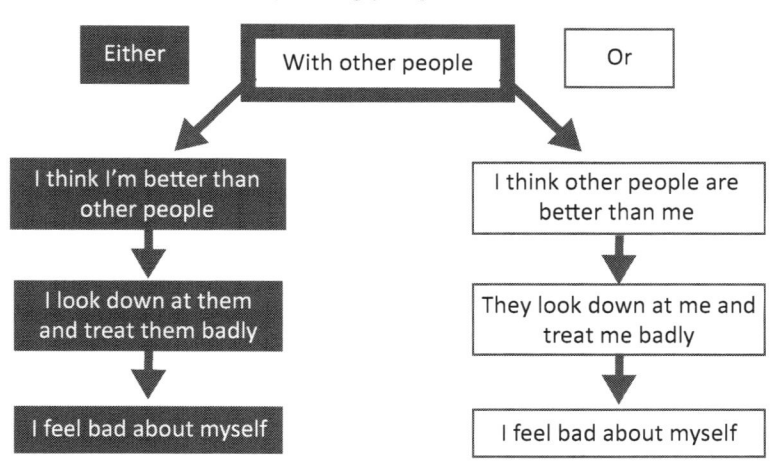

Either — With other people — **Or**

- I think I'm better than other people
  - I look down at them and treat them badly
  - I feel bad about myself

- I think other people are better than me
  - They look down at me and treat me badly
  - I feel bad about myself

Yes / Sometimes / No

6: 'If involved then taken over' dilemma

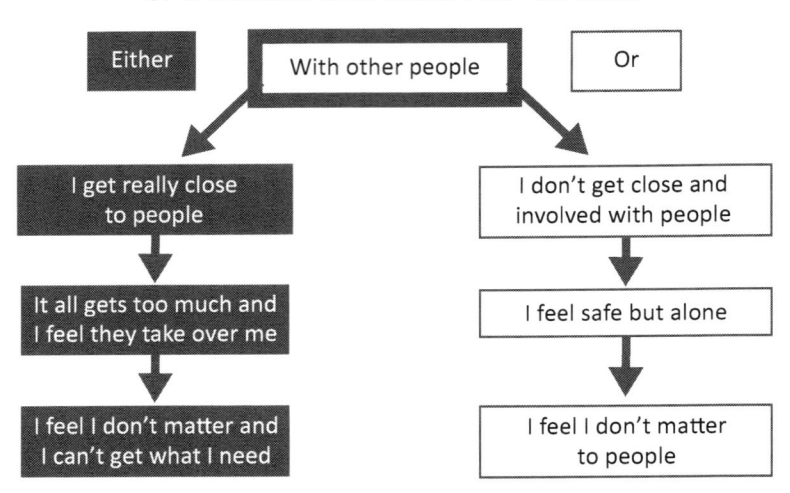

Either — With other people — **Or**

- I get really close to people
  - ↓
- It all gets too much and I feel they take over me
  - ↓
- I feel I don't matter and I can't get what I need

- I don't get close and involved with people
  - ↓
- I feel safe but alone
  - ↓
- I feel I don't matter to people

Yes / Sometimes / No

7: 'If involved then abused' dilemma

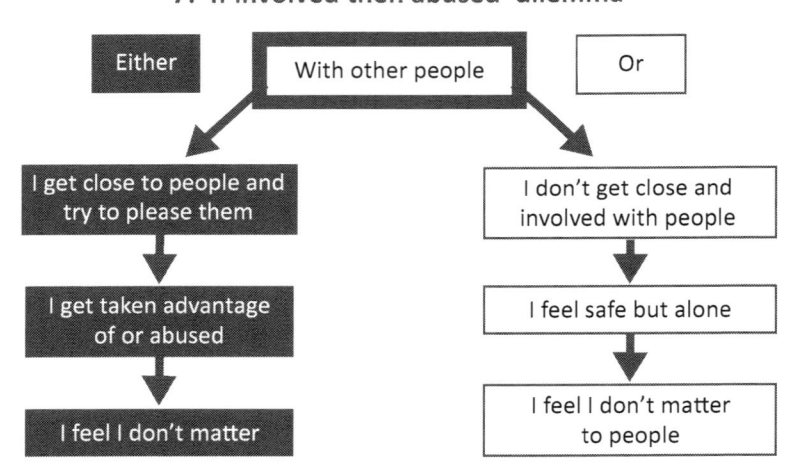

Either — With other people — **Or**

- I get close to people and try to please them
  - ↓
- I get taken advantage of or abused
  - ↓
- I feel I don't matter

- I don't get close and involved with people
  - ↓
- I feel safe but alone
  - ↓
- I feel I don't matter to people

Yes / Sometimes / No

The third type of patterns are called *snags*.

Snags are patterns that get in the way. They stop us doing things that we want to do and stop us making changes in our lives.

Do you have any of these patterns?

I want to...
but...

Appendix 4
Adapted Personality Structure Questionnaire[1]

This questionnaire is about different parts of your personality. Some people feel the same way about themselves most of the time, but other people can feel differently about themselves at different times.

Please tick the box that fits with the way you understand yourself.

I always feel the same				I don't always feel the same
☐ Definitely	☐ Sometimes	☐ Not sure	☐ Sometimes	☐ Definitely

The people I know all think of me in the same way				The people I know all think of me differently
☐ Definitely	☐ Sometimes	☐ Not sure	☐ Sometimes	☐ Definitely

I always think the same about myself				I get confused about who I am
☐ Definitely	☐ Sometimes	☐ Not sure	☐ Sometimes	☐ Definitely

I don't feel like two very different people				I am like two very different people
☐ Definitely	☐ Sometimes	☐ Not sure	☐ Sometimes	☐ Definitely

---

1 (Clayton *et al.* 2003, revised 2013, available at www.acat.me.uk)

My mood never changes suddenly				My mood changes suddenly and makes me feel out of control
☐ Definitely	☐ Sometimes	☐ Not sure	☐ Sometimes	☐ Definitely

I understand why my mood changes				I don't understand my mood changes
☐ Definitely	☐ Sometimes	☐ Not sure	☐ Sometimes	☐ Definitely

I never lose control				I lose control and harm myself/others
☐ Definitely	☐ Sometimes	☐ Not sure	☐ Sometimes	☐ Definitely

I never regret what I have said or done				I regret things I do and say
☐ Definitely	☐ Sometimes	☐ Not sure	☐ Sometimes	☐ Definitely

Thank you for completing the questionnaire.

Your answers will be kept private and confidential.

Appendix 5
'1:1 CAT Care Plan' with Nursing Staff

Rationale

To support the work [Name] is doing in Cognitive Analytic Therapy (with Dr Nicola Murphy) Nicola, [Name] and his Named Nurse have agreed that he will be asked the following in a 1:1 at least three times a week.

Have you got any issues (thoughts/worries/memories) about your family?

Have you felt rejected/disowned by anybody since your last 1:1?

Have you been thinking that 'nobody cares'/nobody loves you?

Appendix 5

Have you been feeling frightened, panicky, unsafe?

Have you been feeling angry?

Have you been feeling lonely/sad/hurt?

Have you 'kicked off' since your last 1:1?

Have you been staying in your room to avoid things?

....
....
....
....
....
....

Have you had a 'happy face'?

....
....
....
....
....
....

Have you been blaming yourself for anything?

....
....
....
....
....
....

Have you been worrying about your relationship with staff?

....
....
....
....
....
....

Appendix 6
The Helper's Dance List
A List of Typical Interactions that can Affect the Helping Relationship

All of us have roles in our lives that involve helping people. Mostly our help is okay but there are a number of unhelpful dances that we, as helpers, can do despite our best intentions. If we can notice them as they happen we have a chance to change. This list adds up to common patterns we have come across in teaching empathy and people skills using Cognitive Analytic Therapy for nurses, doctors, teachers, psychologists, social workers and many others. We call them dances to capture the whole interaction between people of feelings, behaviour and thinking summed up by the adage: 'it takes two to tango'. The list is not set in stone. First, just score your reactions quickly to all the items. Second, go through it again and change or add words to help each item fit your unique variety of experience. Not all the items will strike a chord with you. Add notes such as 'used to be true' or 'true when working at x'. Compare your results by talking them through compassionately with a colleague. Discuss things you might do differently. Keep in mind the rough and ready *one-third* idea that one-third of any dance is led by the person you are helping, one-third is led by you and one-third by the system, model or organisation in which you are embedded whilst helping.

Never good enough: I have high expectations of myself which makes me think my help won't be good enough, others will be disappointed and I will cope by trying even harder.

This could be me: (Please circle)

| not at all | rarely | sometimes | often | always |

When the person I am helping is too demanding: I feel put upon and suffer in silence but won't complain for fear of upsetting them and causing trouble.

This could be me: (Please circle)

| not at all | rarely | sometimes | often | always |

Genuine and vulnerable or safe but less real: Either a) I show feelings and feel genuine but somewhat vulnerable or b) I safely hide feelings, appear professional but less the real me.

This could be me: (Circle for a, underline for b)

| not at all | rarely | sometimes | often | always |

Either it's my way or the wrong way: If I think I am helping in the right way I can stick to it stubbornly and find it hard hearing it could be done another way.

This could be me: (Please circle)

| not at all | rarely | sometimes | often | always |

If at first I don't succeed: I will try and try again to help until I am defeated or successful.

This could be me: (Please circle)

| not at all | rarely | sometimes | often | always |

Lose perspective: I get so involved in the detail I forget the big picture.

This could be me: (Please circle)

| not at all | rarely | sometimes | often | always |

Let it be and wait and see: I am not sure what to do so I tend to let it be and wait and see.

This could be me: (Please circle)

| not at all | rarely | sometimes | often | always |

Silenced or silencing: Either a) I mostly listen quietly and find it hard to interrupt or b) I have lots to say and risk controlling the conversation too much.

This could be me: (Circle for a, underline for b)

not at all	rarely	sometimes	often	always

Tell me what to do: I feel so uncertain about how to help that I can rely too much on reassurance and guidance.

This could be me: (Please circle)

not at all	rarely	sometimes	often	always

Switch off: I can be upset by the suffering of those whom I help, and cope by switching off.

This could be me: (Please circle)

not at all	rarely	sometimes	often	always

Who's who? If I help too many people in a day, my feelings for and understanding of one person can get mixed up with my feelings for and understanding of another.

This could be me: (Please circle)

not at all	rarely	sometimes	often	always

Mostly a hero rarely a villain: When it is going well it is usually thanks to me but when it is not going well I tend to think it must be someone else's fault.

This could be me: (Please circle)

not at all	rarely	sometimes	often	always

Jump in or hold back: Either a) I am in at the deep end as a helper and tend to give my all or b) I am not so involved and hold back, miss the moment to help or watch on from the sidelines.

This could be me: (Circle for a, underline for b)

not at all	rarely	sometimes	often	always

My hands are tied: With a freer hand I could be more helpful but I must follow the rules.

This could be me: (Please circle)

| not at all | rarely | sometimes | often | always |

If I don't help no one will: Other people won't see the need, or have the knowhow to help so it is left up to me to provide the care that someone needs.

This could be me: (Please circle)

| not at all | rarely | sometimes | often | always |

Involved, busy and needed or at a loose end and bored: If I am not busy helping people all the time I can be at a loss to know what to do with myself, feel bored and/or not needed so it's best to keep busy!

This could be me: (Please circle)

| not at all | rarely | sometimes | often | always |

Lack of resources frustrates me: I know what needs doing and how to help but often the money, the treatment or support is not available and I feel frustrated, angry or helpless.

This could be me: (Please circle)

| not at all | rarely | sometimes | often | always |

Looking after others means neglecting myself: I put so much into looking after others that their needs take over and I forget to look after myself enough and am at risk of stress.

This could be me: (Please circle)

| not at all | rarely | sometimes | often | always |

Not here, not now: I see the need to talk about what is happening between us but find it unpredictable or embarrassing and tend to wait and miss the moment to name it.

This could be me: (Please circle)

| not at all | rarely | sometimes | often | always |

Where were we? I can get so involved in sorting out the relationship I forget the reason for meeting.

This could be me: (Please circle)

| not at all | rarely | sometimes | often | always |

Steve Potter © The Helper's Dance List
stevegpotter@gmail.com

Appendix 7
Sequential Diagrammatic Reformulation

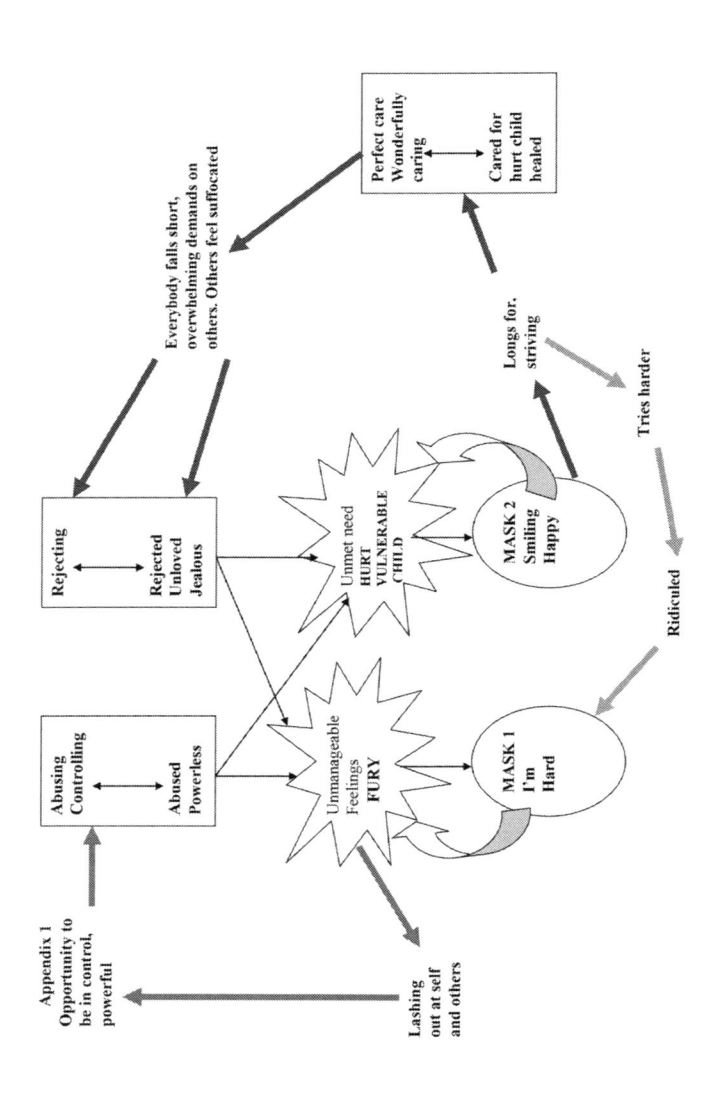

Appendix 8
Reformulation Letter

Dear Jane,

Here is the letter that we discussed last week. It is my attempt to make sense of your life now in relation to the past. We will have an opportunity to look at it, and together we can think about it and make any changes if you would like to do so.

Over the past few weeks you have told me about yourself and how you feel some of the events that happened when you were a child seem to have affected you. The story you tell of your life both within and outside the family is one of abuse, neglect and cruelty. I listened to you tell me about the abuse you experienced not only from your father, but from relationships with other men in your life. This has left you feeling abused and used, but also guilty and very very angry. Although you focus on this abuse as the reason for your 'problems' I am left with a lasting impression of the pain you felt and still feel around your thoughts that your mum never loved you. You described your mum as unloving; she gave you nothing yet blamed you for everything.

Life was difficult from an early age; you had eight siblings which made it difficult to get any attention from your mum. You tried really hard to please her, to make her love you but when this did not happen, you became very jealous and angry and would end up being what you describe as naughty. Because of this behaviour you began to blame yourself for your mum's inability to love you, thinking of yourself as the naughty little girl who nobody loved. You still see yourself as 'bad' and jealous and struggle to find anything about yourself that is 'good'. You feel that this is how everybody else sees you.

As you moved into adult life you entered into several abusive relationships with men and said that you felt you had 'abuse me' written across your forehead. These relationships kept you feeling angry around men. You eventually took this anger out on your last boyfriend J and you told me about the violent attack against him, recognising that all the rage you had inside you due to the repeated abuse was taken out on him. You still carry this rage, and it is difficult not to think about J and the revenge you would like to take on him.

Throughout your life you have been looking for somebody to care for you, somebody to love you for who you are. You talked to me about Mrs B who you said was a lovely lady, she told you that you were a beautiful girl who should have lots of love, yet I was left with the feeling that she too let you down as she never took you away from your terrible life.

The feelings that you cannot have anything good can perhaps explain in some way the incident with your neighbour. You liked her yet you set fire to her flat. Her flat was lovely, you longed for your flat to be the same, but it wasn't, you said it was dirty and horrible, you had no nice things. You told me you felt very jealous of what your neighbour had and it was as though the little girl inside you was saying if I can't have it, neither can she. You understand these feelings and have said how sad and guilty you now feel about the incident.

During these first few weeks of therapy, you have focused on events with J and your neighbour, lingering in the past, perhaps finding it difficult to think about the here and now, and even more so the future as maybe it continues to feel quite hopeless. However in the last session we were able to look at some of the unhelpful patterns that have developed over your life that have helped you cope. We were able to see that sometimes staff can feel like the abusing, controlling and rejecting parent and you find yourself repeating these patterns with others in an attempt to protect yourself.

Here are the patterns that we have discussed.

- When I feel others are rejecting me, I feel unloved and vulnerable; I put on my *happy, smiling mask* and try to please them. I expect in return to be cared for, when this doesn't happen I try harder but others feel overwhelmed and suffocated and end up rejecting me.
- When I feel others are controlling/abusing me, I feel powerless and have a burning fury inside. I put on my *I am hard mask* lashing out at others. I feel powerful and in control but end up abusing others.

Hopefully the task then will be to sit with and think about your story, to create some space for the feelings that you have been left with and to look at the sadness behind the rage. It seems as though all these difficult feelings that you have had throughout your life have been focused on J and your neighbour as if they are representing all the pain and anger you have experienced. We need to try to find a way of helping you stay with the pain without going into a fury, to learn to face it and hold it. Also I feel it is important for you to start to think about yourself, to learn to care for yourself and to begin to accept the good bits others give to you without needing to seek the 'perfect care'.

There may be times during therapy that you will feel angry and disappointed with me. When we last met there was a feeling that I took control of the session and it is possible that you may have experienced me as controlling. You have worked very hard between sessions and perhaps are trying hard to please me maybe fearing rejection. We must be aware of these issues and watch for the patterns being repeated in therapy in order that we can explore them further.

I look forward to the rest of our work together.

Regards,

Michelle

Appendix 9
Goodbye Letter

Dear Jane,

Here is the letter that we talked about last time we met; it is a way of pulling together all the things we have discussed now we are at the end of therapy.

You have already told me that you are feeling sad and anxious at the thought of losing somebody whom you feel you now trust, and you have felt yourself slipping into some of your old, unhelpful patterns of coping. I hope this letter will help you to see the progress you have made during your time in therapy, and at the same time encourage you to continue to develop in your own way.

When you first came to therapy earlier this year, you had so many issues that you needed to talk about that it felt as though we were both overwhelmed. Through your letter writing and poetry, you tried to show me the pain you had experienced in your life. You described the anger and rage at the people who had abused you both in childhood and as an adult. These angry feelings were so intense at the beginning that it was a struggle for us to decide how therapy could best help you, and it was as though the letters and poems were stopping us from understanding the deeper issues. It seemed the only feeling you would allow yourself was anger, anything else was perhaps too dangerous. It was with the introduction of the diagram that the therapy began to change. It was as though the diagram helped contain both of us, and helped us focus.

Although you told me you only felt anger, over time we were able to begin to explore some of the pain behind these angry feelings. You recognised that you have different ways of feeling, you called them your hard mask and smiling happy mask and felt that neither of these were the 'real you', but ways of being that had developed over the years to cope and protect yourself. It became clear that all the years of abuse and rejection had left you feeling hurt and vulnerable, and that most of the time you were trying desperately hard to find somebody to care for you, the 'perfect carer'.

Unfortunately this can never be achieved, and you described the little girl inside who wants more and more, who can never get enough. As a little girl you were rejected and seriously neglected by your mother whom you feel never loved you. This pattern of wanting and demanding more but never getting it seems to have been repeated with the staff on the ward, and at times made relationships with them difficult.

In therapy you have been working really hard at trying to find ways out of these patterns, different ways of coping and feeling that are more acceptable for both yourself and others.

You have begun to understand the importance of caring for yourself, of being in control of your own life and how you feel about yourself. You have worked hard with the staff and your sister at recognising when you have been given enough, to feel content with what others give and to try to respect their needs. You said in one session 'the way I am with others affects the way they are with me' this felt like a very important idea to understand and keep hold of.

The last few sessions have been quite difficult, you have begun to accept that there will not be somebody out there to give you 'perfect care' and that makes you feel very scared but at the same time quite excited at the prospect of independence. For a time perhaps you saw me as the wonderfully caring person, but again this could not be kept up and there were times when I let you down and disappointed you. You did think about ending the sessions, but came back and spoke to me about how it felt to be let down by me.

As the end of therapy came closer, we were able to talk about the sadness you were feeling. You were able to cry not only for the loss you would feel at the ending of the sessions, but also for the loss of your brother who died and whom you have never grieved for, and most importantly for the loss of your own life which you felt had been so damaged and wasted.

I feel you have come a long way in therapy, this is perhaps more difficult for you to see, as you do still return to your old ways of coping when things get very difficult. However you do agree that these times are less frequent, and for shorter periods of time. I hope that through this therapy you can continue to allow yourself some of the more painful feelings of loss and grief, which are so important. You have begun to take some steps to change your life and your relationships with others, and although it is not easy, I hope there is much left in your life to work on and look forward to.

I have really enjoyed working with you and look forward to our follow-up session where we can continue to discuss the progress you have made.

Regards,

Michelle

Appendix 10
Sequential Diagrammatic Reformulation

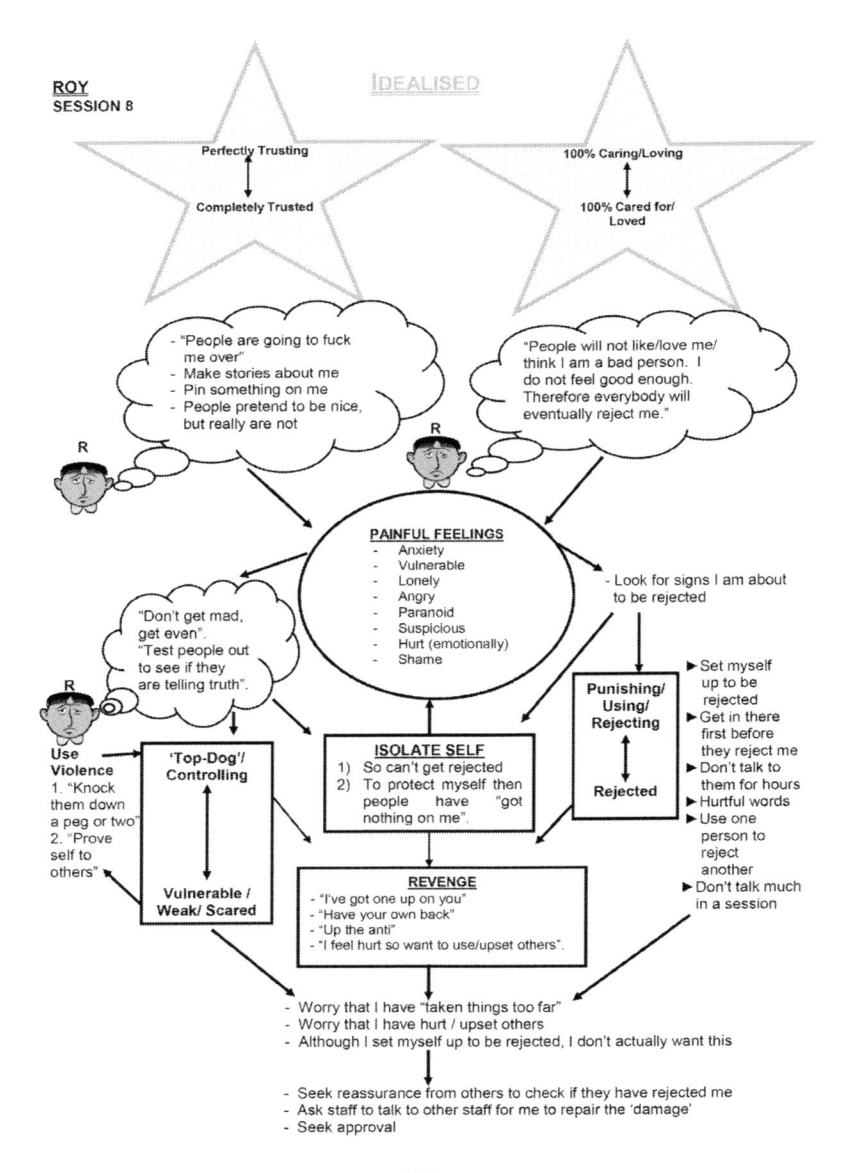

ROY
SESSION 8

IDEALISED

Perfectly Trusting ↕ Completely Trusted

100% Caring/Loving ↕ 100% Cared for/ Loved

Thought (R):
- "People are going to fuck me over"
- Make stories about me
- Pin something on me
- People pretend to be nice, but really are not

Thought (R):
"People will not like/love me/ think I am a bad person. I do not feel good enough. Therefore everybody will eventually reject me."

PAINFUL FEELINGS
- Anxiety
- Vulnerable
- Lonely
- Angry
- Paranoid
- Suspicious
- Hurt (emotionally)
- Shame

- Look for signs I am about to be rejected

Thought (R):
"Don't get mad, get even".
"Test people out to see if they are telling truth".

Punishing/ Using/ Rejecting ↔ **Rejected**

▶ Set myself up to be rejected
▶ Get in there first before they reject me
▶ Don't talk to them for hours
▶ Hurtful words
▶ Use one person to reject another
▶ Don't talk much in a session

Use Violence
1. "Knock them down a peg or two"
2. "Prove self to others"

'Top-Dog'/ Controlling ↕ **Vulnerable / Weak/ Scared**

ISOLATE SELF
1) So can't get rejected
2) To protect myself then people have "got nothing on me".

REVENGE
- "I've got one up on you"
- "Have your own back"
- "Up the anti"
- "I feel hurt so want to use/upset others".

- Worry that I have "taken things too far"
- Worry that I have hurt / upset others
- Although I set myself up to be rejected, I don't actually want this

- Seek reassurance from others to check if they have rejected me
- Ask staff to talk to other staff for me to repair the 'damage'
- Seek approval

Appendix 11
Sequential Diagrammatic Reformulation with Exits

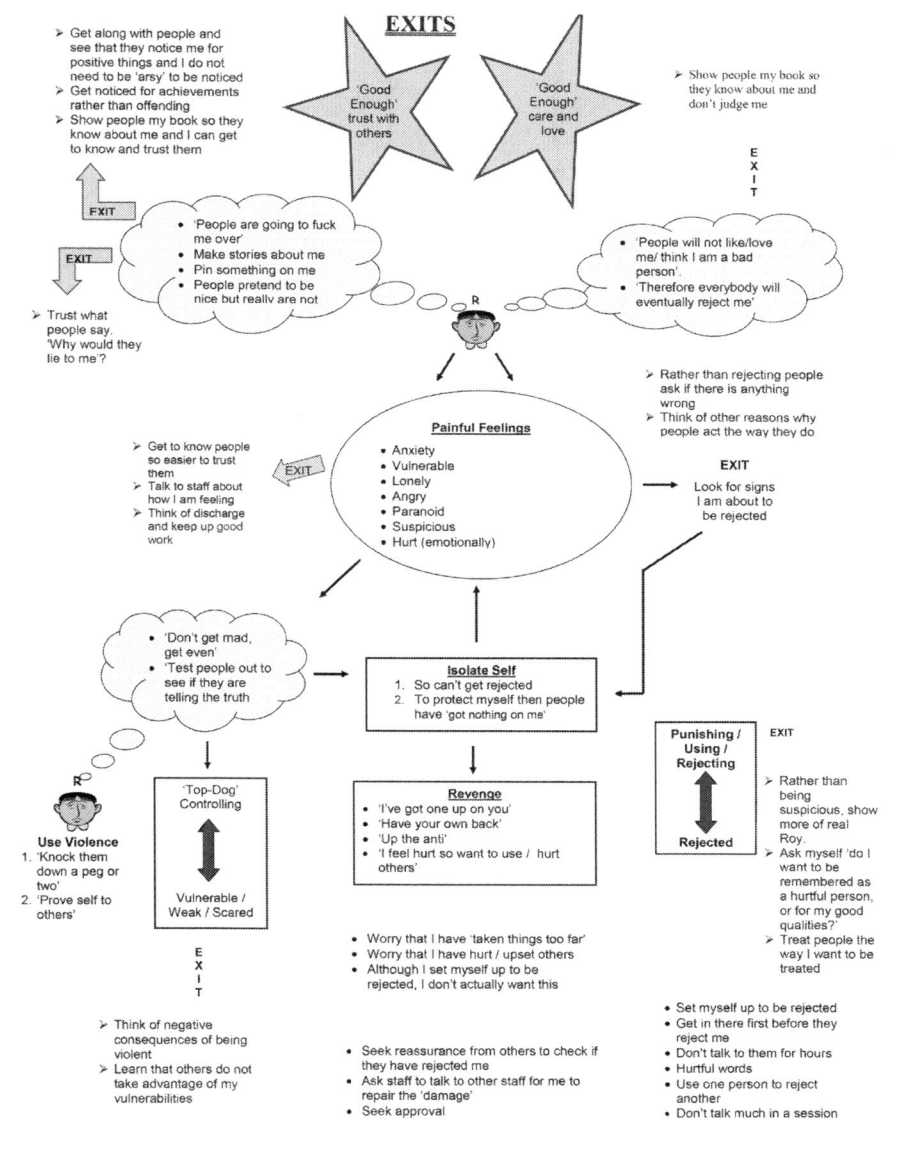

EXITS

- 'Good Enough' trust with others
- 'Good Enough' care and love

- Get along with people and see that they notice me for positive things and I do not need to be 'arsy' to be noticed
- Get noticed for achievements rather than offending
- Show people my book so they know about me and I can get to know and trust them

EXIT

EXIT

- Show people my book so they know about me and don't judge me

EXIT

- Trust what people say. 'Why would they lie to me'?

Thought cloud:
- 'People are going to fuck me over'
- Make stories about me
- Pin something on me
- People pretend to be nice but really are not

Thought cloud:
- 'People will not like/love me/ think I am a bad person'.
- 'Therefore everybody will eventually reject me'

- Rather than rejecting people ask if there is anything wrong
- Think of other reasons why people act the way they do

EXIT

- Get to know people so easier to trust them
- Talk to staff about how I am feeling
- Think of discharge and keep up good work

EXIT

Painful Feelings
- Anxiety
- Vulnerable
- Lonely
- Angry
- Paranoid
- Suspicious
- Hurt (emotionally)

EXIT
Look for signs I am about to be rejected

Thought cloud:
- 'Don't get mad, get even'
- 'Test people out to see if they are telling the truth'

Isolate Self
1. So can't get rejected
2. To protect myself then people have 'got nothing on me'

Punishing / Using / Rejecting ↕ **Rejected**

EXIT
- Rather than being suspicious, show more of real Roy.
- Ask myself 'do I want to be remembered as a hurtful person, or for my good qualities?'
- Treat people the way I want to be treated

Use Violence
1. 'Knock them down a peg or two'
2. 'Prove self to others'

'Top-Dog' Controlling
↕
Vulnerable / Weak / Scared

Revenge
- 'I've got one up on you'
- 'Have your own back'
- 'Up the anti'
- 'I feel hurt so want to use / hurt others'

EXIT

- Think of negative consequences of being violent
- Learn that others do not take advantage of my vulnerabilities

- Worry that I have 'taken things too far'
- Worry that I have hurt / upset others
- Although I set myself up to be rejected, I don't actually want this

- Seek reassurance from others to check if they have rejected me
- Ask staff to talk to other staff for me to repair the 'damage'
- Seek approval

- Set myself up to be rejected
- Get in there first before they reject me
- Don't talk to them for hours
- Hurtful words
- Use one person to reject another
- Don't talk much in a session

Appendix 12
Reformulation Letter

Dear Jack,

This letter is to sum up the important areas that we have discussed so far and to think about how the therapy might progress. At the end of the letter the target problem that we have discussed is named.

We have talked about your family and about memories you have of growing up. You have said how important your brother is to you and described him as the most important person in your life. You told me about the times that your brother stuck up for you when you were being bullied or abused. You have told me that you would like to play the part of the older brother to your younger brother and that you would like to achieve things, like he does. We have talked together about what it was like being bullied or abused by others and we have begun to think about what it might be like to be the bully or powerful person doing the bullying.

(Powerful and bullying to crushed and abused)

We have talked together about how important your parents are to you and you have talked about often being in the position of trying to please them. You have told me that you find it difficult to stand up to your parents and that you often bottle up your own feelings and ignore your own needs. You have said that your dad told you to 'get a life' and that you sometimes cry at night thinking about how you hurt your parents. I imagine that you might feel that you are often disappointing other people, and that you might feel disappointed by other people at times.

(Disappointing to disappointed and let down)

You stated that you attended a special school up until the age of 11, when you then moved into a mainstream school with disabled and able-bodied pupils. You told me that a lot of your difficulties began around the age of 11. I imagine that this change was difficult to adjust to and that it presented lots of challenges for you at that time.

We have often talked about your low mood and your thoughts about ending your life; you have suggested that it would be better for others if you were no longer around. You have told me about wanting to drink yourself to death and have described how you have previously misused alcohol when you were feeling low. You have said that you sometimes wish that you could die in your sleep. I wonder if bottling up your feelings leads to you feeling low and depressed. It seems that your feeling low is connected with your worry that your powerful thoughts might become stronger.

We have talked together about how health difficulties have also caused you distress from an early age and that you have been a frequent visitor to hospital. However, you have also described yourself as a 'tough nut to crack' and as being a 'fighter', which will be great qualities for you to draw on in the remainder of the therapy and into the future.

A difficulty that you have had for many years involves coping with certain kinds of women, who appear attractive or powerful. This difficulty restricts your life significantly and affects where you can go and what you can do.

I wonder if some of the difficult feelings that we have talked about might arise in the course of therapy; you might feel that you are disappointing me or you might feel disappointed in me at different times, or you might feel that I am being abusive or powerful in response to being disappointed in you; you might also try to please me by being a 'good patient' rather than being honest or saying what you really feel. Jack, I look forward to us continuing the work that we have begun and working together to address the target problem that we have identified below.

Best wishes,

Perry

Appendix 13
Sequential Diagrammatic Reformulation

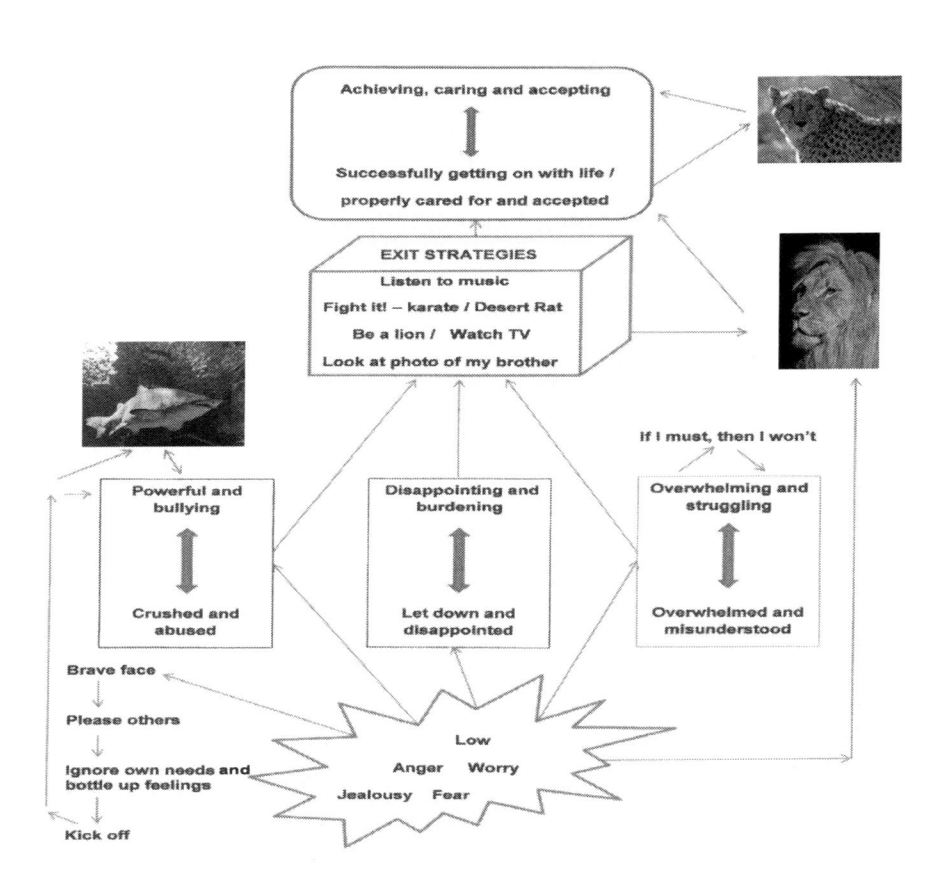

Achieving, caring and accepting ⇕ **Successfully getting on with life / properly cared for and accepted**

EXIT STRATEGIES
- Listen to music
- Fight it! – karate / Desert Rat
- Be a lion / Watch TV
- Look at photo of my brother

Powerful and bullying ⇕ **Crushed and abused**

Disappointing and burdening ⇕ **Let down and disappointed**

Overwhelming and struggling ⇕ **Overwhelmed and misunderstood**

if I must, then I won't

- Brave face
- Please others
- Ignore own needs and bottle up feelings
- Kick off

Low, Anger, Worry, Jealousy, Fear

290

Glossary

Acquiescence: A way of relating that is characterised by submission and/or quiet assent.

Activity theory: An umbrella term for a line of eclectic social sciences theories and research with its roots in Soviet psychological theory. It focuses on what a person does to achieve their goals and accounts for the culture and environmental influences they deal with in their real-life activity. From a CAT perspective it also involves mapping and Reformulation, using signs to introduce clients to new ways of ordering, controlling and representing.

Analytic (psychoanalytic, psychodynamic): Psychological theories, originating from Freud and Jung, defining how personality is developed and organised, particularly around sex and aggression. These are seen as drives that are often 'unconscious' (i.e., the person is unaware of them), so the aim of psychoanalysis is to help the 'patient' to become more aware. From a CAT perspective, see 'object relations' section. The main pioneer of psychoanalytic work with people with intellectual disabilities is Valerie Sinason.

Attachment theory: This describes how the parents' relationship with the child influences development. As a result, adults may have predominantly secure or insecure attachment styles (and insecure attachments are also divided into preoccupied, avoidant and disorganised styles). From a CAT perspective, these attachment styles are refined into a description of reciprocal roles. Many people with intellectual disabilities experience disrupted and chaotic attachments, especially those living in residential or supported living arrangements.

Attunement: Early connectedness with a mother or caregiver, considered to be the template for empathic understanding in later life.

Autism (Autistic Spectrum Disorder): A neurological lifelong disorder in which people have impaired social interactions, poor communication skills and difficulty in appreciating other people's perspectives, and engage in restricted and repetitive behaviours. Autism is on a continuum, with some people far more severely affected than others. Although some people with autism do not have other deficits, it is often found alongside generic intellectual disability. From a CAT perspective, the approach is around helping the system of support to be in dialogue.

Bakhtinian: Ideas from philosopher and literary critic Mikhail Bakhtin (1895–1975) in which he views the human psyche as involving three components; 'I-for-myself', 'I-for-the-other' and 'other-for-me'. This positions people as always in relationship and these relationships involve multiple, simultaneous voices addressed to multiple others. These ideas, central to CAT, are called 'Dialogism', and are illustrated in how working together with people with intellectual disabilities occurs through opening up the space for communication.

Behavioural phenotype: This denotes typical relational and personality characteristics that are associated with various genetic conditions; such as people with autism being typically aloof or people with Down's Syndrome being typically friendly and rigid.

Behaviourism (learning theory): Originating from the work of Pavlov (1849–1936), this approach seeks to understand what promotes learning. By understanding the link between a stimulus (doing to) and response (done to), behaviourism offers a productive method of skills teaching. This enabling skills development approach has transformed the lives of many people with intellectual disabilities through its understanding of how learning can take place. In CAT, new skills are more easily learnt and developed by combining learning theory with a relational approach (also described in 'doing to' and 'done to' terms i.e., reciprocal roles), to enable clients to develop healthier procedures.

Best interest decisions: The Mental Capacity Act (MCA) states that if a person lacks mental capacity to make a particular decision then whoever is making that decision or taking any action on that person's behalf must do this in the person's best interests.

Borderline Personality Disorder: This describes someone who has unstable and extreme emotions and who flits from one extreme mental state to another. The term 'borderline' originated from clinicians who wondered whether such people were on the borders between being 'neurotic' (i.e., worried) or 'psychotic' (outside reality). CAT sees borderline personality disorder as a response to trauma and as a continuum that people move along according to their level of stress.

Bottom end of a reciprocal role: Using Kelly's ideas from Personal Constructs, relationships are described as having two poles ('It takes two to tango'). The bottom end is the done to, impacted on, child position or response.

Boundaries: An idea used in much psychotherapy to describe the contact boundary between either the therapist and the client, or the system and the therapist, or the system and the client. Different therapeutic schools have different views about where they draw this boundary and what constitutes a brick wall or a safe, contained space. In intellectual disability services, thinking about boundaries often involves promoting inclusion against society's tendency to seek exclusion.

Central coherence: A cognitive function in which people are able to put separate sensations together into a big picture i.e., the ability to see the forest as a whole and not just individual leaves. A deficit in central coherence may be a developmental delay, a neurological problem (as in autism) or a response to trauma. A surfeit in central coherence is often a feature found in psychosis.

Challenging behaviour: Behaviour that is 'challenging when it is of such an intensity, frequency or duration as to threaten the quality of life and/or physical safety of the individual or others and is likely to lead to responses that are restrictive, aversive or result in exclusion' (Royal College of Psychiatrists 2007).

Cognitive: Thoughts, language, memory, attention and sensory perception.

Cognitive behavioural therapy (CBT): Problems are seen as being caused by dysfunctional attributional bias that results in self-defeating paradigms. Although CBT can be useful for people with a mild intellectual disability, clients often struggle with differentiating between feelings, thoughts and behaviours; concepts that are necessary to be able to deal with attributional biases. Owing to this, CBT for people with intellectual disabilities concentrates more on cognitive deficits than cognitive distortions.

Communal intelligence: This derives from the core network of intimate relations into which we are born and through which we feel our way to memory and identity. It is the source of strength and quality of our attachment experience; the ways we are validated, held and embedded.

Contextual reformulation: A letter and/or map describing the parallel process going on between staff and organisations in relation to their client.

Counter-transference: The feelings induced in the therapist by their clients; this may come from the easily mobilised Reciprocal Role Procedures of the therapist or from the client's material. The therapist may identify with the client's feelings or be reciprocating to them. For example, if the client is feeling blamed, the therapist may also feel blamed (identifying) or may be blaming (reciprocating towards) the client.

Cross modal sensory correspondence: How the brain knows which stimuli to combine into a single perception. This ability is required to achieve a level of central coherence and from a CAT perspective, in order to perceive reciprocal roles.

Dialogic: An understanding that because 'the self' is always in relation; either to others, wider culture or another part of ourselves, we are a multiplicity of selves and there are many meanings that may or may not be held in dialogue.

Dialogism: The dialogic approach, which in CAT often refers to the approach emphasised by Bakhtin.

Dilemma: A problem procedure in which people are stuck because the number of choices and options are restricted and none of them solves the problem.

Emotional intelligence: The ability to recognise, express and negotiate emotional meaning. It is our entry into participating in and understanding the world. We feel our way into our world. Sometimes this emotional negotiation is seamless, but often it is through tear and repair of the relational fabric around in our community.

Enactment: How the expectations people develop from their early relationships are repeated in ongoing relationships. In CAT, the therapist seeks to respond to enactments by developing a healthier and healing relationship, as well as using relational maps (SDR) to describe the roles that are happening.

Executive functioning: This concept describes an instrumental, intentional, calculating or prefigured sense of purpose and self. It is the ability to know: this is what I need or want and here is a way of going about it that might work.

Functional analysis: This describes the relationship between stimuli and response. It is a behavioural approach used to determine the reason, purpose or motivation behind behaviour. Conducting a functional analysis requires painstaking collecting of data from close environmental observations in order to understand why something is happening that a person cannot describe. It often involves doing momentary time sampling.

Helper's Dance List: A list developed by Steve Potter that describes common relational patterns helpers get into.

Holding environment: The concept of the therapist recreating that which resembles the mother/infant 'dialogue'.

Humanistic: An authentic and collaborative approach to psychotherapy that focuses on healing occurring through warm, genuine and positive therapeutic relationships.

Internalising: The process in which what is learned through interpersonal experience becomes an aspect of the self; a part of the internal dialogue.

Intersubjective: The idea that we are inherently social beings with shared meanings, in contrast with the idea that it is natural to exist as isolated individuals.

Mapping (SDR): The CAT tool of drawing relational patterns. These maps can use words or pictures and describe the routes taken as people move from one position or set of reciprocal roles to another. They are used in CAT to help us know where we are.

Mental Capacity Act (2005): This act seeks to balance the rights of an individual to self-determination and the responsibilities of those around them to step in when people are not able to make decisions for themselves.

Mental Health Act (1983): This act covers the reception, care and treatment of mentally disordered people and the management of their property and other related matters, particularly their detention in hospital or police custody against their wishes.

Narcissistic Personality Disorder: When someone is excessively preoccupied with issues of personal adequacy, power, prestige and vanity. In CAT terms they often seek admiration because, underneath this, they dread contempt. All of us have a healthy narcissistic side; in CAT narcissism is placed on a continuum and becomes a disorder when it is too extreme and egocentrically restricting.

Object relations theory: How we internalise our relationships with other people.

Offence parallel behaviour: Any form of offence-related behavioural (or fantasised behaviour) pattern that emerges at any point before or after an offence.

Other-to-self reciprocal role enactment: How we invite other people to relate towards ourselves in a way consistent with our main reciprocal roles.

Parallel process: How systems, such as the supervisor and therapist, or the community or hospital team, repeat the typical relational patterns that are occurring between the client and therapist. In intellectual disability services, referrals often describe processes that parallel the client's wider life and services can get unwittingly caught up in repeating these patterns.

Personality Disorder: An overall description, which is sub-divided into various categories, of the relational characteristics found in people who are hard to help and often difficult to get along with. People show enduring behaviours and mental traits that appear to deviate from social expectations about relating to other humans and may also experience difficulties with feelings, thoughts, behaviours and controlling their impulses. CAT was developed in the NHS to work with people like this who are hard to help.

Personality structure questionnaire (PSQ): A tool used to help in the identification of switches in mood and states of mind.

Person-centred plan: Approaches designed to assist someone to plan their life and supports to increase their personal self-determination and improve their independence.

Potential space: Where the mother creates an opportunity for the infant/child to play, both in the context of fantasy and reality and enabling playful creative thinking and relating.

Pragmatic solution focused: A realistic and sensible approach about finding solutions to problems. These solutions will not be perfect nor involve insight; they will be practical, creative and useful.

Procedural sequence model: A model describing the idea that reciprocal roles are enacted via a sequence of feelings, thoughts and behaviours.

Procedural sequence object relations model: This refines the procedural sequence model to say that procedures express reciprocal roles that developed out of relationships with other people.

Procedure: The feelings, thoughts and behaviours that are reciprocal roles in action.

Projection: An idea developed in psychoanalysis of how we confuse ourselves with others, resulting in attributing something to others that really comes from ourselves. From a CAT perspective, we are mixing up which pole of the reciprocal role we are – thinking we are in the bottom pole when we are in the top.

Projective identification: In CAT, this originally Kleinian concept (psychoanalytic) is seen as a way of inducing reciprocal roles in other people in which they say, feel or do roles that we want but do not allow ourselves to enact.

Psychotherapy file: A list by Tony Ryle of Reciprocal Role Procedures, i.e., traps, dilemmas and snags. It can be used to pinpoint unhelpful relational patterns. In intellectual disability services we have several adapted accessible versions of this list.

Reciprocal roles: A stable pattern of interaction originating in relationships from our early lives, which determine our current relationships and how we treat ourselves. Playing a role always implies another or the internalised 'voice' of another whose reciprocation is sought or experienced.

Reciprocal Role Procedures: The feelings, thoughts and behaviours that are reciprocal roles in action.

Reflective practice: The opportunity to reflect with a knowledgeable practitioner on actions and processes to promote learning and development.

Reformulation letter: A mutual action between client and therapist. The client's words are used to describe their experience and the therapist makes the progression of actions clear by reflecting on the consequences. Using plain language, the letter traces the links between the detail of childhood relational experiences of emotion, behaviour, body and thought to the 'big picture' current relations between assumptions, roles, identities and self-understanding. The aim is to recap the narrative, concentrating on subjective and restricting conclusions arrived at through repudiated, elapsed or unrecognised meanings of past experience, particularly meanings learnt during formative years.

The letter aims to validate experience, de-pathologise difficulties, elicit repudiated or unappreciated emotion, develop the therapeutic alliance, clarify responsibilities (avoided or incorrectly carried), identify how current procedures are maintaining distress, summarise Reciprocal Role Procedures and relate this communication to the therapeutic relationship.

Relational intelligence: The idea of how the intelligences that operate between us cohere, in contrast with the idea that intelligence is the sole property of an individual. In CAT, four sources of intelligences are focused on: communal, emotional, executive functioning and societal.

Role (see Reciprocal Role Procedures): The types of actions, voices and scripts we typically have that constitute our sense of ourselves.

Ryle, Tony: The founder of ideas about Reciprocal Role Procedures in CAT. He worked as a GP and developed many of the ideas used in CAT from his extensive research, which aimed to integrate the most effective cognitive and analytic tools into a practical therapy useful in the NHS.

Self states: Partially dissociated reciprocal roles.

Self-to-other reciprocal roles: The idea that how we treat other people tends to be in keeping with our main reciprocal roles.

Self-to-self reciprocal roles: This views ourselves as always in relationship; we are a bundle of selves rather than a single self. There is always one part of me that is in relationship with another part of me e.g., 'I say to myself…' implies that one part of me is saying and the other is being said to. These parts of ourselves take on the characteristics developed in important relationships with other people.

Sequential Diagrammatic Reformulation (SDR) or maps: The CAT tool of drawing relational patterns. These SDRs can use words or pictures and describe the routes taken as people move from one position to another. They are used in CAT to help us know where we are.

Six part story method: A technique using structured instructions to identify what we want, the way we perceive and how we habitually react to the world. In intellectual disability CAT work, this drawing tool is a very popular assessment method and another version is also used as a way of marking the end of therapy and saying 'Goodbye'.

Snag: A type of problem procedure in which legitimate and appropriate goals are abandoned because of worries about what others will think or irrational guilt; a 'Yes-but' situation.

Social stories™: Developed by Carol Gray for working with people with Autistic Spectrum Disorders, this tool shares information about how to enact a specific social skill.

Societal intelligence: This is what has been invested in our society over thousands of years in our language, rituals, religions, laws and institutions. It is taught (as rote learning rather than procedural knowledge) in schools, churches and the wider social group.

State shifts: Abrupt changes of mind.

Suggestibility: Capable of being easily influenced by others.

Supported living: An approach to services designed to help people with disabilities live as independently as possible in their local community. This usually involves a contract with an agency whose role is to provide whatever assistance is necessary for the person to live in regular housing.

Systemic: An approach to psychotherapy that views people within relationships, rather than separate individuals. Its roots are in family therapy and involve an understanding of how systems work. Systemic approaches are central to work with people with intellectual disabilities. In CAT it describes how the therapeutic leverage point is often found through working with staff teams.

Target problem: The agreed problem that therapy aims to deal with. A CAT typically involves one to three of these.

Target problem procedure: How a target problem lives on; usually via a trap, dilemma or snag.

Theory of mind: The development of the idea that another's perspective might be different from one's own. This ability is compromised in people with autism, but under stress many people when lose their ability to hold theories about other people's minds being different from their own.

Therapeutic community: An approach to treatment based on a residential model where patients are encouraged to take responsibility for and take a pivotal role in their own treatment.

Top end of a reciprocal role: Using Kelly's ideas from Personal Constructs, relationships are described as having two poles ('It takes two to tango'). The top end is the doing to, active, stimulus or parental position.

Transference: An idea used in therapy to describe how relationships in other (usually early life) situations are brought into the therapeutic relationship. If the therapist spots transference, it is used to offer clues about the client's early, pivotal relationships.

Trap: A problem procedure involving a self-reinforcing vicious circle; negative beliefs generate a choice of actions that produce the very results the belief predicted.

Valuing People (Now): The government's strategy or policy for intellectual disability services.

Vygotsky, Lev: Vygotsky (1896–1934) proposed a theory that the development of higher cognitive functions in children emerged through practical activity in a social environment. He also posited the concept of Zone of Proximal Development. In CAT, Ryle talks about the Vygotskian view that 'What a child can do with its mother today, it can do by itself tomorrow,' becomes, 'What a child did not do with its mother yesterday, it cannot do by itself today,' as a way of understanding relational deficits.

Winterbourne Review: A national response to the serious abuse of people with intellectual disabilities at Winterbourne. There have been many other reviews of systematic institutional abuse, as abuse and neglect are endemic in intellectual disability services (Department of Health 2012). In CAT, awareness of high levels of abuse and neglect is another motivation for working with staff teams.

Zone of Proximal Development (ZPD): This has been defined as 'the distance between the actual developmental level as determined by independent problem solving and the level of potential development as determined through problem solving under adult guidance, or in collaboration with more capable peers' (Vygotsky 1978, p.86).

The Editors

Julie Lloyd is a CAT Practitioner, supervisor and trainer as well as Clinical Psychologist, with over 30 years' experience of working in the NHS, in the community with people with intellectual disabilities and also in hospital with people with severe mental illness. She also edits the journal of the Association of Cognitive Analytic Therapy and chairs the intellectual disability CAT special interest group.

Philip Clayton is a CAT Psychotherapist working for Calderstones Partnership NHS Foundation Trust. His current work involves the integration of CAT into a care pathway that treats people who have great difficulty in their relationships with others, those who have an intellectual disability and a 'personality disorder'. He also works with staff teams, the aim of which is to enable reflective, relational thinking around CAT reformulation and to help think about relapse prevention linked to offending.

The Contributors

Michelle Anwyl is a trained CAT Practitioner and specialises in providing CAT to individuals with intellectual disabilities and forensic histories and supports staff teams using shared CAT formulations and supervision groups. She also leads the Adapted Sex Offender Treatment Programme for learning disabled men who have committed harmful sexual behaviours.

Zoe Ball is a Chartered Clinical Psychologist, having qualified from the University of Liverpool in 2008. She has worked with people with intellectual disabilities at varying stages of her career, from being a support worker in a residential school to her current position in an intellectual disability service in Cheshire and Wirral Partnership NHS Trust, where she works in community and inpatient settings. She has particular passion for attachment theory and intellectual disabilities, hence her interest in CAT work.

Hilary Brown is Professor of Social Care at Canterbury Christ Church University and a specialist in adult safeguarding issues and intellectual disability. She also works as a CAT Psychotherapist with people with intellectual disabilities within the Sussex Partnership NHS Trust and supervises trainee CAT therapists working in this specialty. She has written extensively on issues of disability and safeguarding. Her current work includes the conduct of serious case reviews, many of which hinge on issues of mental capacity, but the decision-making always takes place in a relational context. She has also worked to develop policy and practice in relation to a wide range of abuse over the last 20 years including contributing to the original No Secrets and In Safe Hands drafting policy development for the Council of Europe and working with the Office of the Public Guardian on their engagement in complex cases. She chairs a Safeguarding Adults Board in London and leads the serious case review panel for a large local authority.

Val Crowley, a Consultant Clinical Psychologist and CAT Psychotherapist is also an accredited CAT trainer and supervisor. She is now retired from the NHS, but previously worked with people with intellectual disabilities and mental health problems with CAT therapy for 20 years. She also has a special interest in adults with psychosis and intellectual disabilities. Val continues to be a member of the CAT Special Interest Group and of Midland CAT group and remains interested in developing CAT.

Simon Crowther is a Clinical Psychologist working in forensic setting with adults with intellectual disabilities. He first became interested in CAT through his training in clinical psychology at the University of Liverpool, and is now a CAT Practitioner in training. He has a particular interest in using CAT with groups, staff teams and organisations.

Helen Elford completed a Psychology degree at the University of York in 1999, and following this worked as a support worker and assistant psychologist with adults with intellectual disabilities. She qualified as a Clinical Psychologist at the University of Sheffield in 2007 and as part of this undertook specialist placements using CAT, and working in a community intellectual disability setting. Since qualifying Helen has worked in the NHS in a multidisciplinary community intellectual disability team in Macclesfield. This involves utilising a range of therapeutic approaches, including CAT-informed work, both with individuals and in a systemic context.

Pamela Mount is a Clinical Nurse Specialist working within Psychological Treatment Service of the North West Forensic Intellectual disability Service. She has nearly 30 years' experience within this field, starting her career in the ward environment before undergoing additional expert training for her current post with Calderstones Partnership NHS Foundation Trust. She specialises in CAT for people with intellectual disabilities and also leads the Adapted Sex Offender Treatment Programme for learning disabled men who have committed harmful sexual behaviours.

Perry Morrison is employed by Southern Health Foundation Trust within the Forensic Intellectual disability Service as a Consultant Lead Clinical Psychologist. He is particularly interested in the application of therapies for this client group who tend to be in the borderline intellectual disability range. Therapies need to be engaging and effective, especially for a client group known to be difficult to treat. CAT is one such integrative therapy that can easily facilitate a good degree of engagement by balancing the focus of issues between the *here and now* with the patterns developed historically in the *there and then* of people's experiences.

Dr Nicola Murphy is a Senior Clinical Psychologist and Cognitive Analytic Therapist working with adults with intellectual disabilities; she works two days in a Community Intellectual Disability Team and three days in a regional Secure Service. She qualified as a Clinical Psychologist in September 2001. Qualifications since include a Diploma in Clinical Neuropsychology and Practitioner Training in Cognitive Analytic Therapy (ACAT). She has publications on her work in *Reformulation*, the journal of the Association of Cognitive Analytic Therapy. In addition she has designed two symbolised leaflets to explain CAT to adults with intellectual disabilities either living in a community or inpatient setting, which can be found on the ACAT website. She also regularly presents her work at conferences.

Steve Potter is a psychotherapist, coach, trainer and supervisor who has been doing and using CAT for 20 years. He is keen to take the skills at the heart of psychotherapy beyond the consulting room to the widest range of settings and applications. His main interest is in using simple forms of conversational mapping based on CAT methods to help develop shared understanding and relational intelligence, whether with individuals, groups or teams. He is based in Manchester and is chairperson of the International Cognitive Analytic Therapy Association.

Jo Varela is a CAT Practitioner and Consultant Clinical Psychologist. She has worked with children and adults with intellectual disabilities and mental health problems and challenging behaviour for over ten years. She is interested in adapting psychology and therapy approaches so that they are accessible and meaningful for people with intellectual disabilities and their carers.

David Wilberforce qualified as a Registered Nurse for People with an Intellectual Disability in 1984 and took on various residential and community roles as a nurse in Hull and Holderness. He completed an MA in Integrative Psychotherapy at the Sherwood Institute in Nottingham in 1996, and also trained in Gestalt psychotherapy and CAT. David worked predominantly as a psychotherapist in the NHS for around ten years until leaving in 2012. Now he continues to Lecture at both Hull and York Universities and works privately as a therapist and trainer/consultant.

References

Chapter 1
Goleman, D. (1996) *Emotional Intelligence: Why It Can Matter More Than IQ.* London: Bloomsbury.
Greenberg J., and Mitchell, S. (1983) *Object Relations in Psychoanalytic Theory.* Cambridge, MA: Harvard University Press.
Kelly, G.A. (1955) *The Psychology of Personal Constructs.* New York: Norton.
Psaila, C. and Crowley, V. (2005) 'Cognitive Analytic Therapy in people with learning disabilities: an investigation into the common reciprocal roles found within this client group.' *Mental Health and Intellectual disabilities Research and Practice 2*, 96–98.
Ryle, A. (1995) *Cognitive Analytic Therapy: Developments in Theory and Practice.* Chichester: Wiley.
Ryle, A. (1997a) *Cognitive Analytic Therapy and Borderline Personality Disorder: The Model and the Method.* Chichester: Wiley.
Ryle, A. (1997b) 'The structure and development of borderline personality disorder: a proposed model.' *British Journal of Psychiatry 170*, 82–87.
Ryle, A. and Kerr, I. (2002) *Introducing Cognitive Analytic Therapy: Principles and Practice.* Chichester: John Wiley.

Chapter 2
Bancroft, A. and Murphy, N. (2009) *Specialist Use of Cognitive Analytic Therapy (CAT) with People with Intellectual disability.* Institute Of Psychotherapy and Disability (IPD) conference presentation. Available at www.instpd.org.uk/conf.html, accessed 30 September 2013.
Beail, N. (2013) 'The role of cognitive factors in psychodynamic psychotherapy with people who have intellectual disabilities.' *The psychotherapist UKCP 53.*
Bowlby J. (2005) *The Making and Breaking of Affectional Bonds.* London: Routledge.
Bowlby J. (2008) *A Secure Base.* London, Routledge.
Carradice A. (2004) 'Applying cognitive analytic therapy to guide indirect working.' *Reformulation Theory and Practice in CAT, 23* 16–23.
Clayton, P. (2001) 'Using Cognitive Therapy in an Institution to Understand and Help Both Client and Staff.' In G. Landsberg and A. Smiley (eds) *Forensic Mental Health: Working with Offenders with Mental Illness.* Kingston, NJ: Civic Research Institute.
Clayton, P. (2010) 'From insecure attachment to (partial) inter-subjectivity (fearful aloneness to safely being with others).' *Journal of Intellectual disabilities and Offending Behaviour 1*, 33–43.
Dent-Brown, K. (2011) 'Six-Part Storymaking – a tool for CAT practitioners.' *Reformulation, Summer*, 34–36.

Fisher, C. and Harding, C. (2009) 'Thoughts on the rebel role: its application to challenging behaviour in intellectual disability services.' *Reformulation, Summer,* 4–5.

Gugjonsson, G. in Hollin, C.R. (2001) *Handbook of Offender Assessment and Treatment.* Chichester: John Wiley and Sons Ltd.

Gugjonsson G. (2003) *The Psychology of Interrogations and Confessions: A Handbook.* Chichester: John Wiley and Sons Ltd.

Horowitz, L.M., Alden, L.E., Wiggins, J.S. and Pincus, A.L. (2000) *Inventory of Interpersonal Problems United States of America.* New York: The Psychological Corporation, a Harcourt Assessment Company.

Jacobs, M. (1995) *D.W. Winnicott.* London: Sage Publications.

King, R. (2005) 'CAT, the therapeutic relationship and working with people with intellectual disability.' *Reformulation, Spring,* 10–14.

Kirkland, J. (2010) 'When I'm the dark angel I feel worthless and don't deserve love.' *Reformulation, Winter,* 19–23.

Lahad, M. (1992). 'Storymaking in Assessment Method for Coping With Stress.' In S. Jennings (ed.) *Dramatherapy Theory And Practice II.* London: Routledge.

Lloyd, J. (2013) 'What Aspects of Intelligence are Needed to Understand the Concept of Reciprocal Roles?' In J. Lloyd and P. Clayton (eds) *Cognitive Analytic Therapy for People with Learning Disabilities and their Carers.* London: Jessica Kingsley Publishers.

Lloyd, J. and Williams, B. (2003) 'Reciprocal roles and the "unspeakable known": exploring cat within services for people with intellectual disabilities.' *Reformulation, Summer,* 19–25.

Murphy, N. (2008) 'CAT used therapeutically and contextually.' *Reformulation, Summer,* 26–30.

Potter, S. (2013) 'The Helper's Dance List.' In J. Lloyd and P. Clayton (eds) *Cognitive Analytic Therapy for People with Learning Disabilities and their Carers.* London: Jessica Kingsley Publishers.

Sinason, V. (1992) *Mental Handicap and the Human Condition: New Approaches from the Tavistock.* London: Free Association Books.

Stern, D.N. (1985) *The Interpersonal World of the Infant: A View from Psychoanalysis and Developmental Psychology.* New York: Basic Books.

Sunderland, M. and Armstrong, N. (2011) *Draw on Your Relationships.* Milton Keynes: Speechmark Publishing.

Sunderland, M. and Engleheart, P. (2012) *Draw on Your Emotions.* Milton Keynes: Speechmark Publishing.

Vygotsky, L.S. (1978) *Mind in Society.* Cambridge, MA: Harvard University Press.

Wells, S. (2009) 'A qualitative study of cognitive analytic therapy as experienced by clients with intellectual disabilities.' *Reformulation, Winter,* 21–23.

Winnicott, D.W. (1990) *The Maturational Processes and the Facilitating Environment.* London: Karnac.

Chapter 3

Cormac, I. and Tihanyi, P. (2002) 'Meeting the mental and physical healthcare needs of carers.' *Royal College of Psychiatrists.* Available at http://apt.rcpsych.org/content/12/3/162.full, accessed 6 October 2013.

Colomb, E. and Lloyd, J. (2012) 'Cognitive Analytic Therapy and Dysphagia: using CAT relational mapping when teams can't swallow our recommendations.' *Reformulation (Journal of the Association of Cognitive Analytic Therapy) 39,* 24–27.

Flynn (2012) *Serious Case Review into abuse at Winterbourne View Hospital.* South Gloucestershire Adult Social Care.

Hannush, M. (2002) *Becoming Good Parents: An Existential Journey.* NY: State University of New York Press.

Haydon-Laurelut, M. (2013) 'Internalised-other interviewing, inclusion and the avowal of psychological reality: an anti-disablement action method.' *Context, April,* 7–10.

Haydon-Laurelut, M. and Wilson, C. (2011) 'Interviewing the internalised other: attending to the voices of the "other".' *Journal of Systemic Therapies 30,* 24–37.

Potter, S. (2004) 'Untying the knots: relational states of mind in Cognitive Analytic Therapy?' *Reformulation (Journal of the Association of Cognitive Analytic Therapy) 21,* 14–21.

Sinason, V. (1992) *Mental Handicap and the Human Condition.* London: Free Association Books.

Tomita, S.K. (1990) 'The denial of elder mistreatment by victims and abusers.' *Violence and Victims 8,* 171–184.

Vygotsky, L.S (1978) *Mind in Society: The Development of Higher Psychological Processes.* Cambridge, MA: Harvard University Press.

Wells, S. (2009) 'A qualitative study of cognitive analytic therapy as experienced by clients with intellectual disabilities.' *Reformulation, Winter,* 22–23.

Winnicott, D. (1965) *The Maturational Processes and the Facilitating Environment.* UK: Hogarth Press.

Chapter 4

Bartlett, C. and Bunning, K. (1997) 'The importance of communication partnerships: a study to investigate the communicative exchanges between staff and adults with intellectual disabilities.' *British Journal of Learning Disabilities 25,* 148–153.

Bates, R. (1992) in Waitman, A. and Conboy-Hill, S. (1992) *Psychotherapy and Mental Handicap.* London: Sage.

Beart, S. (2005) '"I won't think of meself as an intellectual disability. But I have": social identity and self advocacy.' *British Journal of Learning Disabilities 33,* 128–131.

Beart, S., Hardy, G. and Buchan, L. (2004) 'Changing selves: a grounded theory account of belonging to a self advocacy group for people with intellectual disabilities.' *Journal of Applied Research in Intellectual Disabilities 17,* 91–100.

Chamorro-Premuzic, T. and Furnham, A. (2005) 'Intellectual competence.' *The Psychologist 18,* 6, 352–354.

Clements, J. (1998) in E. Emerson, C. Hatton, J. Bromley and A. Caine (eds) *Clinical Psychology and People with Intellectual disabilities.* Chichester: Wiley.

Commission for Healthcare Audit and Inspection (2007) *A life like no other: A national audit of specialist inpatient healthcare services for people with learning difficulties in England.* House of Lords, House of Commons Joint Committee on Human Rights, seventh report of session 2007–2008, vol 1. Available at http://www.publications.parliament, accessed 8 November 2013.

Cunningham, C.C., Glenn, S. and Fitzpatrick, H. (2000) 'Parents telling their offspring about Downs Syndrome and disability.' *Journal of Applied Research in Intellectual disabilities 13,* 47–61.

Davies, C. and Jenkins, R. (1997) 'She has different fits to me: how people with a learning difficulties see themselves.' *Disability and Society, 12,* 95–109.

Department of Health (2009) *Valuing People Now: A New Three-year Strategy for Intellectual disabilities.* London: Department of Health.

Department of Health (2012) *Transforming Care: A National Response to Winterbourne View Hospital. Department of Health Review: Final Report.* London: Department of Health.

References

Emerson, E. (1992) 'What is Normalisation?' In H. Brown and H. Smith *Normalisation, A Reader for the Nineties*. London: Routledge.

Fitzsimmons, M. (2000) 'A credit-card sized SDR and its use with a patient with limited language skills.' *Reformulation, Autumn*.

Harvey, L. (1993) 'Towards a greater acceptance of the cognitive in CAT.' *Reformulation, Winter*.

Hatton, C. (1998) 'Intellectual Disabilities-Epidemiology and Causes' in E. Emerson, C. Hatton, J. Bromley, and A. Caine (eds) *Clinical Psychology and People with Intellectual disabilities*. Chichester: Wiley.

Holt, G., Hardy, S. and Bouras, N. (2005) *Mental Health in Intellectual disabilities* (3rd edition). Brighton: Pavilion.

Jahoda, A., Markova, I. and Cattermole, M. (1989) 'Stigma and the self concept of people with a mild mental handicap.' *Journal of Mental Deficiency Research 32*, 103–115.

King, R. (2005) 'CAT, the therapeutic relationship and working with people with intellectual disability.' *Reformulation: Theory and Practice in Cognitive Analytic Therapy 24*, 10–14.

Lovett, H. (1996) *Learning to Listen: Positive Approaches and People with Difficult Behaviour*. London: Jessica Kingsley Publishers.

Lynch, C. (2004) 'Psychotherapy for persons with mental retardation.' *Mental Retardation 42*, 5, 399–405.

Markham, D. and Trower, P. (2003) 'The effects of the psychiatric label "borderline personality disorder" on nursing staff's perceptions and causal attributions for challenging behaviours.' *British Journal of Clinical Psychology 42*, 3, 243–256

Oakes, P. (2012) 'Assessment of intellectual disability: a history.' *Learning Disability Practice 15*, 1, 12–16.

Rapley, M. (2005) 'Won't get fooled again: how might clinical psychology know intellectual disability differently?' *Clinical Psychology 50*, 10–14.

Rapley, M., Kiernan, P. and Antaki, C. (1998) 'Invisible to themselves or negotiating identity? The interactional management of being intellectually disabled.' *Disability and Society 13*, 5, 807–827.

Rice-Varian, C. (2011) 'The Effectiveness of CAT with people with mild intellectual disability and moderate ABI.' *Reformulation: Theory and Practice in Cognitive Analytic Therapy 36*.

Ryle, T. (1991) 'Object relations theory and activity theory: a proposed link by way of the procedural sequence model.' *British Journal of Medical Psychology 64*, 307–316.

Ryle, A. (1994) 'Projective identification: a particular form of reciprocal role procedure.' *British Journal of Medical Psychology 67*, 107–114.

Ryle, T. (1997) 'The structure and development of borderline personality disorder: a proposed model.' *British Journal of Psychiatry 170*, 82–87.

Sinason, V. (1992) *Mental Handicap and the Human Condition: New Approaches from the Tavistock*. London: Free Association Books.

Vygotsky, L.S. (1978) *Mind in Society: The Development of Higher Psychological Processes*. Cambridge, MA: Harvard University Press.

Waitman, A. and Conboy-Hill, S. (2000). *Psychotherapy and Mental Handicap*. London: Sage.

Yeates, G., Hamill, M., Sutton, L., Psalia, K., Gracey, G., Mohamed, S. and O'Del, J. (2008) 'Dysexecutive problems and interpersonal relating following frontal brain injury: reformulation and compensation in Cognitive Analytic Therapy (CAT).' *Neuro-Psychoanalysis 10*, 1.

Chapter 5

Baron-Cohen, S. (2002) 'The extreme male brain theory of autism.' *Trends in Cognitive Science 6*, 248–254.

Donald, M. (1991) *The Origins of the Modern Mind: Three Stages in the Evolution of Culture and Cognition*. Cambridge, MA: Harvard University Press.

Donald, M. (2001) *A Mind so Rare: The Evolution of Human Consciousness*. New York: Norton.

Flynn, J.R. (2012) *Are We Getting Smarter? Rising IQ in the 21st Century*. Cambridge: Cambridge University Press.

Frith, U. (2003) *Autism: Explaining the Enigma*. Oxford: Basil Blackwell.

Gardner, H. (1985) *Frames of Mind: The Theory of Multiple Intelligences*. New York: Basic Books (AZ).

Goleman, D. (1995) *Emotional Intelligence*. New York: Bantam Books.

Knox, J. (2011) *Self-Agency in Psychotherapy*. New York: W.W. Norton.

Reddy, V. (2008) *How Infants Know Minds*. Cambridge, MA: Harvard University Press.

Rubenstein, J. and Merzenich, M. (2003) 'Model of autism: increased ratio of excitation/inhibition in key neural system.' *Genes Brain Behaviour 2*, 255–267.

Stern, D. (1998) *The Interpersonal World of the Infant: A view From Psychoanalysis and Developmental Psychology*. London: Karnac.

Trevarthen, C. (2001) 'The Neurobiology of Early Communication: Intersubjective Regulations in Human Brain Development.' In A.F. Kalverboer and A. Gramsbergen (eds) *Handbook on Brain and Behavior in Human Development*. Dodrecht: Kluwer.

Chapter 6

Potter, S. (2012) 'Speed supervision.' *AUCC Journal UK, March*.

Ryle, A. and Kerr, I. (2002) *Introduction to Cognitive Analytic Therapy*. Chichester: Wiley.

Chapter 7

Arscott, K., Dagman, D. and Kroese, B. (1998) 'Consent to psychological research by people with an intellectual disability.' *Journal of Allied Research in Intellectual Disabilities 11*, 1, 77–83.

Dagnan, D., Chadwick, P. and Proudlove, J. (2000) 'Toward an assessment of suitability of people with mental retardation for cognitive therapy.' *Cognitive Therapy and Research 24*, 627–636.

Damasio, A. (1994) *Descartes' Error: Emotion, Reason, and the Human Brain*. New York: Putnam Publishing.

Dunn, L., Dunn, D., Styles, B. and Sewell, J. (1997) *The British Picture Vocabulary Scale: Second Edition (BPVS-II)*. Windsor: NFER.

Ekman, P. and Davidson, R. (1994) *The Nature of Emotion; Fundamental Questions*. Oxford: Oxford University Press.

Frank, J. (1961) *Persuasion and Healing*. Baltimore: John Hopkins University.

Luborsky, L., Singer, B. and Luborsky, L. (1975) 'Comparative studies of psychotherapies: is it true that "everybody has won and all must have prizes"?' *Archives of General Psychiatry 32*, 995–1008.

Mackintosh, N. (1998) *IQ and Human Intelligence*. New York: Oxford University Press.

Oathamshaw, S. and Haddock, G. (2006) 'Do people with intellectual disabilities and psychosis have the cognitive skills required to undertake cognitive behavioural therapy?' *Journal of Applied Research in Intellectual Disabilities 19*, 35–46.

Psaila, C. and Crowley, V. (2005) 'Cognitive Analytic Therapy in people with intellectual disabilities: an investigation into the common reciprocal roles found within this client group.' *Mental Health and Intellectual disabilities Research and Practice 2*, 96–98.

Raven, J., Raven, J.C. and Court, J.H. (1998) *Manual for Raven's Progressive Matrices and Vocabulary Scales. Section 2: The Coloured Progressive Matrices.* San Antonio, TX: Harcourt Assessment.

Ryle, A. (1975) 'Self-to-self, self-to-other: the world's shortest account of object relations theory.' *New Psychiatry, April* 12–13.

Shapiro, D.A. and Shapiro, D. (1982) 'Meta-analysis of comparative therapy outcome studies: a republication and refinement.' *Psychological Bulletin 92*, 581–604.

Wells, S. (2009) 'A qualitative study of cognitive analytic therapy as experience by clients with intellectual disabilities.' *Reformulation: Theory and Practice in Cognitive Analytic Therapy 33*, 22–23.

Whitaker, S. and Laird, C. (2011) *Error in the measurement of low intellectual ability: Implications for research.* International Joint Congress of the European Association for Mental Health in Intellectual Disability and IASSID Challenging Behaviour and Mental Health SIRG Conference, 1–3 September 2011, Manchester, UK.

Chapter 8

Arendt, H. (1958) *The Human Condition.* Chicago: University of Chicago Press.

Bakhtin, M. (1981) in Holquist, M. (ed.) (1981) *The Dialogic Imagination: Four Essays.* Austin and London: University of Texas Press.

Blackwell, R. (1997) 'Holding, containing and bearing witness: the problem of helpfulness in encounters with torture survivors.' *Journal of Social Work Practice 11*, 2, 81–89.

Bloom, S. and Farragher, B. (2011) *Destroying Sanctuary: The Crisis in Human Service Delivery Systems.* New York: Oxford University Press.

Corbett, A. (2009) 'Words as a Second Language: the Psychotherapeutic Challenge of Severe Intellectual Disability.' In T. Cottis, T. (ed) *Intellectual Disability, Trauma and Psychotherapy.* London. Routledge.

Dudley-Marlin, C. (2004) 'The social construction of intellectual disability.' *Journal of Learning Disabilities 37*, 6, 482–489.

Erikson, E. (1950) *Childhood and Society.* New York: Norton.

Fannon, F. (1961) *The Wretched of the Earth,* translated by Farrington, C. (1963). New York: Grove Weidenfeld.

Hannam, C. (1975) Reprinted in Blackman, B. (ed.) *Living With Loss: Helping People with an intellectual disability Cope with Bereavement and Loss.* Brighton: Pavilion.

Holquist, M. (1990) *Dialogism: Bakhtin and his World* (2nd edition). London: Routledge.

Kierkegaard, S. (2000) *The Secret to the Art of Helping. Kierkegaard's Writings* (Volume 22) H.V. Hong and E.H. Hong (eds). Princeton, NJ: Princeton University Press.

King, R. (2005) 'CAT the therapeutic relationship and working with people with a Learning Disability.' *Reformulation, Spring,* 10–14.

Lloyd, E. (2009) 'Speaking Through the Skin: the Significance of Shame.' In T. Cottis (ed.) *Intellectual Disability, Trauma and Psychotherapy.* London: Routledge.

Mclean, K.C., Pasupathi, M. and Pals, J.L. (2007) 'Selves creating stories creating selves: a process of self development.' *Personality and Social Psychological Review 11*, 262–278.

Rogers, C. (1958) 'Characteristics of a helping relationship.' *Journal of Personal Guidance 37*, 6–16.

Sinason, V. (1992) *Mental Handicap and the Human Condition: New Approaches from the Tavistock.* London: Free Association Books.

Stokes, J. and Sinason, V. (1992) 'Secondary Handicap as a Defence.' In A. Waitman and S. Conboy-Hill (eds) *Psychotherapy and Mental Handicap.* London: Sage.

Suzuki, S. (1973) *Zen Mind, Beginner's Mind.* New York. Weatherhill.

Symington, M. (1981) 'The psychotherapy of the subnormal patient.' *British Journal of Medical Psychology 54*, 187–199.

Szivos, S. and Griffiths, E. (1992) 'Coming to Terms with Intellectual disability: the Effects of Group work and Group Processes on Stigmatised Identity.' In A. Waitman and S. Conboy-Hill (eds) *Psychotherapy and Mental Handicap.* London: Sage.

The Journals of Soren Kierkegaard, vol 22 (1854) Translated by Hong, H. and Hong, E. Princeton, NJ: Princeton University Press.

Van der Veer, R. and Valsiner, J. (1991) *Understanding Vygotsky, a Quest for Synthesis.* Oxford: Blackwell.

Van der Veer. R. and Valsiner, J. (eds) (1994) *The Vygotsky Reader.* Oxford: Blackwell.

Chapter 9

Department of Health (2012) *Transforming Care: A National Response to Winterbourne View Hospital. Department of Health Review: Final Report.* London: Department of Health.

Emerson, E. (1995) Cited in Emerson, E. (2001) *Challenging Behaviour: Analysis and Intervention in People with Severe Intellectual disabilities.* Cambridge: Cambridge University Press.

Maslow, A.H. (1943) 'A theory of human motivation.' *Psychological Review 50,* 4, 370–396. Available at: http://psychclassics.yorku.ca/Maslow/motivation.htm, accessed on 22 June 2013.

Royal College of Psychiatrists, British Psychological Society and Royal College of Speech and Language Therapists (2007) *Challenging Behaviour: A Unified Approach.* London: British Psychological Society.

Ryle, A. and Kerr, I.B. (2002) *Introducing Cognitive Analytic Therapy Principles and Practice.* Chichester: Wiley.

Chapter 10

Addison, M. (2013) *Finding the Causes of Challenging Behaviour: Part 2.* Available at www.challengingbehaviour.org.uk, accessed 2 October 2013.

Ball, T., Bush, A. and Emerson, E. (2004) *Psychological Interventions for Severely Challenging Behaviours Shown by People with Learning Disabilities.* Leicester: British Psychological Society.

Bancroft, A., Collins, S., Crowley, V., Harding, C., Kim, Y., Lloyd, J. and Murphy, N. (2008) 'Is CAT an island or solar system?' *Reformulation, Summer,* 23–25.

Byrne, A., Morton, J. and Salmon, P. (2001) 'Defending against patients' pain: a qualitative analysis of nurses' responses to children's post operative pain.' *Journal of Psychosomatic Research 50,* 2, 69–76.

Campbell, M., Robertson, A. and Jahoda, A. (2012) 'Psychological therapies for people with intellectual disabilities: comments on a matrix of evidence for interventions in challenging behaviour.' *Journal of Intellectual Disability Research* [Epub ahead of print: doi: 10.1111/j.1365-2788.2012.01646.x.].

Carradice, A. (2004) 'Applying cognitive analytic therapy to guide indirect working.' *Reformulation, Autumn,* 18–23.

Department of Health (2001) *Valuing People: A New Strategy for Learning Disability for the 21st Century.* London: Department of Health.

Department of Health (2007) *Services for People with Learning Disabilities and Challenging Behaviour or Mental Health Needs: Report of a Project Group (The Mansell Report)* (revised edition). London: Department of Health.

Department of Health (2009) *Valuing People Now: A New Three-year Strategy for Learning Disabilities.* London: Department of Health.

Dunn, M. and Parry, G. (1997) 'A reformulated care plan approach to caring for people with borderline personality disorder in a community mental health service setting.' *Clinical Psychology Forum 104* 19–22.

References

Duxbury, J. (2002) 'An evaluation of staff and patient views of and strategies employed to manage inpatient aggression and violence on one mental health unit: a pluralistic design.' *Journal of Psychiatric and Mental Health Nursing 9*, 3, 325–337.

Duxbury, J. and Whittington, R. (2005) 'Issues and innovations in nursing practice: causes and management of patient aggression and violence.' *Journal of Advanced Nursing 50*, 5, 469–478.

Emerson, E. (2001) *Challenging Behaviour: Analysis and Intervention in People with Intellectual Disabilities* (2nd edition). Cambridge: Cambridge University Press.

Emerson, E. and Einfield, L. (2011) *Challenging Behaviour.* Cambridge: Cambridge University Press.

Emerson, E., Kiernan C., Alborz, A., Reeves, D., Mason, H., Swarbrick, R., Mason, L. and Hatton, C. (2001) 'The prevalence of challenging behaviors: a total population study.' *Developmental Disabilities 22*, 1, 77–93.

Farrell, G.A., Shafiei, T. and Salmon, P. (2010) 'Facing up to Challenging Behaviour: a model of training for staff-client interaction.' *Journal of Advanced Nursing 66*, 7, 1644–1655.

Felce, D. (1988) 'Behavioural and social climate in community group residences.' In M.P Janicki, M.K. Krauss and M.M. Seltzer *Community Residences for Persons with Developmental Disabilities.* Baltimore, MD: Paul H Brookes.

Felce, D., de Kock, U. and Repp, A.C. (1986) 'An eco-behavioural comparison of small community based houses and traditional large hospitals for severely and profoundly mentally handicapped adults.' *Applied Research in Mental Retardation 7*, 393–408.

Felce, D. and Perry, J. (1995) 'The extent of support for ordinary living provided in staffed houses: the relationship between staffing levels, residents characteristics, staff: resident interactions and resident activity patterns.' *Social Science and Medicine 40*, 6, 799–810.

Felce, D., Repp, A.C., Thomas, M., Ager, A. and Blunden, R. (1991) 'The relationship between staff: client ratios, interactions and residential placement.' *Research in Developmental Disabilities 12*, 3, 315–331.

Fisher, C. and Harding, C. (2009) 'Thoughts on the rebel role: its application to challenging behaviour in intellectual disability services.' *Reformulation: Theory and Practice in Cognitive Analytic Therapy 32*, 4–5.

Greenhill, B. (2011) 'They have behaviour, we have relationships?' *Reformulation: Theory and Practice in Cognitive Analytic Therapy 37*, 10–15.

Hall, J. (1990) 'Towards a psychology of caring.' *British Journal of Clinical Psychology 29*, 124–144.

Harper, D.C. and Wadsworth, J.S. (1993) 'Grief in adults with mental retardation: preliminary findings.' *Research in Developmental Disabilities 14*, 313–330.

Hastings, R.P. (1997a) 'Staff beliefs about the challenging behaviours of children and adults with mental retardation.' *Clinical Psychology Review 17*, 75–90.

Hastings, R.P. (1997b) 'Measuring staff perceptions of challenging behaviour: the Challenging Behaviour Attributions Scale (CHAB).' *Journal of Intellectual Disability Research 41*, 495–501.

Hastings, R.P. and Remminton, B. (1994) 'Staff behaviour and its implications for people with intellectual disabilities and challenging behaviour.' *British Journal of Clinical Psychology 33*, 423–428.

Hill, C. and Dagnan, D. (2002) 'Helping attributions, emotions and coping style in response to people with intellectual disabilities and challenging behaviour.' *Journal of Learning Disabilities 6*, 4, 363–372.

Kroese, B.S. (1997) 'Cognitive-behaviour therapy for people with learning disabilities: conceptual and contextual issues.' In B.S. Kroese, D. Dagnan, and K. Loumidia(1997) *Cognitive Therapy for people with Learning Disabilities.* London: Routledge.

Lloyd, J. and Williams, B. (2003) 'Reciprocal roles and the "unspeakable unknown": exploring CAT within services for people with intellectual disabilities.' *Reformulation: Theory and Practice in Cognitive Analytic Therapy, Summer,* 19–24.

Lloyd, J. and Williams, B. (2004) 'Exploring the use of cognitive analytic therapy within services for people with intellectual disabilities and challenging behaviour.' *Clinical Psychology and People with Learning Disabilities 2,* 2, 4–5.

Lovett, H. (1996) *Learning to Listen: Positive Approaches and People with Difficult Behaviour.* London: Jessica Kingsley Publishers.

Markham, D. and Trower, P. (2003) 'The effects of the psychiatric label "borderline personality disorder" on nursing staff's perceptions and causal attributions for challenging behaviours.' *British Journal of Clinical Psychology 42,* 3, 243–256.

Moss, A. (2006) 'The application of CAT to working with people with learning disabilities.' *Reformulation, Summer,* 20–27.

Murphy, N. (2008) 'CAT used therapeutically and contextually for a client with intellectual disability and Aspergers Syndrome.' *Reformulation: Theory and Practice in Cognitive Analytic Therapy 30,* 26–30.

Qureshi, H. and Alborz, A. (1992) 'Epidemiology of challenging behaviour.' *Mental Handicap Research 5,* 130–145.

Royal College of Psychiatrists (2007) *Challenging Behaviour: A Unified Approach. Clinical and Service Guidelines for Supporting People who are at Risk of Receiving Abusive or Restrictive Practices.* College Report CR144. London: Royal College of Psychiatrists.

Ryle, A. (1991) 'Object relations theory and activity theory: a proposed link by way of the procedural sequence model.' *British Journal of Medical Psychology 64,* 307–316.

Ryle, T. and Kerr, I (2002) *Introducing Cognitive Analytic Therapy: Principles and Practice.* Chichester: Wiley.

Sharrock, R., Day, A., Quazi, F. and Brewin, C. (1990) 'Explanations by professional care staff, optimism and helping behaviour: an application of attribution theory.' *Psychological Medicine, 20,* 846–855.

Sinason, V. (1992) *Mental Handicap and the Human Condition: New Approaches from the Tavistock.* London: Free Association Books.

Wanless, L.K. and Jahoda, A. (2002) 'Responses of staff towards people with mild to moderate intellectual disability who behave aggressively: a cognitive emotional analysis.' *Journal of Intellectual Disability Research 46,* 6, 507–516.

Whittington, L.K. and Wykes, T. (1994) 'An observational study of associations between nurse behaviour and violence in psychiatric hospitals.' *Journal of Psychiatric and Mental Health Nursing 1,* 2, 85–92.

Wodehouse, G. and McGill, P. (2009) 'Support for family carers of children and young people with developmental disabilities and challenging behaviour: what stops it being helpful?' *Journal of Intellectual Disability Research 53,* 7, 644–653.

Chapter 11

Clarkson, P. (1995) *The Therapeutic Relationship.* London: Whurr.
Klein, J. (1987) *Our Need for Others: And its Root in Infancy.* London: Routledge.
Mahler, M. (1949) 'Clinical studies in benign and malignant cases of childhood psychosis – schizophrenia-like.' *American Journal Orthopsychiatry 19,* 297.
Reddy, V. (2008) *How Infants Know Minds.* London: Harvard University Press.

Trevarthen, C. (2001) 'The Neurobiology of Early Communication: Intersubjective Regulations in Human Brain Development.' In A.F. Kalverboer and A. Gramsbergen (eds) *Handbook on Brain and Behavior in Human Development.* Dodrecht: Kluwer.

Williams, D. (1992) *Nobody Nowhere.* London: Jessica Kingsley Publishers.

Chapter 12

Brown, H. (2011) 'The role of emotion in decision-making.' *Journal of Adult Protection 13*, 4, 194–202.

Brown, H. and Marchant, E. (2011) *Best Interests Decision-making in Complex Cases.* London: Office of the Public Guardian. Available at www.canterbury.ac.uk/social-applied-sciences/ASPD/documents/BestInterestDecisionMakinginComplexCasespaperJune2011.pdf, accessed on 23 June 2013.

Brown, H. and Marchant, E. (2013) 'Using the Mental Capacity Act in complex cases – Tizard.' *Learning Disability Review 18*, 2, 60–69.

Damasio, A. (2010) *Self Comes to Mind: Constructing the Conscious Brain.* New York: Pantheon.

Flynn, M. for Cornwall Social Services (2011) *Serious Case Review into the death of Steven Hoskin.* Truro: Cornwall Safeguarding Adults Board. Available at http://www.pkc.gov.uk/CHttpHandler.ashx?id=14720&p=0, accessed 26 September 2013.

Holland, A. and Wong, J. (1999) 'Genetically determined obesity in Prader-Willi syndrome: the ethics and legality of treatment.' *Journal of Medical Ethics 25*, 230–236.

Kahneman, D. (2011) *Thinking, Fast and Slow.* St Ives: Clays Ltd.

Mental Capacity Act (2005) 'Chapter 9.' Available at legislation.gov.uk, accessed 6 October 2013.

Mental Health Foundation (2012) *Best Interests Decisions Study.* London: Mental Health Foundation. Available at www.mentalhealth.org.uk/publications, accessed on 23 June 2013.

Chapter 13

Department of Health (2005) *Responding to Domestic Abuse.* London: Department of Health.

Lund, E.M. (2011) 'Community-based services and interventions for adults with disabilities who have experienced interpersonal violence: a review of the literature.' *Trauma, Violence and Abuse 12*, 4, 171–182.

Walby, S. and Allen, J. (2004) *Domestic Violence, Sexual Assault and Stalking: Findings from the British Crime Survey.* London: Home Office Research, Development and Statistics Directorate.

Chapter 14

Cappleman (2013) 'Preventing another Winterbourne: lessons from a therapeutic community for people with intellectual disabilities.' *The Psychotherapist UKCP 53.*

Clarke, S., Thomas, P. and James, K. (2013) 'Cognitive analytic therapy for personality disorder: randomised controlled trial.' *The British Journal of Psychiatry 202*, 129–134.

Clayton, P. (2010) 'From insecure attachment to (partial) inter-subjectivity (fearful aloneness to safely being with others).' *Journal of Intellectual disabilities and Offending Behaviour 1*, 33–43.

Jacob, C. and MacAllister, P. (eds) (2010) *Standards for Psychotherapy in Medium Secure Units.* London: Royal College of Psychiatrist Centre for Quality Improvement.

Jones, L. (1997) 'Developing Models for Managing Treatment Integrity and Efficacy in a Prison Based TC: The Max Glatt Centre.' In E. Cullen, L. Jones and R. Woodward (eds) *Therapeutic Communities for Offenders.* Chichester: Wiley.

Kellett, S. (2005) 'The treatment of dissociative identity disorder with cognitive analytic therapy: experimental evidence of sudden gains.' *Journal of Trauma and Dissociation 6*, 3, 55–81.

Kerr, I.B. and Gopfert, M. (2006) 'Cognitive Analytic Therapy: Informed Model of the Therapeutic Community: Implications for Work in Forensic Settings.' In P. Pollock, M. Stowell-Smith and M. Gopfert (2006) *Cognitive Analytic Therapy for Offenders*. London: Routledge.

Livesley, J.W. (2003) *Practical Management of Personality Disorder*. New York: Guildford Press.

Morrissey, C., Taylor, J. and Bennett, C. (2012) 'Evaluation of a therapeutic community intervention for men with intellectual disability and personality disorder.' *Journal of Learning Disabilities and Offending Behaviour 3*, 1, 52–60.

National Institute for Mental Health in England (2003) *Personality Disorder: No longer a Diagnosis of Exclusion: Policy Implementation Guidance for the Development of Services for People with Personality Disorder*. London: National Institute for Mental Health in England.

Pollock, P. and Stowell-Smith, M. (2006) 'Cognitive Analytic Therapy Applied to Offending: Theory, Tools and Practice.' In P. Pollock, M. Stowell-Smith and M. Gopfert (2006) *Cognitive Analytic Therapy for Offenders*. London: Routledge.

Ryle, A (1997) *Cognitive Analytic Therapy of Borderline: The Model and the Method*. Chichester: Wiley.

Ryle, A. and Kerr, I. (2002) *Introducing Cognitive Analytic Therapy: Principles and Practice*. Chichester: Wiley.

Shannon, K. (2009) 'Using what we know: cognitive analytic therapy's contribution to risk assessment and management.' *Reformulation, Winter*, 16–21.

Shine, J. (2011) 'Working with offence paralleling behaviour in a therapeutic community setting.' In M. Daffern, L. Jones and J. Shine (eds) *Offence Paralleling Behaviour: A Case Formulation Approach to Offender Assessment and Intervention*. Chichester: Wiley.

Taylor, J. (2011) *Cheltham Democratic Therapeutic Community: A Treatment Model for Offenders with Intellectual disability and Personality Disorder*. Nottingham: Nottingham Healthcare NHS Trust.

Taylor, J., MacKenzie, J., Bowen, J. and Turner, K. (2012) 'The development and accreditation of a treatment model for prisoners with a learning disability and personality disorder.' *Journal of Intellectual disabilities and Offending Behaviour 3*, 1, 44–51.

Vygotsky, L. (1978) *Mind and Society: The Development of Higher Psychological Processes*. Cambridge, MA: Harvard University Press.

Withers, J. (2008) 'Cognitive analytic therapy (CAT): a therapy in a medium secure hospital for a mentally disordered offender with a personality disorder.' *British Journal of Forensic Practice 10*, 3, 24–32.

Chapter 15

Carr, A. (2003) *The Handbook of Child and Adolescent Clinical Psychology: A Contextual Approach*. London: Brunner-Routledge Publications.

Champion, P. (2010) *Attachment. Complex Learning Difficulties and Disabilities Research Project (CLDD)*. Christchurch, New Zealand: The Champion Centre. Available ar www.championcentre.org.nz, accessed 30 October 2013.

Golding, K. (2008) *Nurturing Attachments: Supporting Children who are Fostered or Adopted*. London: Jessica Kingsley Publishers.

Maniglio, R. (2012) 'The role of parent–child bonding, attachment, and interpersonal problems in the development of deviant sexual fantasies in sexual offenders.' *Trauma, Violence and Abuse 13*, 2, 83–96.

Marshall, W.L. (2010) 'The role of attachments, intimacy, and loneliness in the etiology and maintenance of sexual offending.' *Sexual and Relationship Therapy 25*, 1, 73–85.

McCormack, J., Hudson, S.M. and Ward, T. (2002) 'Sexual offenders' perceptions of their early interpersonal relationships: an attachment perspective.' *The Journal of Sex Research 39*, 2.

Psaila, C.L. and Crowley, V. (2006) 'Cognitive analytic therapy in people with intellectual disabilities: an investigation into the common reciprocal roles found within this client group.' *Reformulation, Winter*, 5–11.

Ward, T. and Beech, A.R. (2005) 'An integrated theory of sexual offending in rehabilitation, etiology, and self-regulation: the comprehensive good lives model of treatment for sexual offenders.' *Aggression and Violent Behaviour 11*, 77–94.

Ward, T. and Stewart, C.A. (2003) 'The treatment of sex offenders: risk management and good lives in rehabilitation, etiology, and self-regulation: the comprehensive good lives model of treatment for sexual offenders.' *Aggression and Violent Behaviour 11*, 77–94.

Chapter 16

Bancroft, A. (2010) 'The psychotherapy file as dialogue-adaptations and modification of the psychotherapy file when working with people with an intellectual disability.' (Unpublished conference presentation). *The Practice of Cognitive Analytic Therapy with People with Intellectual disabilities*. Birmingham University, 28 May 2010.

Vygotsky, L.S. (1978) *Mind in Society: The Development of Higher Psychological Processes*. Cambridge, MA: Harvard University Press.

Chapter 17

Bancroft, A., Collins, S., Crowley, V., Harding, H., Youngsuk, K., Lloyd, J. and Murphy, N. (2008) 'Is CAT an Island or a Solar System? The dilemmas in the therapeutic frame when working with people in learning disability services.' *Reformulation 30, Summer*, 23–25.

Potter, S. (2010) 'Words with arrows: the benefits of mapping whilst talking.' *Reformulation: Theory and Practice in Cognitive Analytic Therapy 34*.

Stern, D.N. (2004) *The Present Moment in Psychotherapy and Everyday Life*. New York: Norton.

Sunderland, M. and Engleheart, P. (1993) *Draw On Your Emotions*. Bicester: Winslow Press.

Vygotsky, L.S. (1978) *Mind in Society: The Development of Higher Psychological Processes*. London: Harvard University Press.

Afterword

Bender, M. (1993) 'The unoffered chair: the history of therapeutic disdain towards people with a learning disability.' *Clinical Psychology Forum 54*, 7–12.

Linington, M. (2002) 'Whose handicap? Psychotherapy with people with a learning disability.' *British Journal of Psychotherapy 18*, 3, 409–414.

Glossary

Department of Health (2012) *Transforming Care: A National Response to Winterbourne View Hospital. Department of Health Review: Final Report.* DoH.

Royal College of Psychiatrists (2007) *Challenging Behaviour: A Unified Approach. Clinical and service guidelines for supporting people who are at risk of receiving abusive or restrictive practices.* College Report CR144. London: Royal College of Psychiatrists.

Vygotsky, L.S (1978) *Mind in Society: The Development of Higher Psychological Processes*. Cambridge, MA: Harvard University Press.

Subject Index

abstract thinking 46
acquiescence 291
active (recognition) phase 29, 35–7, 44, 147, 150, 186–7, 195, 199, 221–3, 229–30
activity theory 19, 75, 291
analytic 291
anger management 198, 233
Applied Behavioural Analysis 58, 165
art therapy 199
Asperger's syndrome 203
assessment 29, 30, 55, 97–9, 122–3, 139–40, 183–5
Association of Cognitive Analytic Therapy (ACAT) 38–9
Association for the Severely Handicapped (TASH) 137
attachment theory 45, 204–6, 291
attunement 45, 86, 142, 154, 291
Auden, W.H. 112–3
audio recordings 46
Augmented Interaction 165
autism 85–7, 153–67, 203, 291
'autistic' therapist 159

Bakhtin, Mikhail 27, 60, 291
behavioural phenotype 292
behavioural theory 145, 149, 165, 292
best-interests decisions 176, 292
'big brain' 81

borderline personality disorder 74, 192, 292
boundaries 292
Bowlby, John 204
British Picture Vocabulary Scale (BPVS) 98
Brooklands Offender Relationship Treatment Programme 203–15
'building blocks' framework 133–4
bullying 61
burnout 200
buttons 49–50

capacity 168–77, 294
'care' 112–4
care plans 50–1, 272–4, 294
carers
  attitudes of 140, 151
  and challenging behaviour 139–40
  support for 139
  see also family members; mothers; parents; staff team
'caring' 110, 111
central coherence 85, 157, 292
challenging behaviour
  carers and 139–40
  definitions of 123, 137–9, 141–3, 292
  misdiagnosis of cause 69
  reciprocal roles in 138–40, 143–5
  reformulating 142–3
  target problem procedure in 145–6
  in traditional models 141–2

Challenging Behaviour, A Unified Approach 138
character, reciprocal roles as 20
child derived role 20
cognitive 292
cognitive analytic therapy
  1:1 care plan 50–1, 272–4
  active (recognition) phase 29, 35–7, 44, 147, 150, 186–7, 195, 199, 221–3, 229–30
  adapting to intellectual disability context 48, 51, 56–8, 270–1, 294
  assessment 29, 30, 55, 97–9, 122–3, 139–40, 183–5
  autistic clients 163–7
  in Brooklands Offender Relationship Treatment Programme 206–7
  'building blocks' framework 133–4
  challenging behaviour reformulated in 142–52
  contra-indications to 60
  deciding when to offer 58, 60, 125–6
  development of 18–9
  ending phase 29–30, 37–8, 57–8, 188–9, 214, 223–4, 230–1
  goodbye letters 37–8, 57–8, 149–50, 189, 224, 284–5

314

Subject Index

personality disorder
 models 192
reformulation phase 29,
 30–1, 46–7, 52, 70,
 142–3, 149–50,
 185–6, 196, 218–9,
 229, 281–3, 288–9,
 293, 295
relational approach of 18,
 20, 26–7, 77–9,
 110–1, 130, 132,
 138, 209–14
Special Interest Group 38,
 45, 56, 235
structure of a 28–38
training in 38–9, 125,
 126, 127, 196, 200
using to assess mental
 capacity 169–77
cognitive behavioural therapy
 105, 292
communal intelligence 82–3,
 293
communication
 accessible 28
 with autistic clients 165
 see also language; Makaton;
 pictures
community
 community forensic
 outpatient 227–34
 community mental health
 team 183
 Therapeutic Community
 (TC) approach 192–
 202, 297
consent *see* Mental Capacity
 Act (2005)
contextual reformulation 293
'core pain' 32
counter-transference 58, 92,
 115, 161, 200, 293, 297
'cover stories' 116–7,
 118–21
cross modal sensory
 correspondence 293
curiosity 195
 see also autism

dance, helper's 50, 89–95,
 275–9, 293
decision-making 171–7

dependency 46
development *see* Zone of
 Proximal Development
diagnosis 111
'diagnostic over-shadowing'
 69
dialogic approach 19, 27,
 58, 60, 70, 77–9,
 110–1, 293
dilemmas 23, 24–5, 26, 61,
 148, 260–8, 293
disability transference 115
discharge planning 130–32
domestic violence 181–90
Down's syndrome 118–9
'Draw On Your Emotions'
 232
drawings 28, 43–4, 46, 165,
 232
duration of therapy 48, 57
dysphagia 55–6

emotional intelligence 76,
 82–3, 164, 293
emotions
 autistic people 156
 carers' 140, 151
 and decision-making
 171–2, 172–3
 and 'traps' 123–4, 134
empathy 146, 149, 154–5
enactment 293
ending phase 29–30, 37–8,
 57–8, 188–9, 214,
 223–4, 230–1
 see also goodbye letters
executive functioning 83–7,
 293
exits 35, 44, 59, 66, 187,
 287
experience, reductions in
 74–5

'facilitating environment' 45
 see also Zone of Proximal
 Development
family members 62–7, 117,
 139–40
Fanon, Franz 111
flattening of hierarchy
 196–7

follow-up phase 189–90,
 225
forensic settings *see* offenders
functional analysis 146–7,
 293

Glasgow, David 48
Good Lives Model-
 Comprehensive
 (GLM-C) 207–8
Good Thinking Groups 231
goodbye letters 37–8, 57–8,
 149–50, 189, 224,
 284–5
 see also ending phase
Gray, Carol 31

handovers 57–8
helpers, of autistic people
 158–67
helper's dances 50, 89–95,
 275–9, 293
helpfulness 110
helplessness 113
heroic therapist 159–60,
 165
hierarchy of needs 133
holding environment 293
Hoskin, Steven 175
How Infants Know Minds
 (2008) 83
humanistic 293

identity, self- 71, 111,
 155–6, 214
inpatients
 admission 122–3
 units 123–5
instrumental action 36
Integrated Theory of Sexual
 Offending (ITSO) 207
intellectual competence 75,
 76
intellectual disability
 accessible communication
 28
 adapting CAT to 56–8
 as an identity 111
 changing nomenclature
 62, 68
 as a cognitive impairment
 71–5

intellectual disability *cont.*
　as a coping strategy 43, 76
　definitions of 46, 76–7
　as label 27, 68–71, 112
　relational model 77–9
　as a social construct 111, 113
　as a social role 76–7
　stigma of 77
intellectual disability clients
　changes in services approach to 61–2
　choosing to be recipient of care 111–2
　'done-to' 60
　self to self talk of 61
　sense of reciprocal roles 96–105
　as vulnerable group 136
intelligence
　communal 82–3, 293
　emotional 76, 82–3, 164, 293
　measurement 71, 75–6, 80, 98
　relational 18, 55, 77–9, 80–8, 88, 154–5, 156–7, 166, 235, 295
　societal 83–4, 296
internalising 294
International Cognitive Analytic Therapy Association (ICATA) 38
intersubjective 294
Inventory of Interpersonal Problems (IIP) 52

King, Roz 45

label, intellectual disability as 27, 68–71, 112
language
　Bakhtin on 27
　in challenging behaviour definitions 141
　changing nomenclature 62, 68
　client 'parroting 60
　in reformulation letter 31
　simplifying 42–3, 57

using client's own 70
　see also label
leaflets (adapted) 51, 58
learning theory 36, 145, 149, 165, 292
Leiman, Mikael 19, 27
letters *see* goodbye letters; reformulation

macho image 221
McNamara, Nicola 48
Makaton 31, 98–9
mapping *see* Sequential Diagrammatic Reformulation (SDR) (mapping)
measurement 51–2
Mental Capacity Act (2005) 168–77, 294
Mental Health Act (1983) 203, 294
metaphor 47, 231
middle ground, as therapeutic goal 61–2, 124–5
misdiagnosis 69
misunderstandings 42–3
monitoring sheets 51–2, 186–7, 190
'moral holidays' 61
mothers 62

naming, noticing and negotiating 95
narcissistic personality disorder 192, 294
narrative approach 19, 27, 58, 60, 70, 77–9, 110–1, 293
National Health Service 114
National High Secure Intellectual disability service 192
negotiating, naming and noticing 95
neuropsychology 72
Nobody Nowhere 156
noticing, naming and negotiating 95

object relations theory 19, 20, 72, 294

objects, working with 49–50
occupational therapy 195
Offence Parallel Behaviour 195, 198–9, 294
offenders
　attachment problems and 206
　Brooklands Offender Relationship Treatment Programme 203–15
　cognitive analytic therapy with 209–14, 227–34
　Secure Service CAT case study 216–26
　Therapeutic Community approach 192–3, 195, 198–202
　see also sex offenders
other-to-self reciprocal role enactment 294

parallel processing 56, 294
parentally derived role 20
parents 113, 117, 117–8, 151, 228
patterns
　in Psychotherapy File 239–43, 247–55
　see also helper's dances; procedures; Ravens Coloured Progressive Matrices (RCPM)
perspective taking 155
person-centred plan 73, 294
Personal Construct Theory 18
personal vs. professional 90–1
personality disorders 191–3, 203, 294
　see also borderline personality disorder; narcissistic personality disorder
Personality Structure Questionnaire (PSQ) (adapted) 48, 270–1, 294

Subject Index

Picture Exchange Communication System (PECS) 165
pictures 28, 43–4, 46, 165, 232
pie chart 48, 230
polarised thinking *see* traps
potential space 45, 294
power 211–2
pragmatic solution focused 295
pre-formulation phase 52
presenting problems 54–6
prisoners *see* offenders
pro-social behaviour 195, 197, 202, 206
problems
  presenting 54–6
  Target Problem Procedures (TPP) 49, 69, 145–6, 148, 185–6, 220–2, 296, 297
Procedural Sequence Object Relations Model (PSORM) 19, 20, 72, 295
procedures 22–6, 30–1, 35–6, 145–6, 295
  see also patterns; Target Problem Procedures (TPP)
process focus vs. task focus 90
professional vs. personal 90–1
projection 295
projective identification 295
psychoanalytic approach 18–9, 27, 45–6, 62, 92
psychometric testing 71, 75–6, 80, 98
psychotherapy file 45, 217, 237–43, 244–55, 256–69, 295

rating scales 35–6
rating sheets 51–2, 186–7, 190
Ravens Coloured Progressive Matrices (RCPM) 98, 104
reality orientation 195

reciprocal roles 19–24, 32–3, 297
  autistic clients 163–7
  caring-cared for 114–5, 118
  challenging behaviour and 138–40, 143–5
  definitions 292, 295
  in forensic setting 197, 198, 212–3, 229–30
  humiliating/controlling-humiliated/controlled 201–2
  in inpatient admissions 124–5
  intellectual disability client's sense of 96–105
  as parallel processing 56, 294
  unhelpful 60
recognition 29, 35–7, 44, 147, 150, 186–7, 195, 199, 221–3, 229–30
referrals 54–5
reflective practice 91–3, 127–8, 200, 225–6, 295
  see also recognition
reformulation 29, 30–1, 46–7, 52, 70, 142–3, 149–50, 185–6, 196, 218–9, 229, 281–3, 288–9, 293, 295
relapse prevention 195
relational approach 18, 20, 26–7, 77–9, 110–1, 130, 132, 138, 209–14
relational intelligence 18, 55, 77–9, 80–8, 88, 154–5, 156–7, 166, 235, 295
  see also dialogic approach
relationships
  in autism 156, 158–67
  therapeutic 36, 96–7
  see also relational approach
responsibility, shared 91
revision 29, 150, 195, 199, 221–3, 230
risk 195, 197, 198, 203, 227–33

roles
  child derived 20
  parentally derived 20
  unhealthy 21–2, 112
  see also reciprocal roles
ruptures 36, 221
Ryle, Tony 18–9, 21, 48, 296

'secondary handicap' 43, 76
secure service 192, 216–26
Self Agency in Psychotherapy (2011) 83
self-awareness 22, 92–3
self-identity 71, 111, 155–6, 214
self-self reciprocal role 21, 211, 296
self-states 33, 173–4, 296
self-to-other reciprocal roles 197, 296
Sequential Diagrammatic Reformulation (SDR) (mapping) 31–5, 55–6, 59–60, 70, 88, 104–5, 128, 142–3, 150–1, 185–90, 196, 199, 200, 219–20, 294, 296
  abusing-neglecting 64
  abusing-rejecting 280
  'bullying-bullied' 44
  controlling-vulnerable 287
  disappointing-disappointed 290
  heroic and stoic therapist 162
  loving-loved 286
  overwhelming-overwhelmed 290
  powerful-abused 290
  rejecting-rejected 287
  relationship with staff team 73
  trusting-trusted 286
service culture 61–2
sex offenders 197, 205, 228–9, 233
shame 117–8
Six Part Story Method (6PSM) 37–8, 47, 48–9, 296

317

snags 23, 25, 148, 175–6, 221, 269, 296
social construct, intellectual disability as 111, 113
social story writing 31, 296
social style, reciprocal roles as 20
societal intelligence 83–4, 296
Special Interest Group 38, 45, 56, 235
speech therapy 55–6, 199
Speed Supervision (2012) 93
splits 173
splitting 52, 200
staff team
  attitudes of 140
  awareness sessions 222–3
  change in practice of 36–7, 128–9
  and endings 57–8
  hierarchy within 196–7, 198, 211–2
  in inpatient unit 123–5
  joint working within 130–2
  personal vs. professional self 90–1
  reflective groups 127–8
  relational intelligence in 88
  sharing information within 129, 233–4
  training in CAT 38–9, 125, 126, 127, 196, 200
  traps in 134–5
  unhelpful reciprocal roles 60
  Zone of Proximal Development within 132–3
state shifts 296
step down psychotherapy 233
stoic therapist 160–3
storytelling 31, 37–8, 47, 48–9, 116–7, 118–21, 296
suggestibility 296
summarising 43

supervision 47, 93, 196, 200, 208, 219
supported living 296
symbolised leaflets 51, 58
systemic 296

Target Problem Procedures (TPP) 49, 69, 145–6, 148, 185–6, 220–2, 296, 297
task focus vs. process focus 90
theory of mind 156, 297
Therapeutic Community (TC) approach 192–202, 297
therapeutic relationship 36, 96–7
time-limited therapy 48, 57
training 38–9, 125, 126, 127, 196, 200
transference 58, 92, 115, 161, 200, 293, 297
traps 23–4, 59, 123–5, 134–5, 148, 174, 221, 257–60, 297

unhealthy roles 21–2, 112
unknowability 27
'unmanageable emotions' 32
'Unoffered Chair, The' 235

Valuing People (Now) 297
vicious circles (traps) 23–4, 59, 123–5, 134–5, 148, 174, 221, 257–60, 297
Vygotsky, Lev 27–8, 36, 297

Winterbourne View Hospital 61, 297

Zone of Proximal Development 27–8, 45, 60, 75–6, 132–3, 199, 217, 232, 297

Author Index

Addison, M. 142
Alborz, A. 136
Allen, J. 181
Antaki, C. 70
Arendt, H. 118
Armstrong, N. 49
Arscott, K. 97

Bakhtin, M. 110
Ball, T. 137
Bancroft, A. 47, 52, 53, 143, 217, 232
Baron-Cohen, S. 85, 86
Bartlett, C. 69
Bates, R. 78
Beail, N. 45
Beart, S. 69, 70, 77, 79
Beech, A.R. 207
Bender, M. 235
Bennett, C. 192
Bloom, S. 112
Bouras, N. 76
Bowlby J. 45, 46
British Psychological Society 123
Brown, H. 170, 171
Buchan, L. 70, 77
Bunning, K. 69
Bush, A. 137
Byrne, A. 140

Campbell, M. 136, 146
Cappleman 193
Carr, A. 204
Carradice, A. 52, 53, 144, 152
Cattermole, M. 71
Chadwick, P. 105
Chamorro-Premuzic, T. 75
Champion, P. 204

Clarke, S. 192
Clarkson, P. 161
Clayton, P. 47, 52, 53, 192
Clements, J. 71
Colomb, E. 55
Commission for Healthcare Audit Inspection 77
Conboy-Hill, S. 76
Corbett, A. 115
Court, J.H. 98
Crowley, V. 21, 97, 212
Cunningham, C.C. 78

Dagnan, D. 97, 105, 148
Damasio, A. 104, 171
Davidson, R. 98
Davies, C. 71, 77
de Kock, U. 139
Dent-Brown, K. 49
Department of Health 77, 133, 136, 181, 297
Donald, M. 81
Dudley-Marlin, C. 111
Dunn, L. 98
Dunn, M. 144
Duxbury, J. 140

Einfield, L. 137
Ekman, P. 98
Emerson, E. 70, 123, 136, 137, 138, 144
Engleheart, P. 49, 232
Erikson, E. 117

Fannon, F. 111, 112
Farrell, G.A. 137, 151
Felce, D. 139
Fisher, C. 52, 144, 146
Fitzsimmons, M. 70
Flynn, J.R. 61, 81

Flynn, M. 175
Frank, J. 96
Frith, U. 85
Furnham, A. 75

Gardner, H. 80
Golding, K. 204
Goleman, D. 33, 82
Gopfert, M. 194, 198
Greenberg, J. 19
Greenhill, B. 146
Griffiths, E. 115
Gugjonsson, G. 43

Haddock, G. 105
Hall, J. 140
Hannam, C. 117
Hannush, M. 66
Harding, C. 52, 144, 146
Hardy, G. 70, 77
Hardy, S. 76
Harper, D.C. 140
Harvey, L. 72
Hastings, R.P. 139, 140, 151
Hatton, C. 76
Haydon-Laurelut, M. 58
Hill, C. 148
Holland, A. 173
Holquist, M. 110
Holt, G., 76
Horowitz, L.M. 52
Hudson, S.M. 206

Jacob, C. 200
Jacobs, M. 45
Jahoda, A. 71, 77, 136, 151
James, K. 192
Jenkins, R. 71, 77
Jones, L. 199

Kahneman, D. 172
Kellett, S. 192
Kelly, G.A. 18
Kerr, I. 20, 21, 89, 93, 123, 132, 142, 146, 149, 192, 194, 198
Kierkgaard, S. 109
Kiernan, P. 70
King, R. 47, 49, 75, 78, 121
Kirkland, J. 46
Klein, J. 153
Knox, J. 83
Kroese, B. 97, 140

Linington, M. 236
Livesley, J.W. 191, 192
Lloyd, E. 117, 139, 144, 148, 152
Lloyd, J. 46, 52, 53, 55
Lovett, H. 69, 78, 137, 140, 144
Luborsky, L. 96
Lund, E.M. 182
Lynch, C. 71

MacAllister, P. 200
McCormack, J. 206
McGill, P. 136, 151
Mackintosh, N. 98
Mclean, K.C. 119
Mahler, M. 153
Maniglio, R. 205
Marchant, E. 170, 171
Markham, D. 69, 140
Markova, I. 71
Marshall, W.L. 205
Maslow, A.H. 133
Mental Health Foundation 176
Merzenich, M. 85
Mitchell, S. 19
Morrissey, C. 192
Morton, J. 140
Moss, A. 146
Murphy, N. 50, 52, 53, 142

National Institute for Mental Health in England 192

Oakes, P. 71, 77
Oathamshaw, S. 105

Parry, G. 144
Perry, J. 139
Pollock, P. 198
Potter, S. 63, 93, 151, 229, 279
Proudlove, J. 105
Psaila, C. 21, 97, 212

Qureshi, H. 136

Rapley, M. 70
Raven, J. 98
Raven, J.C. 98
Reddy, V. 81, 83, 153
Remmington, B. 139, 140
Repp, A.C. 139
Rice-Varian, C. 72
Robertson, A. 136
Rogers, C. 115
Royal College of Psychiatrists 62, 123, 136, 137, 138, 139, 141, 142–3, 144, 152, 292
Royal College of Speech Language Therapists 123
Rubenstein, J. 85
Ryle, A. 20, 21, 22, 33, 72, 74, 75, 89, 93, 104, 123, 132, 142, 145, 146, 149, 191, 192

Salmon, P. 137, 140
Shafiei, T. 137
Shannon, K. 198
Shapiro, D. 96
Shapiro, D.A. 96
Sharrock, R. 140
Shine, J. 195
Sinason, V. 43, 62, 68, 76, 113, 141, 149
Singer, B. 96
Stern, D.N. 45, 85, 232, 234
Steward 47
Stewart, C.A. 207
Stokes, J. 113
Stowell-Smith, M. 198
Sunderland, M. 49, 232
Suzuki, S. 111
Symington, M. 114
Szivos, S. 115

Taylor, J. 192, 196, 197
Thomas, P. 192
Tomita, S.K. 61
Trevarthen, C. 81, 153
Trower, P. 69, 140

Valsiner, J. 110
Van der Veer, R. 110
Vygotsky, L.S. 47, 60, 78, 194, 217, 232, 297

Wadsworth, J.S. 140
Waitman, A. 76
Walby, S. 181
Wanless, L.K. 151
Ward, T. 206, 207
Wells, S. 46, 59, 104
Whitaker, S. 98
Whittington, L.K. 140
Williams, B. 52, 53, 139, 144, 148, 152
Williams, D. 156
Wilson, C. 58
Winnicott D.W. 45, 66
Withers, J. 192
Wodehouse, G. 136, 151
Wong, J. 173
Wykes, T. 140

Yeates, G. 72

Printed in Great Britain
by Amazon